After Long Silence

Helen Fremont

After Long
Silence

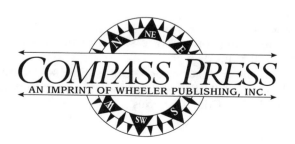

COMPASS PRESS
AN IMPRINT OF WHEELER PUBLISHING, INC.

Published in Large Print by arrangement with Delacorte Press, a division of Random House, Inc. in the United States and Canada.

Compass Press Large Print Book Series.

Set in 16 pt Plantin.

Library of Congress Cataloging-in-Publication Data

Fremont, Helen.
    After long silence / Helen Fremont.
       p. (large print) cm.(Compass Press large print book series)
    ISBN 1-56895-740-8 (hardcover)
    1. Children of Holocaust survivors—United States—Biography.
2. Holocaust, Jewish (1939–1945)—Poland—Personal narratives.
3. Large type books. I. Title. II. Series
[E184.37.F74A4 1999b]
940.53/18/092 B 21   99-031906
                                                          CIP

For Donna

Author's Note

This is a work of nonfiction. I have changed the names, locations, and identifying characteristics of a number of individuals in order to protect their privacy. In some instances, I have imagined details in an effort to convey the emotional truths of my family's experiences.

Prologue

The first time I heard about the bomb that killed my mother's parents, I was five years old, and my sister Lara was eight, and we each clasped a batter-drenched beater in our hands while working our tongues around the stainless-steel blades. My mother had spread raspberry jam over the pan of linzer torte dough, using a scarred wooden spatula that looked like it had survived the Pleistocene Era.

"When I was your age," Mom said, screwing the lid back on the Stop & Shop jar, "my mother used to cook huge pots of raspberry jam. The whole apartment smelled of it." She broke off a small piece of dough and rolled it into a long noodle between the palms of her hands. "Now, watch," she said, draping it across the pan like a plump worm. "See, this is how you make the lattice top."

Her hands worked quickly, forming a criss-cross pattern.

"What happened to your mother?" Lara asked.

My mother pinched the corners of the lattice and slipped the pan into the oven. She glanced away as she wiped her hands on her floral print apron. "Oh, she died," she said.

"When? What happened?"

"It was a long, long time ago. Before you were born."

"What happened?"

1

My mother didn't answer right away. "They died," she said slowly, "in a bomb." Her eyes looked so dark and full of memories, Lara and I grew quiet.

"What do you mean?" I whispered. "Where were you?"

My mother took a deep breath. "I was living at home, in Poland, but I would take the trolley each morning into town. And one day...one day I took the trolley into town—" Her lips quivered; a single tear drew a shiny trail down her cheek.

"And when I came back at the end of the day..." My mother's voice seemed to lurch on creaky wheels. I'd never seen her like this before, and it seemed to me that the words themselves were hurting her. "Everything was gone..." she said, "the whole block was bombed out! There was nothing left, no trace of them." She wiped her eyes.

I stared at her. It terrified me, the thought that I might find my parents' house bombed out, that I might go to school one day and come home and find nothing there. How could my mother manage to live without her parents, to lose them and continue her life?

"How old were you?" I asked.

Tears poured down my mother's face. "I was twenty."

"Oh," I said, greatly relieved, "you were already a grown-up. You didn't need them any-more."

Lara shot me a glare that I will never forget. "Helen!" she snapped.

2

"I loved them very much," my mother said, breaking into thin sobs.

My discovery that my father's mother, too, had died in a bomb was much less horrifying. We were sitting at the dining room table, I think, and either Lara or I asked, "How did your mother die?"

I remember my father's terse response: "A bomb." He sounded angry, and we let it drop.

PART
One

1

Lara and I were raised Catholic in a small city in the Midwest. In 1960, at the age of three, I went to nursery school at the convent of the Saint James Sisters, and at six I wore Lara's hand-me-down itchy white petticoat dress to my First Communion. It was the first and last time I would ever swallow a wafer, however, since our family always tiptoed out of church every Sunday before Communion. "It's not an important part of Mass," my mother explained, and for a long time we believed that Communion was a curious American addition to Catholicism.

My sister and I knew that our parents were from a distant and dangerous world, that they had come out of a war, and that no one else had come with them. Although we could not hear their accents, our playmates told us our parents spoke funny English; and when our schoolmates asked about our grandparents and aunts and uncles, we said we didn't have any. Except, of course, our auntie Zosia, who lived across the ocean in a place called Italy.

I also knew that my parents had been in concentration camps. I misunderstood the meaning of *concentration* and assumed that in prison, the inmates were consumed by intensely focused mental activity. I believed that these camps were so deadly that they had sewn my parents into pockets of complete silence. And so I understood that two things could happen to you in a war: either you were suddenly, breathlessly, swept off the streets by a bomb, or you were scooped into a concentration camp, where you swallowed a terrible silence.

My mother, I knew, was finally sprung from the camp by her sister, Zosia, who baked goodies and buttered up the camp warden. My father had it worse—he was off on a sheet of ice somewhere in Siberia for six years, until he escaped. I never knew how he escaped, except that he had managed to jump a train and hang on for days. I pictured him dangling from his one good arm, long, tattered legs swinging an arc each time the train banked a curve.

Their love story I had been fed early and often, until it seemed part of my bones. I knew that they had fallen in love before the war, and they had been separated for six years without knowing if the other was alive; my mother escaped Poland dressed as an Italian soldier, and my father walked across Europe after the war, found my mother in Rome, and married her ten years to the day after they had first met. This was the tale they liked to tell and retell, the story they used to summarize their lives. It was a good story, because it ran a thread across the war and connected the two lovers before and after. It tied a knot in their tongues at the end, and the war remained silent; the intervening six years could never be spoken.

My father, Kovik Buchman, was a self-employed family doctor with a sharp Slavic accent, pure white hair, and a chip on his shoulder the size of a Soviet tank. He was forty-two when I was born, twice as old and almost twice as tall as other daddies. He built a little office downtown, having drawn up the blue-prints and supervised the construction him-self. He bought all the latest equipment, an X-ray machine and elaborate instruments, lab equipment and simple furniture. His office was dark and smelled of medicine, with floor-to-ceiling bookcases, textbooks, and illus-trated medical periodicals. My mother sewed the curtains—bold op-art designs without a trace of heritage.

His patients poured in, Poles and Lithuanians, Czechs and Hungarians. They liked bantering with him in their home tongues, liked his European approach, his punctuality, his efficiency, his dry sense of humor. He worked from early morning until late at night, six days a week. He made house calls on a moment's notice, day or night. You could almost hear him click his heels as he marched from one patient to another. His stride was enormous, his smile brief, his gaze intense. "Sit," he would command, slapping on a blood-pressure band. "Inhale deeply." "Cough." "Say 'Aaah.' " His exam was quick and thorough. "All set," he would snap. "You may dress. Call me tomorrow." In a flash he would be down the hall, ushering the next patient into his other examining room.

My mother was a more slippery figure. Slender and supple, she was half my father's size and twice as elusive. She spent the day at home up to her elbows in yellow Playtex living gloves, cleaning house. She smelled of ammonia and lemons. "Be a doctor," my mother always instructed us. "Don't marry one."

In the fall she tied her hair in an aqua-green surgeon's cap and began rearranging nature, brandishing a rake that was taller than she was. She stuffed leaves into barrels, dragged them from one end of the property to the other, and dumped them over the cliff behind our house. In the spring she planted an elaborate rock garden under the white pines, using rocks she had kidnapped from nearby streams. Kneeling in dirt for hours, she separated and reunited plants from the woods and the rock garden, until it was hard to tell where her garden ended and the woods began.

Our house itself was a crazy-shaped glass-and-brick affair surrounded by a small forest— a swank fifties Frank Lloyd Wright knockoff. My parents had fallen in love with it instantly because it looked like nothing they'd ever seen before. We moved in just after I was born, after they'd changed their name to Bocard and settled into their new American identity.

It was a loud house. The sun danced through the pines and smashed through our floor-to-ceiling windows. An overbearing sky trumpeted each new day and tossed us out of bed. From the living room, violins wept on the hi-fidelity. A fat medical text lay open on my father's lap, the Sunday *Tribune* spread at his feet. The dog a respectful distance away, banished from the Oriental rug.

Kazakhstan followed my father to the new world in the form of floor covering. He wiped his feet on Middle Asia. Solzhenitsyn lined his bookshelves. *The First Circle, Cancer Ward, One Day in the Life of Ivan Denisovich. The Rise and Fall of the Third Reich* by William Shirer. *The Gathering Storm,* volume after volume after volume, by Churchill. Books soared for the ceiling: *The Art of Florence, The Operas of Puccini, The Roman Ruins.* Dictionaries in every color and language. Volumes of German grammar, *Duden.*

From the moment my mother moved to the States, she and her sister, Zosia, wrote each other three or four times a week. Pale blue aerograms with every millimeter of available space filled in elite type, with handwritten notes squeezed into the margins. The Italian post was terrible, and my mother would go days without mail and then get a bonanza of letters. Sometimes the letters arrived in little plastic bags, charred, torn, and taped back together.

They wrote of the same things day after day: the weather, their bridge games, the children, books, movies, opera—or so my mother claimed whenever I asked her to translate the letters. From the excerpts she read to me, I couldn't fathom why my mother's face lit up every time she found a letter from my aunt in the mailbox. "Zosia!" she would exclaim, and race up the driveway to make her-

11

self a celebratory cup of pale tea with lemon. Then she gently pried open the aerogram with a knife, careful not to lose any words clinging to the inside edge of the folds, and settled into the chaise longue in her bedroom to read.

When I was small, maybe five or six, my mother came to my bed every night to tuck me in. She would teach me the sign of the cross in six languages: Polish, Russian, German, Italian, French, and English. Each night I selected a language, and we said the sign of the cross in that language: *In the name of the Father, the Son, and the Holy Spirit, Amen.* Then she taught me the prayer Our Father in these languages, and I rehearsed them until I knew them by heart. I loved the way gumdrop syllables rolled off the tongue in Italian and the way consonants crashed in German; I loved the tongue-twisting sounds of Polish and the fur-lined purr of French and Russian. And of course, I loved our conspiracy—my mother's and mine. It was our time alone, our time together, and she was sending me into a night of sleep, protected by a God who could respond to me in any language, under any sky.

What I didn't understand was that my mother was equipping me with the means of survival: proof of my Catholicism to anyone in a dozen countries.

Like most little kids, I considered my parents perfect. That is, I twisted in any direction necessary so that they always remained absolutely perfect in my mind.

My father suffered from the realization that his life had been unbearable. My mother, on the other hand, suffered from the illusion that hers was not so bad as it really was.

And so my sister and I grew up between the trunks of these two old trees, twisted and tough, throwing enough shade to shelter three or four continents. Childhood was a strange place to find oneself after so much history.

As the baby of the family, I was the tail end of that history, and by the time I would try to make sense of it, it had been erased by my elders.

In grade school my classmates and I marched single file into the blue-windowed gymnasium under the howling horn of Civil Defense drills, the heels of our patent-leather shoes clacking over the polished wood floors like the patter of rain. Our teachers lined us up in rows, then ordered us down on our knees; obediently, we offered our heads to the floor, clasping our little hands over the nape of our necks, elbows poking the shiny floor like praying mantises. I prayed the drill would last forever, cut into class time, splash the day with emergency and adventure. I never equated those drills with war or with the bombs that had wiped out my grandparents, my history, my identity. I loved Civil Defense drills for the distraction from my daily life as a first-grader.

I was free to skip church once I'd made

my First Communion. Consequently, as a youngster I came to associate Catholicism with *The NFL Today,* which I watched on TV every Sunday while my mother and sister were at church. Highlights of the prior week's games were replayed in slow motion, set to rock and roll music, with voice-over narration by Frank Gifford. The moments of impact were like a dream: Half a ton of heavenly bodies, jerseys, and cleats collided soundlessly in exquisite slow motion. This is how I worshiped my Catholic God each Sunday at noon, through the miracle of television.

My mother never really paid attention to what I watched; she was under the spell of America, and everything American, she believed, must be good for me. I ate Fritos, Scooter Pies, and Fluffernutter sandwiches on Wonder bread and watched *The NFL Today.*

My mother always emphasized that one's relationship with God was personal. She had private tête-à-têtes with God from time to time, I later discovered; my mother and God would bargain a little, and she would extract from Him a promise of our well-being in exchange for her vow to go to Catholic church each week.

There was no doubt in my mind that my mother's churchgoing was a sacrifice. "Ach!" she would shout, storming into the kitchen and slamming the garage door behind her. "It's a *sin* the way that priest speaks English!"

I would creep out from the TV room, glance up at the clock, and realize that once again my mother had come home early from church.

"'Jesus died for you and I!'" she would exclaim. "'For you and *I*!'" She would shake her head in a rage. "An idiot he is!" She would yank off her gloves and march into the bedroom, peeling off her dress, her stockings, her slip. "A waste of time!" she'd mutter. "I have better things to do than listen to someone who doesn't even know basic grammar!"

The following week, of course, she'd dutifully powder her face, apply her Cherry Blossom lipstick, don one of her postwar Italian dresses, and poke the nose of the Dodge Dart down the driveway and out to church. She'd made a vow, she told me later, a deal with God, and she did not dare back down.

I did not have that sort of relationship with God. I glimpsed bits of Him here and there, but I never talked directly to Him. I could usually find His beauty on the TV, during particularly eloquent moments of grace and violence on *The NFL Today*. But I never thought of God during the elbow-scraping fights I got into on the playground, when Jimmy Delaponti's knee was crushing my ribs, or when I smashed my knuckles in Jimmy's face. My everyday life was unencumbered by religious concerns.

It occurs to me now that my parents were not keen on organized religion or orthodoxy of any sort. It was as if they had read the *Cliff Notes* on Catholicism, just as they subscribed to the family architectural principle of form over function. From the outside we looked like a typical happy family; it was an image that we all worked hard to achieve.

When I was nine my parents sent me to a summer camp on a remote island off the coast of northern Maine. My cabinmate and soulmate was Twinky James, a hefty lion-haired maiden straight out of the Valkyrie, with solid white calves and smooth, milky skin. She had the beginning nips of breasts, a tuft of pale yellow fuzz between her legs, which made me feel boyish and lucky. The others have slipped from my memory, except our counselor, Katherine, a tall, graceless teenager shaped like an ironing board, with thick glasses magnifying her brittle self-righteousness. She once turned me and Twinky in for eating a pack of M&M's after lights-out.

On Sunday mornings we were expected to get up before dawn, pull on our little white skirts and blouses and socks and shoes, and assemble in the gravel parking lot behind the dining hall in the dark. Yawning and nodding, we were herded onto a school bus, which began the long, bumpy journey across the bay to a church in the town of Dragamond. There we could worship to our heart's content, file back on the bus, and ride back to camp in the afternoon, thereby blowing more than half of a perfectly good day.

Nearly all of my cabinmates were Protestants, and our counselor, a devout Catholic, urged them to go to church as good Christians; to

16

my amazement, nearly all of them did—if not eagerly, then at least obediently. As for me, the only other Catholic in the bunch, Katherine simply ordered me to attend church.

"But church is optional," I whined. "I don't want to go! Pleeeease!"

"God is not discretionary!" Katherine informed me coldly. "It's your obligation as a Catholic to go to church." Her enormous eyes seemed to pop out from behind those octagonal plastic frames. "I will see to it that you are on the bus," she continued. "I will not stand by and watch you commit a mortal sin."

I sneaked a glance at Twinky, pigtailed, Protestant, eyes squinting like slit envelopes. She flashed me a smile behind her pink hands.

"But, Katherine," I pleaded, "I don't even have to go to church at home!" It struck me as the height of injustice that I should be forced to attend church now that I was on vacation.

Katherine sent me to see the Directors of the camp—two large, middle-aged sisters in stretch pants, one of whom I felt strangely fond of, perhaps because her name was also Helen. I sat in a rough-hewn straight-back chair, feet dangling a few inches above the pinewood floor, and stated my case. The Directors seemed reasonable and agreed to write my parents, asking their wishes.

Did I suffer pangs of doubt? I don't think so. Still, I was skeptical of the Camp Directors' ability to interpret my parents' wishes in my absence. A tense week trickled by. My mother finally rescued me, sending the Directors written permission for me to skip church. Joyously relieved, I pranced around my cabin, dangling my mother's letter in Katherine's enraged face. "I don't have to go to chuu-urch," I sang gleefully, over and over. It was my most delicious religious experience.

The following summer I finally confessed to Twinky what the Russians had done to my father. We were walking to our cabin in the woods from the lavabo after brushing our teeth. I don't remember what we were talking about—but for some reason the story about my father in Siberia was weighing on me.

"Listen, Twinky," I said, "I want to tell you something." We were holding our toothbrushes in front of us like candles.

"My father was put in a concentration camp by the Russians," I said. "For six years. In Siberia. That's a really cold part of Russia. A bunch of prisoners ganged up on him and broke his arm—" Suddenly I was fighting back tears, alarmed, and ashamed of my inexplicable need to tell someone. Twinky stared at me with horror, and the two of us were speechless for several seconds while I looked down at the ground and blinked my eyes.

"Gee," Twinky said helplessly. "Gee, that's—what did they—why did they do that?"

My lip started trembling. I shrugged but couldn't speak. Night was falling softly, the air cooled, and the woods darkened. Mosquitoes found us, landed softly on our arms and legs. We slapped at them and walked back to the cabin. I was amazed and embarrassed by my emotion, which seemed to have arrived like an alien invasion, and I realized that I must never speak of our family, that our story must be kept a secret. I clutched my elbows in front of me. My smooth arms had grown from his shattered life.

In the eighth grade many of my friends were getting middle names. They were going through a ritual called Confirmation, which, I gathered, had something to do with the Church and Catholicism. The middle names captured my imagination. I was trying to decide what name I would pick for myself. My friends were all getting stupid names, like Mary and Elizabeth and Christina. I already had a stupid name—Helen. I wanted something dashing and adventurous, like Gonzalez or Vladimir.

I asked my mother about this business of Confirmation and whether I, too, could choose a middle name. My mother had never heard of Confirmation and scoffed at the idea. "We didn't have anything like that in Poland," she said with great disdain. "It must be some American invention."

This made sense to me, since there were a great many foolish American institutions that did not exist in Poland. Among these were frat parties and cheerleaders, homecoming queens and prom nights, drive-in movies and back-seat sex. Confirmation, I concluded, was simply one more mindless American ritual like the Miss America Pageant. I never thought of it again but was grateful that I didn't have to go through the ordeal, which obviously involved more Sunday school attendance and more dressing up. The only thing I missed was the chance to acquire a more exciting name.

What I didn't realize was that all our names had been recently invented. My mother had survived the war using a false name and papers; she had escaped from the Nazis dressed as an Italian soldier, under yet another name and false papers. My parents had changed our family name upon applying for citizenship in the United States. To this day I don't even know what my mother's real name is.

2

When I was sixteen or seventeen, our family was invited to Susie Janiczek's wedding. Her parents were Auschwitz survivors and close friends of our parents'. They'd met in rural Michigan in 1953, when Dr. Janiczek helped my father set up his medical practice.

Dressed in our Sunday best, our family piled into my father's forest-green Chrysler New Yorker and followed the stream of big boxy American cars from the temple to the Sheraton hotel for the reception.

"My parents survived," Susie addressed the hundreds of Holocaust survivors in the ballroom, "and have given me this, a new life, new friends, the future." Flashbulbs snapped, and a hush fell over the room. "We have conquered the past," Susie added triumphantly to the nodding hairsprayed heads. "We have conquered Hitler! We will survive. We will flourish." She raised her white-gloved arms over her head, and the crowd cheered. A band of musicians in electric-blue tuxedos lifted their instruments from black cases behind her.

Lara and I and the handful of other American-born youngsters were paraded around and shown off by the older generation, who chattered among themselves in impenetrable Polish. Middle-aged ladies with layers of hair coloring and penciled eyebrows, sumptuously retouched lips, glossy fingernails in shades of berries. They clasped my hand with their diamond-studded fingers, smiled and assessed my figure, talking the whole time in Polish to my mother, who beamed with pride.

The men clustered together—solid black-and-white islands in the sea of colorful women. Unbuttoning their jackets, they smoked filterless cigarettes and drank champagne from slender flute glasses, their cheeks growing redder and redder.

I was used to seeing tattooed numbers on wrists and hearing Polish- and German-peppered accents—many of my parents' closest friends were survivors. I liked the way the wedding celebration was turning into a joyous, arrogant in-your-face to history, to gas chambers and ghettos and starvation and mass murders, as if it were my personal mission to fly in the face of oppression. I was proof of the tenacity of my parents, and I was fiercely proud of them. The only glaring gap in my understanding of the war against the Jews was my family's precise role in it.

It didn't bother me that Lara and I were the only non-Jews at that wedding. We were the children of survivors in an ocean of survivors, and it seemed the most natural thing in the world for us to celebrate—religion didn't seem to enter into it. My mother explained the Jewish traditions—the *chuppah,* the chairs, the broken champagne glass, so that I understood what was happening. I never questioned how she knew so much. I was used to my mother's complete fluency with the world.

It never occurred to me that someone in my family might actually be Jewish, until a few years ago, when I was already in my thirties and working as a public defender in Boston. One evening, at a Bar Association cocktail party, I was introduced to a statuesque high-heeled, slim-hipped woman, the wife of a partner in a Boston firm. She told me she was the daughter of a distinguished family of Philadelphia WASPs, and only after she had married and had three children did she discover that her mother was in fact Jewish. We exchanged family stories over a glass of wine, and she threw back her head and laughed. "You're Jewish!" she said.

"No," I insisted, "Catholic. Polish Catholic."

"Then why were your parents in concentration camps?" Her eyes gleamed a beautiful emerald-green, and she tried to suppress a smile. She did not look the least bit Jewish. When she laughed, her yellow hair seemed to break around her shoulders like waves on a beach.

"Lots of Poles were imprisoned during the war or taken by the Germans," I explained. "They—"

"Of course," she interrupted, "but if they were Catholic they wouldn't have had to escape and emigrate to the States. I bet your parents were Jewish. Or at least your mother."

It didn't take more than half a glass of wine for me to grow fond of the idea. This would explain so much, I thought—all those mysteries of childhood, my endless tiptoeing around a jigsaw-puzzle past in which all the pieces were missing except my parents. As a child my questions about our family had always elicited strange, winding soliloquies that led to bedtime or, worse, dinner, the two most dreaded events of my day. And when Lara and I had fought as children, my mother sometimes fell to her knees, sobbing, "I should have died with my parents! I shouldn't have lived! *Bosze, Bosze, Bosze.*" God, God, God. This was always a shoe-in to make Lara and me stop fighting and turn into perfect children before her eyes. But by the time Mom had called upon *Bosze,* she was beyond noticing us.

Perhaps, I now thought, all these mysteries could be explained: Maybe we were Jewish.

A few months later I ran the idea past Lara, who was living in San Diego and working as a psychiatrist. "I have this theory," I told her over the phone. "What if Mom and Dad were Jewish? Or maybe one of their parents was Jewish."

A long silence. "I really doubt it," she finally said.

"Well, I know it sounds crazy," I said quickly. "I mean, it's just this idea I have. But think about it. I mean, Mom escaped from Poland *dressed as an Italian soldier*! Why would she have to do that if she was Catholic? And why wouldn't *any* other relatives be alive? This would explain so much."

"I just can't see it," Lara said. "Why would they hide their religion now?"

I was disheartened by her lack of interest. "I know," I agreed, "it's pretty strange. But still..."

I couldn't let go of the idea. Believing we were Jewish offered me the possibility that my parents were still in hiding, that we were all in hiding, that all the underground emotional tunnels in our house were not just figments of my imagination.

But the more I thought about it, the less I could justify my suspicions. Lara had a point— why would my parents deny their Judaism here in America, fifty years later? Perhaps, I thought, we were Jewish, or partly Jewish, but my parents didn't even know *themselves* that they were Jewish.

I tried this idea out on them at Christmas

a year later. Lara had flown in from San Diego for the holiday, and I had arrived from Boston after finishing a legal ethics report for my office. Before dinner I found my mother in the kitchen, hoisting the twenty-two-pound turkey to the counter.

"Hey, Mom," I said. She muscled the bird onto the cutting board. Her forearms were covered with little notchlike burns from years of cooking.

"Want some help?" I asked. I knew she never accepted help with anything.

"No, no," she said.

"So here's my theory, okay?"

She rustled through the drawer for a serving spoon.

"Maybe your mother was Catholic, and your father was Jewish, okay? Something like that. Big taboo. So when they married, your grandparents went through the roof, and that's why you don't know anything about them. Huge mega-rift in the family. And you wouldn't even have known about it."

My mother was hacking up the turkey now, twisting its legs with her bare hands. The bone and cartilage broke, and steam poured from the leg sockets.

"So what do you think?" I prodded her.

She shrugged and took a butcher's knife to the wings, then started on the breast. Juice streamed down the sides of the turkey and gurgled in the pan. Her eyes narrowed, examining the turkey's exposed pink breast. "I don't know," she said. "Why do you think so?"

"I'm just guessing," I said. "But it would make sense. It would make sense if someone in your family was Jewish."

Thin slices of meat curled off the knife blade and onto her palm. She placed them on four waiting plates of white china.

"I doubt it," she said, pushing her bifocals back up her nose. "But I don't know. The Germans would have known about that, I wouldn't."

Her cheeks gleamed under the bright kitchen lights, and slight folds of skin gathered under her chin. She'd grown self-conscious about this lately and had taken to wearing turtlenecks.

"Put some broccoli on here," she said, pointing with the knife to a steaming pot. "And some of these baby potatoes." She swung the pot of boiled potatoes from the burner toward me in a swift, fluid motion: Mikhail Baryshnikov in oven mitts. It was hard to believe she was in her mid-seventies.

"That one's for Dad," she said, pointing to the plate in my left hand. "Now, take that in before it gets cold."

It's crazy, I told myself—these wild guesses of Jewish roots—as if I were casting about for some adventure to beef up my ordinary American existence. I carried the plates into the dining room, and our family sat down to dinner.

My mother brought in the last plate and passed the salt and pepper. "But what is it with you girls," she said, puzzled and slightly annoyed. "What is it with all this Jewish business?" She turned from me to Lara. "All I hear now for months from you is about the past, our family, and so on. What is it all about?"

I glanced across the table at my sister, but she avoided my eyes. She was researching our family history for her fellowship in child psychiatry, and now I wondered whether she, too, was beginning to think we were Jewish.

"I don't know," I said, "but I have the feeling that I'm Jewish. I don't know why, exactly."

My mother stabbed a piece of turkey with her fork and smothered it with dressing.

"Like that time," I said, "I went to visit Rachel after my first year of law school."

Rachel's mother was a Jewish Holocaust survivor. I'd spent a weekend at their house twelve years earlier. "Remember what I told you when I came back? That it was just like being at home. With her father listening to a violin concerto in the other room, and the living room filled with books, and all her mother's plants in the windows. And we sat at the kitchen counter, Rachel and her mother and I, and sipped coffee and talked and talked—and for a moment I thought I was with you and Dad—it was just so much like *home*. I can't explain it—but I remember I told you about it—there was a deep resonance somehow."

My mother snorted with disgust.

"It's not as if we discuss religion or anything," I said quickly, "but it just so happens that most of my closest friends are Jews. I can't help noticing it." My mother was chasing a bit of cranberry

27

relish around her plate with a piece of roll. When she finally captured it, she chewed thoughtfully. "And most people assume I'm Jewish," I added. "It's always a surprise to them when I tell them I'm not." I named some of my closest friends in recent years: Kari and Allen, Sue Klein, Annie and David.

"Oh, I suppose next you're going to tell me that Jean Sacks is Jewish," my mother spat out.

I wasn't prepared for the hostility in her voice. Jean Sacks was my boss. African-American.

"I'm not saying my *only* friends are Jewish," I said quietly. "It's just that—"

"What about Paula?" my mother said, glaring at me. "She's not Jewish!"

"Yes," I agreed, adding irrelevantly, "but she married a Jew."

As soon as I said this I winced. I was undermining my own argument by descending to a finger count of the number of my friends who were Jewish and Gentile. Instead, to my surprise, it gave my mother pause.

"Yes, that's true," my mother said thoughtfully, pondering the fact of Paula's marriage to a Jew, as if this somehow compromised Paula's non-Jewish identity. "You're right about that." Amazingly, this seemed to carry great weight with my mother. She thought about it awhile and remained quiet.

Oh, I thought, what a ridiculous argument.

We finished our turkey in silence, and my mother returned to the kitchen and brought out the salad.

She placed the bowl on the table, a bit too abruptly, and it teetered before righting itself. The serving utensils jumped against the wooden sides of the bowl with a dull clatter. "What difference does it make!?" my mother suddenly exclaimed. "What difference does it make?" She was shaking with anger. I stared at her, dumbfounded.

"What difference does it make whether you're Jewish or Catholic or Protestant or Buddhist?!" she screamed. "Who cares?"

I felt my eyes widen. Across from me, thin flames from our dinner candles gleamed in the framed Emilio Greco sketches on the wall. There was a story behind those drawings, but I didn't understand it yet. I looked at my mother, unable to speak. "I care," I said finally, "*I* care."

"Then I've failed as a mother!" she cried. "I've failed! I brought you up to be tolerant, not to size everyone up by their religion or color, or—" Her voice broke, and she exploded with emotion, tears streaming.

"I *am* tolerant," I tried to reassure her, suddenly aware of how ridiculous this sounded. My father and sister waited to see how I would dig myself out of this. Dinners in our family are often a kind of spectator sport.

"Oh, look—I'm sorry, Mom," I said. "I didn't mean to upset you. Really, I'm sorry." I was stunned by her reaction. I vowed never to raise the subject again.

The following evening my mother showed Lara and me a postcard written by Dad's mother in 1943, shortly before she was killed. We'd never seen this card before. Zosia had brought it with her on a recent visit.

The postcard was addressed to Zosia in Rome, and dated April 29, 1943. It was post-marked *Galicia*. A twelve-pfennig German postage stamp clung to the right-hand corner—Hitler's face. His right profile, with a bright ear against dark hair, a stern expression on his lips. His hair combed over the left forehead, his mustache short, his cheeks haggard. Below this stamp was Zosia's Rome address, written in calligraphy with blue ink by Dad's mother. I picture her now, putting pen to paper, and I see my father—the steel-blue eyes, the slight smile, the pride with which he carves letters like rhapsodies of pen and ink.

The return address on the postcard was filled out by Dad's Ukrainian music teacher: *Anya Karelewicz, Musiklehrerin, in Buczacz, Galizien, Frankengasse Nr 15.* Beneath her address were various stamps and signatures of censors, as well as the stamp of the Italian censor: *Commissione Provinciale di Censura.* On the reverse side the message, first written in the elegant handwriting of my grandmother Helen, and then an additional few lines added by Anya.

Kochana Pani! my grandmother writes.

Dear Madam:
On the 28th of this month, I received the greetings sent to me along with the news from you indicating that you are in good

30

health and think of us. So I take this oppor-
tunity to convey to you all my sincerest greet-
ings. You must have passed Easter
happily...but I am not complaining since
the holiday went pleasantly and quietly here.
Now here, too, it is getting warmer and we
expect a warm spring.

If it does not cause any great inconve-
nience, I would appreciate a rosary or a
similar item consecrated by the church in
Rome. Even without it I have you in my
prayers and wish you good health.

I kiss you all.

Beneath, scribbled in blue ink, are a few words from Dad's music teacher:

I, too, include my best wishes and again
beg for news. Have you heard anything
about Kovik?

Anya K.

The next night, back in Boston, I couldn't sleep. At midnight it finally dawned on me. The postcard was proof: My grandmother was Jewish. My grandmother, a woman named Helen Buchman under the Nazi occupation, was writing a postcard that would be read and stamped by the censor, writing for a shred of hope, the trappings of a Catholic cover. She must have been desperate by then. I didn't begin to know the whole story. But the card, for all its Catholic dressing, was the clearest proof we had that she was Jewish. I called Lara up.

"Lara," I said, "you know that postcard? Dad's Mom was Jewish. I know it. And you know what? She didn't die in a bomb as Mom and Dad always said. She was killed at Auschwitz. Or on the way to Auschwitz. Or somewhere. She was killed by the Nazis, I'm sure of it. If you write to the Red Cross, I bet you anything she was killed in Auschwitz, not in her hometown. That's why Dad never found her grave. She wasn't bombed in Buczacz."

I was right, and I was wrong. All I knew was Auschwitz. I had a lot to learn.

3

The phone was ringing when I came in the door three months later. I'd spent the day arguing with lawyers, insisting that they could not bill more than twenty-four hours in one day, but no one seemed to believe me. "Helen, it's true," Lara said when I picked up the phone. "I just got a packet of documents in the mail. Our grandparents were Jewish. You and I are Jewish."

It was raining outside in Boston, a bitter, gray March drizzle—they'd been predicting flash floods for the Cape—and I was standing in the kitchen, still holding my soggy black briefcase in one hand, watching a delicate ring of rainwater drip from the hem of my coat to the oak floor.

"...this rabbi in Israel," Lara was saying. "After Christmas I wrote to Yad Vashem—it's a Holocaust museum in Israel—and their rabbi sent me these documents, pages of testimony. Mom and Dad's parents were gassed by the Nazis in 1943."

It took a moment for her words to sink in. I cradled the receiver against my ear and closed my eyes. "You're sure?" I asked. Slowly I leaned over the kitchen counter, resting my elbows on the white Formica. Excitement flushed my face, and something else—a sense of horror slowly seeped through.

"...Mendel Goldberg," she said. "He was Mom's cousin. He survived. He wrote down what happened to her parents. They were gassed at a camp called Belzec."

I pushed the mail aside and struggled to concentrate, to line the words up in a neat row that led directly from Lara to me, but I kept stumbling over them. I began to rock back and forth, slowly grinding my elbows into the counter.

"So what...did you find out?"

"It was one of the worst camps," she said. "I've been reading about it. Our grandparents were gassed in May 1943. May 23, 1943."

I had never heard of Belzec. I tried to focus on the idea that they were Jewish, that I was Jewish. In spite of everything, I felt a strange surge of elation.

"One hundred percent?" I asked. "We're one hundred percent Jewish? All of them?"

"All of them," Lara said. "One hundred

percent. There isn't a single non-Jew in the family."

"So why didn't they say anything?"

"I don't know, Helen. It's incredible. Mom and Dad are Jewish. You and I are Jewish. They've been hiding everything. Everything."

I tried to say something, to fill the space, to tell her I was with her. "Wow," I said.

"I'll make copies of this stuff and send it to you. It's really—it's hard going, reading these pages of testimony, I'm warning you."

I nodded. Pages of testimony. Were they court records? Witness statements were my métier.

"There's two different witnesses," Lara said. "This guy Mendel Goldberg, who lives in Brooklyn. And a woman, Elsa Sonderling, in Israel. We've got to get in touch with these other survivors."

Mendel Goldberg and Elsa Sonderling. Mom never told us she had any cousins.

I hung up the phone and took off my raincoat, letting it drip over the banister. Why had they hidden this from us? I yanked open the refrigerator and scanned the shelves, half-expecting to find the answer in a carton of left-over moo shu pork. Everything was just the same as it had always been, I told myself, except suddenly everything was different. HAPPY EAT! said the red lettering on the carton. I flipped it open, examined the contents, and replaced it in the refrigerator.

I had been living my life with flawed vision,

stumbling in the dark, bumping into things I hadn't realized were there. No one acknowledged anything. Yet each time I walked into my parents' house, I fell over something, or dropped into something, a cavernous silence, an unspoken, invisible danger. Now everything sprang into sharp focus. My parents were transformed from unfortunate bystanders, swept up in the horror of war, to targeted victims, specifically hunted for annihilation. This line of distinction was the tightrope that my parents had been walking for fifty years.

In the living room I sank into the black leather chair. Drumbeat of rain on the sidewalk, occasional slosh of car wheels moving down the street. I was stunned by the magnitude of the secret—its endurance, its stubbornness. After all my parents had been through— the war, the camps, the escapes, the lies—perhaps they wanted to protect me from it. Or perhaps they wanted to protect themselves, to put it behind them forever.

Still, I was exhilarated by the revelation. I had to admit, I wanted to be Jewish—if for no other reason than because it simply made *sense*. I began to recognize myself as a person with roots and a past, with a family history, with an identity. The stories of my childhood suddenly took on new meaning—everything seemed to be shifting, an underground movement of tectonic plates slowly clicking into place, finally *fitting*.

But an unsettling feeling gnawed at me

when I thought about my parents. What had kept them in hiding all these years? What had made them hide from me?

Lara Express-Mailed me a copy of the rabbi's packet—crude handwritten statements in Hebrew and Yiddish, listing names, dates, and locations. Here, at last, was our family. Zalman Schmuel Tannen and his wife, Basia. Their children Moshe (my grandfather!) and Mendel and Schlomo and Rivka and Zhenia— names of people whom Lara and I had never even heard of before. We never imagined we'd had so many relatives. The pages, scribbled in Yiddish and translated by the rabbi, described how our grandparents had been killed; our great-aunts, uncles, cousins, everyone.

Jackpot, the rabbi had written on the pages of testimony next to the names of my grandfather and his brothers, nephews, and nieces. Jackpot.

How do you tell your parents you know how their parents were killed? Post-traumatic stress was Lara's specialty, for which growing up in our household had been excellent hands-on training. "We can't just rip off their new identity," Lara told me over the phone. "If we confront them with the truth, it could shatter them."

"Okay," I said. "Well, maybe we should start with these witnesses, then. The two survivors who wrote these pages of testimony."

The rabbi had already looked up Elsa Sonderling in the Tel Aviv phone book, but there was no one listed. *She may be dead already,* he wrote us; *she filled out these pages so long ago. Move quickly,* he added, *most of these survivors are in their eighties, or older. They are dying out, and with them, the information about your family.*

Lara searched for Mendel Goldberg in Brooklyn phone books, without success. But I seemed to remember a Mendel from my childhood. An old man with horn-rimmed Coke-bottle glasses, thin wild gray hair, and pants that he wore too high on his waist. He was short and wheezy, and half blind, or so it seemed to me. I thought he wore a yarmulke, although I might have been wrong about that. I remembered him walking down our front steps with difficulty, first pausing at the top of them, staring silently, as if reflecting on the Talmudic meaning of descent. He came to visit us on Glendale Road when I was very young, but I had no idea that he was family.

Now I called up my mother and chatted for a while, trying gradually to steer the conversation toward the past. "I was trying to remember this guy," I said as nonchalantly as I could, "Mendel Somebody. Who was Mendel?"

The conversation seemed to skip a beat, and then my mother quickly said, "Oh, he's dead."

My heart sank. "Mmm," I said, "but who was he?"

"Oh, no one, a friend of a friend, no one."

"I remember him."

"No, you wouldn't have known him. I'm sure you don't."

"But I do! I remember he came to visit us at Glendale Road."

"No, no, he never came to Glendale Road," my mother insisted. "He lived in Brooklyn, I think. He came to visit me once in Irvington." My mother spoke quickly, and I sensed an edge in her voice, an impatience. "He heard that I'd escaped from Lvov in 1942," she said, "and so he came to Irvington to ask me if I knew anything about his relatives. But I didn't know anything, so that was it. I couldn't help him. It was before you were born."

"Bingo," I told Lara, calling her back. "But stop looking up Mendel in all the phone books. Mendel is dead. Mom said so."

A few months later the Red Cross completed our search. Mendel, it turned out, had been a rabbi. My mother's cousin, son of her father's brother, Mendel had been an Orthodox rabbi.

Lara and I spent days and nights on the phone, examining our lives from every angle, finding clues and hints scattered across our childhood and adolescence. We plunged into history books and met with survivors, historians, and rabbis— black-capped, neckless men with beards to their navels, and Reform rabbis in Yves Saint Laurent and fishnet stockings. I called Lara every day and we exchanged information, ricocheted reactions; we were bubbling with ideas and leads.

In our separate cities Lara and I started going to synagogue on Saturdays. Embarrassed by our ignorance, we stood blankly, listening, watching, wondering whether we would ever feel comfortable in temple. We couldn't read the language; we couldn't understand the words. We felt left out of a world.

Some things, of course, were familiar. Lara and I laughed with recognition: the challah bread of our youth (Zosia had always made us two braided loaves); the smoked fish that my father loved; potato pancakes. The matzos that we had always eaten at Easter. The fact that we had never gone up for Communion in church after that first time. And we had never gone to Confession, a Catholic ritual that my mother had always held in the highest contempt. Confession, she'd said, had enabled Catholics to commit atrocities throughout history with a clear conscience.

After some debate Lara and I decided to contact our parents' friends the Janiczeks, now in their late seventies. Twenty years had passed since we had attended their daughter Susie's wedding celebration of Holocaust survivors. Our parents, we knew, had lost touch with the Janiczeks in recent years, but when Lara called Dr. Janiczek to arrange a meeting, he seemed delighted to hear from us.

Lara and I met at the Detroit airport on a clear April evening and drove to the Janiczeks' suburban home, a low-slung ranch house that looked like a bedroom slipper.

Over dinner we told them how we had discovered that our parents were Jewish.

Mrs. Janiczek shot a glance at her husband and leaned over the table, pouring coffee. Her perfectly manicured fingernails gleamed fire-engine red.

"Have you told your parents?" Dr. Janiczek asked.

We shook our heads. Dr. Janiczek rubbed his chin thoughtfully and looked out the window, his smoky-blue eyes glistening.

"We always worried for you girls," Mrs. Janiczek said carefully. "We always wondered how you girls would take it if you ever found out." She glanced again at her husband, who seemed lost in thought.

"Then you knew they were Jewish," Lara said. "You knew all along."

Dr. Janiczek nodded. "Yes," he said quietly, "of course we knew, although none of us ever spoke of it." His wife cleared the plates from the table, and Lara jumped up to help, but Mrs. Janiczek motioned her to sit.

"I think that's why your parents and we were so close," Dr. Janiczek continued. "I think they trusted us. They knew that we knew, you see? And they knew we would never tell." He paused, stirring a dot of cream into his coffee. A tiny strand of white swirled around the cup like a pinwheel.

"And as far as we were concerned," he continued, "we respected their wishes. We never questioned their decision. After what we had been through, we understood." He shook his head slowly.

I looked at Lara, who was folding her paper napkin into a tiny accordion. "So what did they tell you, that they were Catholic?"

Dr. Janiczek nodded, then tipped his head back and drained his coffee cup. "One time," he said, "I had friends visiting me in Irvington, other survivors who were from your mother's hometown." He turned from me to Lara, raising his eyebrows. "They knew your mother's parents; they were from the same neighborhood. And my friends told me, 'But they're Orthodox!'

"Your grandmother," Dr. Janiczek said slowly, looking me in the eye, "shaved her head and wore a wig! You understand?"

Lara was nodding. "Orthodox women wear a wig after they marry," she explained to me. "The most religious women shave their heads."

I looked at her with surprise. When had she picked this up?

"But," Dr. Janiczek continued, "I told my friends, 'No, the Bocards are Catholic.' And my friends were outraged that your parents were pretending not to be Jewish, and I remember I got very angry with them. 'What difference does it make?' I told them. 'This is their choice, leave them alone! What business is it of ours?' "

He fell silent for a moment. "You see, I have a great deal of respect for your parents, for both your parents. They have had very hard lives.

41

We have all suffered a great deal. I fought in the Warsaw Uprising, you know. My wife survived Auschwitz. We have lost everyone, everything, and the same is true with your parents. No one has a right to judge them. They did this to protect you. You must understand this," he said solemnly. "They did this for your sake, to protect you."

Lara drew a little family tree, or to be more accurate, a family twig. It had a spattering of names, half a dozen, and we began from there. We tried to find witnesses, people who had known our parents before or during the war. Mendel Goldberg was dead, and Elsa Sonderling was probably dead, but perhaps there were others. Lara and I became detectives, calling and writing around the world for a trace of our past.

During one of her conferences in Washington, Lara went to the Library of Congress and photocopied maps of prewar Poland and street maps of my parents' hometowns: Lvov, Busk, Buczacz. She found maps of provincial Galicia before, during, and after the Soviet occupation.

Researchers at the Holocaust Memorial Museum gave her the name of a survivor in Chicago, Saul Rosenfeld, who was from our father's hometown. I called him up. An energetic man in his late seventies, Saul spoke a galloping English. "Kovik Buchman, Kovik Buchman," he muttered. "I don't know....It's been so long."

He asked for dates, a description, details. "Ah, yes!" he said. "Of course! The violinist! I remember hearing him play in the movie theater! He was quite a smart kid, your father, he was in *Gymnasium,* right? Yes, yes, I went to shul with him! He was without a father. He went everywhere with his mother. She was a beautiful woman, with a round face and blue eyes. And he, too, he had a round face. And he was very tall, yes, I remember him!"

Saul Rosenfeld told me about my father's hometown. "Before the war," he said, "there were ten thousand Jews in Buczacz. Most of the Jews were rounded up and shot in the Fodor. And the rest were rounded up and taken to Belzec. Only one hundred survived the war. And of those, only fifty are still living. We are a tight group, the Buczaczers— we get together in Israel."

Why had my father cut himself off from this handful of survivors?

"...a Pole named Altinsky," Saul was saying, "owned the movie theater. He employed a Jewish boy to run the movies. And he hired your father to play the violin as background music. He was a good man, Altinsky. He even hid some Jews during the war. Me, I hid in the Jewish cemetery, with my mother and brother." Saul paused. "We hid in the graves."

In the background I heard the whistle of a teakettle. "My mother was killed by the Germans," he said. "Don't go to Buczacz. In Buczacz there are only tears. Go to Israel. In Israel you will celebrate."

"Should we tell our father?"

He took a deep breath. "Your father will cry when you tell him," he said. "But what does it matter? He has been crying inside all these years. When you tell him, tell him I remember him. Tell him Saul Rosenfeld remembers him!"

Lara and I sent Rosenfeld our photographs. He wrote us and called a few times. "I feel we are family," he said tearfully. "We are all Buczaczers. You will be my nieces. I will be your uncle."

He gave us other names and I began dialing.

"Listen, honey," Mala Scheiman, another survivor from Buczacz, told me, "I raised my children in yeshiva. My son is a rabbi in Colorado....He says I didn't tell him enough about the Holocaust. But I told him enough. Listen, sweetheart, maybe your mother can't tell you because she had a very, very tough time. That's why. But I'm touched that you're doing this. Roots, roots, the tree, sure, I know. What else can you do?"

4

My mother's coffee cake lay in ruins on the serving tray. A damning trail of powdered sugar led directly from it to my plate. Dad had risen from the table, bundled the newspaper under his good arm like a surfboard, and retreated to the bedroom to read.

I felt Lara's green eyes fasten on me from

across the table; *Get on with it,* she seemed to say. We had rehearsed this moment for months, but she could see I was stalling. A Boston rabbi had warned me not to confront my parents with our Jewish identity. "Don't tell them," he had urged me. "It could destroy them! At their age...the trauma may be too great, and you'll only make your parents relive the Holocaust all over again."

"Mom," I finally said.

My mother's lips were pressed together in a minus sign. She seemed to sense what was coming; her eyes glared with a ferocity that unnerved me.

"Mom," I repeated, "we—Lara and I—we wanted to talk with you, and maybe—"

"What about?" my mother asked impatiently. Her wrists bore down on the table edge, then slowly slid forward: a boxer's stance. Her mouth was set hard, jaw clenched.

I took a deep breath. "Well," I said, "about your past. We wanted to—"

"Ah, no!" she said, pushing back her chair and throwing up her hands. "I told you, I don't want to talk about that! I told you! It's too painful for me! I cannot do it!" She jumped up from the table and marched across the living room. For a moment it seemed she would blast right through the opposite wall. I shot a glance at Lara, who shook her head and sighed.

My mother was rummaging through her desk. "I want to show you something," she called, very businesslike. "I cut it out of the

Times the other day. I want you to read this."

"Mom," I said as she strode back to the table, carrying the article in her hand. "Mom, look, we'll read it, but we still want to talk with you."

My mother ceremoniously slapped the paper down on the dining room table and tapped it angrily with her index finger. "Read this," she commanded. "It's exactly how I feel about all this business of the past, all this cultural baggage. Read it."

We glanced at the article, a clipping from the Sunday *Times* magazine. CULTURAL BAGGAGE read the title in bold black letters.

"We'll read the article," Lara said, "but we need to talk to you, okay?"

My mother sat down and read the article over herself. "Look here," she said, "you see, she feels exactly the same way I do! Until I saw this I was beginning to think I was crazy! But here, she says the same thing! Who needs all this *balooney* about the past?" A bullet of saliva hung at the edge of her lip and shot off with her next words. "Enough with the past! Forget about the past! Look forward! Enjoy today! Think about tomorrow!"

"Listen, Mom," I said, "we've done a lot of research, and we don't want to hide this from you. We know—"

At that moment my father absentmindedly wandered into the dining room. He took one look at our faces and froze in his tracks. His eyebrows shot up, and for a moment it seemed he would turn on his heel and run out of the room. Instead, quietly, he slipped into the seat

46

next to Lara. I tried to continue as if nothing had happened, but my father's look of alarm registered in the pit of my stomach.

"All our lives," I said, "we've sensed that something just didn't fit, it didn't make sense. And, well, finally…it's—this is all we have, you and Dad and—" I hadn't realized it would be so hard to tell my parents that we knew we were Jewish. It seemed like an accusation.

"I wrote away for information," Lara said, "and I got back documentation about our family. We know what happened to your parents. We know what happened to Dad's mother."

"What happened?" my mother suddenly cried. Her hands started trembling with a terrible urgency, while her face remained frozen—a wide-eyed mask of incomprehension. "Then you know more than I do!" she exclaimed.

Lara nodded slowly, confused by my mother's sudden shift from anger to bewilderment.

"Tell me," my mother cried. "What happened? I don't even know what happened to my parents!" She turned desperately from Lara to me and back again, her hands shaking. "What happened?"

I hadn't been prepared for this. I had expected my mother to refuse to talk about it; I had been prepared for her to deny it, to get angry, to scoff at me and dismiss it, but I did not expect her to beg us to tell her how her parents were killed.

"Tell me!" my mother repeated. "What happened to them?"

I screwed up my courage, looked directly in my mother's eyes, and spoke as calmly as I could: "We found out," I said evenly, "that your parents were gassed in Belzec."

My sentence dropped like a bomb into a terrible silence. I bit my tongue. I hadn't meant to be so blunt, so harsh. Lara kicked me under the table, and with growing panic I waited for my mother's reaction. Seconds ticked by, and I was consumed by an excruciating sense of guilt that I had just shattered my mother's world.

But my mother did not react. She stared at me with the same puzzled look on her face, as if I hadn't spoken. "Tell me what happened to them," she repeated, hands outstretched.

I kept quiet, shaken. I can't continue with this, I thought. I can't bear to do this.

I glanced at my father sitting perfectly still across the table from me, listening closely. His body was hunched forward, eyebrows raised. I knew he'd heard what I said about Mom's parents, but his eyes didn't meet mine.

"I don't even know what happened to my parents!" Mom cried. "Tell me!"

"Look, Mom," Lara said, reaching for her hand. "We have a lot of information, we'll go over everything with you, okay?" She signaled to me with her eyes, and I remembered what she had told me earlier over the phone. "Trauma victims," she had said, "are splintered people, and you have to be careful. It's got to be done gently."

My mother looked attentive now, cooperative, like a good student.

"We have documents," Lara explained. "We have testimony of witnesses, other survivors."

"Who?" my mother asked defiantly.

Lara took a deep breath. "Elsa Sonderling."

My mother leaned forward, trying to catch the name.

"Elsa Sonderling," I repeated.

My mother shook her head blankly. "No," she said with frank openness, "never heard of her. I don't know who she is." She looked across to my father, to see if he recognized the name.

My father also shook his head.

"And Mendel Goldberg," Lara added, turning to my mother. "He was your cousin."

"Yes, but he wouldn't know a thing!" my mother blurted out. "He was in Russia during the war! He missed the whole thing! He wasn't even there!"

My father shrugged with exaggerated calm. "They're lies," he said dismissively.

"We've talked to survivors," Lara persisted. "We've found people who remember you, people from your hometown."

My father's eyebrows jumped, planting furrows in his forehead, but he remained silent and glanced at my mother.

"We don't want to hide this from you," Lara continued. "We wanted to let you know that we know, we understand. We admire

49

you. We're proud of you. If you ever are able to talk about it, we want to talk with you."

My father crossed his long, bony legs and took a deep breath, his signal that he would now deliver a lecture. I was momentarily distracted by the sheer length of his left leg, which rose like a wrecking crane from under the table, swung across the rear end of the dog lying on the carpet, and finally settled on top of his other knee. "We have two options," he said pedantically, pointing to the fingers on his left hand. "We can either confirm this or deny it. Either way you won't know whether we are telling the truth, so it won't matter what we say."

He shrugged, having made his point, as if there were nothing further to be said.

"Dad," I said. "Look, this is not a game of wits. We've done this research because it was important to us. We needed to know—"

"And what difference does it make?" my mother snapped angrily.

"For Lara and me, things are starting to make sense."

My father's lower lip clasped his upper lip—the same as it did whenever he studied a game of chess, working out his strategy while his opponent cautiously moved his piece. I could see my father was already planning his next move.

"All our lives," I said, "there's been something that just didn't fit. This explains so much about who we are, our childhood, our family. We appreciate you so much more."

"Don't try to tell me you're doing this for me!" my mother burst out. "You're not doing this for me!"

"Mom," I said, "we just want to be able to speak openly with each other, drop the barriers between us. We're all grown up. We appreciate what you've been through—"

"What difference does the past make?" she cried. "You are who you are today, that's all that matters! Forget about the past! Look forward! Live for today!"

"It's not that simple," I said. "We need to know who we are, where we come from. For me, it's—"

"Ach." My mother waved her hand in disgust. "Everybody has to jump on the bandwagon," she said. "All these young people, digging, digging for their roots—it's just another American fad, and you girls are stupid enough to get swept up—"

"You know why I finally wrote to Yad Vashem?" Lara interrupted, looking steadily into my mother's eyes. "You know what finally triggered it? After all those months of getting names and dates of relatives?"

My mother nodded with irritation. "Yes," she said impatiently, "well?"

"Because I had a dream," Lara said. "I dreamed that your mother came to me and told me I had to find out. She told me I had to do this research, find out what had happened to her, to the family. And that's why I sent off the letters to Yad Vashem and to the American Red Cross."

"And so?" my mother demanded. "What has it changed?" Outside, the day was yawning bright with sun. It was ten-thirty, Saturday morning. Rosebuds pushed their way into the sunlight. The lawn glowed green. The magnolia tree had burst into pink-and-white blossoms, and petals lay scattered around its skirts.

"Nothing," Lara said quietly, her hand resting on my mother's forearm. "It hasn't changed anything." She took a deep breath and continued. "But you know," she said cautiously, studying my mother's eyes, "we're thinking of going to Jerusalem."

My mother didn't miss a beat. "Don't waste your money!" she snorted. "I've been to Jerusalem!" She waved her hand with disgust. "If you want to know about our roots, you don't need to go to Israel! Right here, go to Brooklyn! The Lubavitchers, in Brooklyn!"

Lara's face melted with amazement. "I've read about the Lubavitchers," she said brightly. "Yes, I've heard about them!"

This was too much. I couldn't believe my ears. In one instant my mother denied everything with such force and vehemence that she couldn't even hear our words. The next instant she was essentially insisting that she is Hasidic, Orthodox, *Ostjude*.

"There's a big debate nowadays," Lara said energetically, "about whether the old traditions ought to continue—the long beards and hats, the long black coats—"

"Yes!" my mother agreed. "It's so ridiculous! So stupid!"

The sun sparkled through the windows and the grass gleamed. We talked for nearly three hours. "Exactly," my mother said, satisfied that we had finally understood her point. "Forget about the past."

For the next two months Lara and I were on the phone, piecing together the puzzle. The Buchmans grew with each new letter from the rabbi. The mail was full of death. We found out we had aunts and uncles we'd never heard of. Starved in the ghetto; shot in the Tartokower Forest. Gassed at Belzec. Those little pale blue air-letter envelopes from Yad Vashem sent chills down my spine.

Through various connections I contacted a survivor in New York who was organizing a trip to Galicia for survivors and their families. Four days in Lvov, four days in Tarnopol, with side trips to people's hometowns. Lara and I immediately booked our reservations to join the group.

Mom, in the meantime, was rattling through some hard months of sleepless nights and sudden flashbacks. She kept falling into holes, as she put it later. Without any warning she suddenly found herself back in the ghetto, under the Germans, making up stories to save her life, spinning a tale of herself, shifting colors and sequences to suit her needs. She had invented herself a hundred times over by the time the war was over; it was nothing to sew a new identity onto the old ones and present it to an unsuspecting America. Compared to the Russians and Poles, Ukrainians and Italians, Americans were a cinch.

But once Lara and I started chipping away at her facade, my mother was flooded with memories. Events she had wiped out for fifty years sprang back to life, she later told me. Even her childhood drifted back to her with painful clarity—her family's poverty, their constant concern for food, their cramped living quarters, without running water, electricity, or heat.

Lara and I grew worried. My mother was taken over by nightmares. She stopped eating and grew tinier by the day. Lara and I started calling her once a week to check in on her. She was tense, on edge. Her daughters were playing with fire, stepping right into the flames of the Holocaust with our goofy American gumshoed sneakers. Hot on the track of our discovery, we were dragging her back across the burning coals.

Finally, in June, my mother opened up a bit. "Now, look," she said testily over the phone. "I made a vow a long time ago. It involves Zosia, and I want to wait until Zosia is here with us this summer."

"Sure," I said, "of course she should be included."

"July Fourth," my mother suggested. "Zosia will already be here, and you girls come for that weekend, and we'll talk about it then."

5

A relentless, nail-biting rain battered my parents' house. Zosia, in mismatched pajamas, hovered over the stove, heating milk for her coffee. Her white hair erupted like a tornado from her head, and every so often she patted it, as if to make sure it was still there. Lara and I sat at the kitchen counter, staring out the window at chipmunks burrowing into my father's lush green lawn.

"Change in plans," my mother whispered, pulling Lara and me out of the kitchen. "I decided not to tell Zosia." We huddled in the hallway. "I don't think she can take it."

Mom glanced toward the kitchen to make sure Zosia couldn't hear. "Here's what we'll do," my mother said conspiratorially. "At noon we'll go out, just the three of us. I told Zosia we were invited to a barbecue."

Lara winced. "In the rain?" she asked.

"It's the Fourth of July," my mother said, shrugging. "Dad will stay with Zosia. All right?"

We drove to the end of the driveway, windshield wipers slapping maniacally back and forth. "Go to the Melrose shopping mall," my mother directed. "We'll talk there."

A bolt of lightning separated the sky as I nudged the car onto Glendale Road. I felt like a burglar, sneaking off with my mother and sister to talk about our dirty little history.

We sat at an orange Formica booth at the food court under blinding fluorescent lights. A gluey Muzak version of "Yesterday" piped through the air vents as if from an ironic God, and my mother launched into her story. It seemed she had rehearsed it. She spoke smoothly, in full paragraphs, for nearly four hours.

What she told us that day would eventually help me piece together the story of her life. But it would take me several more years before I could begin to understand it, to arrange it into a narrative that led from her to me. Telling her story, I discovered, is not a simple act.

When Lara and I interrupted with questions, she breezed past them. I had the uneasy feeling that huge chunks of the story were still missing, or altered, that although we were being given more information than we'd ever had before, certain topics remained taboo. Such as the issue of religion.

"How religious were you?" I asked my mother.

"Not at all!" she exclaimed. "We were completely assimilated."

"Well, did you ever go to synagogue as a child?"

"Never!" she said.

I glanced at Lara, trying to see if she bought this.

"Did you celebrate any holidays?"

"No, never," my mother insisted. "We weren't the least bit religious!"

"What about Friday night?" I persisted.

"Didn't you light candles? Did your mother?" (The rabbi had told me to ask her that.)

"No."

"Never? Not even once? You never went to synagogue for the High Holy Days? What about your father?"

She shook her head vehemently.

"Your father never set foot in a synagogue?"

"No."

Wouldn't know a synagogue if it fell on him.

"Look," Dad told me months later when we were alone in the living room, "you have to understand what Mom and Zosia left behind. They turned their backs on their faith."

"But Mom said they never even went to synagogue," I said, "they—"

My father shook his head. "Her father was Orthodox," he said solemnly. "You know what that means? *Orthodox*."

Long beard. Black coat. The works.

"As a youth, Zosia was an active Zionist," my father continued, "very deeply committed—at one time, she nearly emigrated to Palestine. You have to understand, Mom and Zosia turned their backs on their faith, on their family."

Soon after the Fourth of July Lara told our parents that we were going to Ukraine for two weeks with a group of Holocaust survivors.

"No!" my mother gasped over the telephone. "You mustn't go! There's nothing there!" She sounded desperate. *"No!"*

It took several weeks for her to realize she

could not prevent us from going. Finally she and my father reluctantly agreed to go over prewar Polish maps of their hometowns with us.

Lara and I flew home and spread our maps across our parents' picnic table. With a strange mixture of fear and excitement, our parents pointed out their homes and schools, the streets they'd walked as children, the parks where they'd held hands as teenagers.

6

Our group leader stepped off the bus on the outskirts of my mother's hometown. Built like the Empire State Building topped with a cloud of white hair, Leo moved slowly, with a pronounced limp, but seemed to cover twice as much ground as everyone else. When he smiled, his eyes gleamed with a warmth that could roast chestnuts.

"The water in the ravine was red," he said, pointing at the drop-off to our left. Armed guards stared at us from wooden towers of the Janowska camp as our group walked along a narrow ledge beside the original brick walls topped with coils of barbed wire. At the lookout point over the ravine sat a few squalid shacks, a pigsty with rotting garbage, and two or three muddy pigs. Two shirtless Ukrainian workmen stared at us, scowling. Dust-colored pants with questionable closings drooped around their bony hips, knees worn dark and shiny.

Our group consisted of eight families—three generations of survivors, ranging in age from fifteen to ninety-four. Lara and I were the only members of the group unaccompanied by our parents, which inspired the survivors to claim us as their own, tell us their stories, and lecture us on the ignorance of young people.

"Two hundred thousand Jews were killed here," Leo said. "Every day, they took prisoners out to the sands there"—he pointed at dirt cliffs in the ravine— "and shot them." He kicked a rusted beer can with his good leg and limped on. "Actually," he said, looking around with an assessing eye, "actually, they've cleaned this area up quite a bit since I was here last year. It's much improved."

Suddenly a frenzied high-pitched shriek behind us. Henry Klein, a stocky survivor from Dniepa, had burst into wild, piercing sobs. Turning away from us, he began to howl Kaddish, his voice shrill. His children stood by, stunned.

He was doubled over now, hands on his knees, yelping. His brother had been killed in the sands in the ravine fifty years ago. Our group swayed on the narrow perch of land, on piles of decomposing garbage. Heads bent, we stood in agonized silence, unable to look and unable to walk away. It seemed as if the whole wide planet had been sucked into the knife of that ravine. The air filled with Henry's screams, and he clasped his children around him and cried, "This is all there is! So that you children will know and live right! It's all there is!"

Lara and I met the only surviving Jew in my father's hometown—a tough, square-built woman with deep lines in her forehead and steel-gray eyebrows that met over the bridge of her nose. She was too young to remember Dad, but she took us to the Jewish cemetery on a hill above the town. Dozens of tall tombstones leaned among charred remains of burned garbage overlooking a deep valley.

"Buczacz was a Jewish town," the woman kept telling us. "Over half of the town was Jewish."

The cemetery was quite large, and as we trudged up and down rows of broken tombstones, knee-deep in weeds, we realized how hopeless it would be to try to find our great-grandmother's stone.

"Here is where they lined the Jews up and shot them," the woman said, pointing above us. "They fell down the hill, past where we're standing."

Lara and I were getting used to this story, a never-ending refrain throughout all of Ukraine. Every little hamlet, every little town, has its own desecrated cemetery, its site of mass killings, its huge mass graves. Lara and I climbed the steep hill, sending the woman back to the car to wait for us. The soil was wet with reddish clay and mined with scores of nettles. We cleared a spot and laid three gladiolus at the point where the Jews were killed—which, of course, was not where Erna Rosenbaum was buried, nor where our grandmother Helen Rosenbaum was killed. Nevertheless, we allowed our grief to mix and let history be general and geography generous. This was, after all, the site of death of our family, and we commemorated it with our flowers and stinging flesh.

The Ukrainian trucker we met on the outskirts of town offered to show us the Fodor, another place where Jews were killed. He climbed into the backseat of our taxi, and we bumped and jostled along an unmarked clay road until the mud got too deep. We walked the rest of the way through a beautiful forest— thin-trunked trees flashed their leaves like a halo of green. The Ukrainian led us deeper and deeper into the woods. Finally he stopped and pointed at an enormous rectangular pit in the ground. Lara reeled backward. A memorial stone, cracked in two, lay on the ground next to the pit. Immediately beside the stone was a pile of human bones—the femur and parts of the pelvis.

"Here," he said.

When we staggered off the plane at the airport back home, Dad was standing on the sidewalk, alone against the pitch-black sky. It was 1:15 A.M. With his good arm he helped us heave our bags into the trunk and drove us home. Mom was waiting for us in bathrobe and slippers, proffering heated broccoli soup and rolls. Zosia was asleep in my bed.

Cautiously, anxiously, they asked for news of Buczacz and Busk, of Lvov, their homes, their schools. "I'm glad I didn't go," Mom said, but she sounded uncertain.

A few days later we showed them our slides of Lvov. "Oh, that was our grade school!" Zosia called out. "The Sobieskego School! If you stand at that corner there"—she jumped up and touched the screen to point out the building—"your friend Tanya lived right there," she said to my mother, "in that apartment with the little balcony on the second floor, remember?"

My mother studied the screen. "Yes!" she exclaimed, jumping up and running to the screen. "And right here, this is where I turned left to walk to my *Gymnasium*!"

Her face broke into an excited grin. She pointed out buildings that had been cafés and boutiques during her teenage years. "Right here, on the ground floor of the Intourist Hotel at Platz Mariacki," she cried, "remember that café, Zosia? Oh, yes, and over there—there used to be a huge synagogue, the Goldene Rose, topped with an enormous round dome."

Then she found the small street on which their friends, the wealthy Blumenthal family, had lived. "Remember I told you about them?" she said. "They took Dad in under the Russians. And then we tried to hide them under the Germans...."

She motioned us forward. "Enough of Lvov," she said brusquely. "What about Busk?"

We changed the slide tray and showed pictures of the resort where she'd spent her summers as a child. "No!" she cried, horrified. "It's a different town. It can't be! It used to be so beautiful, with gardens everywhere, flowers and—"

When the slides of the Busk cemetery flashed on the screen, Mom and Zosia gasped. "Enough," my mother said tersely.

Lara flipped on the lights. Zosia slipped off to bed without a word.

After packing up the slides I found my father in the other room. "Dad," I said, "a man called me this morning, someone who knows you. He went to high school with you in Buczacz, and he wants to see you. He lives nearby, in Dobb's Crossing."

My father's eyebrows went up in amazement, but he said nothing.

"When Lara and I went to your *Gymnasium* in Buczacz, I left my business card with the headmaster. Apparently a few days later this classmate of yours showed up at the school. He hadn't been back in fifty years—he emigrated to the States in 1949."

My father stared at me. "What's his name?" he finally whispered.

"Stefan Rezywyszki."

My father did not react at first. Then very slowly, his head began to nod. "Rezywyszki," he said, with a mixture of disappointment and relief. "Yes, I remember him. He was a Ukrainian. But a very decent fellow. Yes, I would like to talk to him."

The next morning I woke to the sound of Dad's voice, excited, at the telephone stand, speaking in Ukrainian to his high-school classmate.

"What does Zosia think of our trip to Ukraine?" I asked my mother later in the kitchen. "Don't you think she has some inkling that we know we're Jewish, that we understand what happened?"

"*No!*" my mother whispered. "No, she mustn't find out! I told her you simply wanted to go see our hometowns, where we were from."

I shrugged. "But it's obvious we went with a group of Jewish survivors," I said. "I mean, they're all in the pictures, with their yarmulkes, bent over Hebrew gravestones. She must know we're on to something. Doesn't she suspect—"

My mother interrupted by raising her hand, as if in a classroom. I stopped talking to let her speak, but she didn't lower her arm. She smiled and nodded, then rolled up the sleeve on her wrist with her other hand. "See this?" she said. "I have no number. I wasn't in the camps. I was never in Auschwitz." Her pale forearm was still raised, like a white banner.

I waited for her to finish, but she grew more desperate, her voice quivering. Tears came to her eyes. "I'm not a survivor!" she cried, shaking her arm, pointing to her smooth, unblemished wrist. "You see? I have no numbers! I'm not a survivor!"

PART
Two

7

Over the next several months I gradually pieced together the story of my family: from my mother, anecdotes stripped of context, shrouded in mystery; from libraries, museums, and other survivors, I was able to fill in and add color to my mother's outline. And so the story began to take shape with information from several sources, stacked high like an enormous building, overlapping layers of history and family, fact and omission.

Naively, I had hoped to arrive at an understanding of my own identity by recovering that of my grandparents. But in digging up the past I exposed the hole that lay like an enormous crater at the center of my mother's heart.

Let out the rope then, slip into the crater: back to the time when my mother was not a mother, but a child, and even before that, when her mother was not a mother or grandmother, but a child, nothing but a child.

My grandmother Sarah was born in eighteen eighty-something in Busk and raised by parents of whom I know nothing—traditional, poor, and uneducated, they scraped together a living and raised two daughters: my grandmother and her older sister, Godja, who was married and widowed before the age of twenty-five.

When my grandmother Sarah reached the age of twenty, she was matched up with a young man from a neighboring village and they were married in 1911. "In those days," my mother explained, "marriages were arranged by a broker." A year later my aunt Zosia was born in a tiny thumbnail of a shtetl not far from Lvov in the province of Galicia, famous for its poverty. Poland had ceased to exist, swallowed up by Prussia in the northwest, Austria-Hungary in the southwest, and Russia in the east. Kaiser Franz Josef was the ruler of the Habsburg dynasty, controlling the province of Galicia with scarcely the interest or means to inspire its economy. Lvov looked and smelled and sounded like a shabbier cousin of Vienna; my parents were raised on German.

And Yiddish, of course.

Three-quarters of a century ago my aunt Zosia was five years old. According to my mother she was a battery pack of pure unbridled energy, an impatient, impulsive little fireball whom my grandmother had to peel off the ceiling every five minutes. It was 1917. Zosia's father—my grandfather Moshe—had been away at war for three years already, fighting in the trenches for the Austrian emperor during the First World War.

There are no photos of Zosia as a child, but I can see her in a pair of lace-up boots, a blue-and-white dress with ruffles on the sleeves, and a conquering look of trouble on her face. Her eyes a brazen blue with just a glint of gray, a gaze of rascally delight. Falling over her forehead was a burst of sandy hair, which would darken with age and settle into a coppery red by the time she was a teenager. Mom has always said Zosia was a blonde but now admits she bleached her hair.

In the spring of 1917 the front swept past their town and back again—hordes of mud-spattered Cossacks on horseback, dizzy with vodka. They raided and looted, raped women and killed at random. Once, my mother told me, while Zosia and her mother were hanging white-sailed sheets on the line behind the house, a gray cyclone of soldiers thundered up. Bleary-eyed and unshaved, the Cossacks leapt to the ground. Their sabers clattered against muddy thighs. Horses' bellies heaved close enough for Zosia to touch. My grandmother yanked Zosia by the arm and held her close to her skirts. "Get out of here," she said, eyeing the Cossacks with cool detachment. "Go to your business, there's nothing for you here."

Perhaps it was the tone of her voice or the brutally calm look on her face that stopped them, or maybe it was her child's face peeking from behind folds in her skirt. For whatever reason, they turned and left, regaining their spirit in the street, where they chased other women—juicier, squealing women—and tore them from the arms of husbands.

By the time Zosia met her father again when she was six, she had become accustomed to this: the raids, the screams, the loss of balance, the world tilted on its side. In 1918 her father came home one day on furlough and never returned to the front. He seemed old and tired after four years of fighting. He had lost much of his hearing in the trenches, and now shells whistled to him sometimes when he was asleep at night.

The war in the east was still raging, but my grandmother convinced Moshe to desert. The family fled west to Warsaw to escape the front, which was forever approaching, receding, and returning again. It had become a familiar rhythm for the family; all their lives they'd been buffeted by waves of advancing troops. Now my grandfather waited out the war with his wife and daughter in a small rented room in Warsaw. There, in March of 1919, my mother was born.

Warsaw was an inhospitable city with scalding high prices and no jobs, and my grandparents did not speak a word of Polish. The family struggled to survive until the Russian front moved farther east; in the summer of 1919 they picked up and moved back to Galicia. But my grandmother refused to return to the shtetl. "She was a women's libber," my mother says. "She was born a century too soon." This appears to be a recurring problem in our family; everyone seems to have been born at the wrong time.

Instead, my grandmother insisted that they settle in the cultural capital of Galicia—Lvov, city of lions—surrounded by twelfth-century walls and towers. Baroque palaces and onion-domed churches gazed dreamily over elegant downtown shops, the opera house and theater.

Poland was emerging as a country for the first time in over a century: street signs turned Polish, the money changed names, and the language was a nightmare of endless nominal declensions and unpronounceable syllables. But my grandparents did their best to adjust to the new government and the new language and resumed their lives on the same land as their parents.

The family rented a tiny street-level apartment in Zamarstynowska, the poor Jewish section on the outskirts of Lvov, north of the city. Two small rooms, one in which to cook and eat, the other in which the family slept, rolling out a mattress for the two girls; my grandparents shared a narrow bed in the corner. The apartment was dark and cramped, overlooking the dingy rear alley where the sun never shone.

The neighborhood kids attended the local Yiddish grammar school in Zamarstynow, but Sarah had bigger plans for her children and marched them off to the state schools run by the Polish government. "Every morning Zosia and I had to get up very early and walk from our house in the dark all the way down Zamarstynowska Street to the public school," my mother told me. By the time she was old enough to go to grade school in 1925, Marshal Pilsudski, the leader of Poland, had ordered the removal of all religious symbols from the state schools. On the walls of each classroom, my mother could see the clear outline where the crucifix used to hang.

As children, Zosia and my mother spent their summers in the country with their aunt, Checha Godja, who lived in the little town of Busk, its gardens ablaze with flowers, freshwater streams sparkling through pine woods behind their house. Checha Godja took them into the fields to collect berries, and they spent long, hot summer afternoons swatting at flies and filling their baskets with raspberries and plums. The raspberries gleamed red and purple, peeking out from under frocks of leaves, and Zosia pulled them from their scratchy stalks and ate them greedily, eyeing her little sister. Batya was such a baby, so skinny and insignificant, with twigs for legs and a head like a brussels sprout. She had no interest in running through the fields with Zosia but preferred to curl up in the lap of their aunt or mother, gazing at the pattern of leaves and branches overhead.

The sun strolled lazily across the sky; in the afternoons Zosia and my mother ran home to Checha Godja, who was already firing up the stove. Soon a huge pot of raspberry jam was bubbling in the kitchen, filling the house with a sweet acidic smell. Hands in the berries, Zosia squeezed, forming a hard sticky ball. She eyed my mother across the room, drew a careful bead on my mother's forehead, and let loose with a gleeful shriek.

In September the family returned to Lvov, as they did every fall—to the damp gray walls and stiff wooden chairs of the classroom, the oily windows and cobblestoned courtyards. Books and candles and cold dark nights, the stove that smelled black with coal, and the early mornings of frost before winter fell with a thud on their shoulders. My mother lay curled under blankets, while Zosia grumbled and looked for her socks. She helped her mother start the fire in the kitchen stove and boiled water for coffee. They lived the entire winter with the smell of coal, the feel of it in their hands, the taste of it in their mouths. They had little money for food, and even less for clothes. But money appeared whenever it was time to enroll in a new grade, apply to a private school, or find a language teacher—money that had been tucked in the mattresses, sewn into the linens, or planted in shoe soles. For school, wadded bills came out of hiding.

My grandfather Moshe remains fuzzy. I have nothing to suggest his appearance— no photographs, no token of his dress or his habits. All I have is my mother, who, she says, takes after him. Both had dark soft eyes and serpent-black hair, long willowy fingers, with elegant fingernails and deep cuticles. They were both on the quiet side, self-effacing and bookish; they got along with people but were content to be by themselves. They both adored my grandmother, feared her strength, and admired her energy.

Like all fathers at the time, my grandfather left child-rearing to his wife. At her urging, he started a small business selling religious pictures—the Crucifixion, the Virgin Mary—on installments to peasants in the countryside.

His business slowly improved, and after ten years, the family moved closer to town, to Owacowa Street on the edge of Zamarstynow, a few blocks from respectability. Their new second-floor apartment faced the street, where the sun gleamed through windows and glanced off pinewood floors. Down the hall they shared a toilet with the other tenants in the building.

My mother was ten at the time, and she ran through the new apartment with glee. Zosia was already in high school; at seventeen, she was fiercely independent and flooded with friends. She cruised the streets with large gangs of teenagers, parading through parks, sitting in cafés, talking politics, fashion, books, movies. People fell under her spell, as they still do. Quick-witted and fast-moving, Zosia has no patience for long-winded pretentious babble. She has her feet on the ground and her fists on her hips. Either a kaleidoscope of impressions, or nothing. She has the shortest attention span in history.

My mother, on the other hand, liked to sleep late and read books, study languages and memorize long passages from Mickiewicz and Goethe. To this day she cannot begin a discussion without reaching for a book or an article to bolster her argument.

In the thirties Poland began tilting toward militant nationalism. Beatings, break-ins, rocks thrown through shop windows and religious buildings. Gangs of thugs roamed the streets with homemade harpoons of razor blades attached to poles. Here and there a killing. Lvov found itself on the crest of a new wave of anti-Semitic violence and pogroms supported by the National Socialist political party, or "Endeks," encouraged by teachers and university professors, condoned by the government, ignored by the police.

My mother was still a child but knew that her parents worried about the violence; the more they worried, the more she studied. In 1933 she was admitted to the private girls' high school in the city at the ninth-grade level.

Zosia had graduated from the same school three years earlier, but because of the strict quotas for Jews, she could not enroll in the University of Lvov. Instead, she went to college in Prague, a sophisticate's paradise. In the fall of 1930 she stepped off the train at the Prague station, carrying her suitcase of clothes, a jar of her mother's jam, and notebooks and pencils. At the age of eighteen, she somehow had achieved lift-off.

8

My sister Lara left for college when I was fifteen. We loaded up her '67 Chrysler till the trunk wouldn't shut and the back window was a wall of clothes. Forty thousand skirts and slacks, blouses and sweaters, nylons, pumps, and running shoes. Hair curlers, manicure kit, stuffed animals, and record player; posters, books, records, lamps, and pillows. All the detritus of a sixties girlhood, piled high until the body of the car barely cleared the driveway.

My parents and I followed behind in my father's car, loaded with whatever wouldn't fit in Lara's. At her college we made fifty trips, ferrying her stuff into her modern dorm room. "They're charging me by the minute for these lawns," my father muttered, walking up the stone steps to the monumental brick building in which my sister would spend the next four years. Each tree and bush had been carefully placed to create an atmosphere of peace and prosperity. This was my father's way of expressing his pride.

On the ride home, my parents were silent. I caught a glimpse of a tear on my mother's cheek. "Hey, Mom," I said. "Can I have a party this Friday night?"

"We'll see," my mother said. "Lara may be coming home for the weekend."

Lara returned home not only that weekend

but also the following weekend and the one after that. In fact, she came home nearly every weekend for the next few years. "Just wait," Lara told me one evening during her sophomore year. "You may not appreciate Mom and Dad now, but just wait till you get out there. You'll wish you'd spent more time with them while you could."

I thought she must be crazy.

"I'll never forget it," Mom told me, "when Zosia came home from Prague that first time on her college break. She'd undergone a complete transformation— her hair, her clothes, her figure: We didn't even recognize her!" Zosia had become a blonde, self-possessed—like a fashion model. Her eyes sparkled, her lips were a deep peach, and from her ears, clusters of fake stones dangled like grapes. She wore shiny high heels and a black skirt with a long, slim line, curving around her thigh. She walked with an air of confidence, her leather jacket thrown casually over her shoulders as if she tolerated its wish to accompany her on a walk across town.

"The whole neighborhood was in shock. And she even brought home a tennis racket, something completely unheard of—we'd never even seen a tennis racket before, except in the movies!"

Some things, however, Mom never mentioned: by the time Zosia hit Prague she had become a hip-fisted, tradition-trashing Zionist.

And what happened later is even harder to explain—Zosia's ultimate transformation from Zionist to Roman Catholic.

Zosia graduated from the Czech university in 1933 and decided to pursue a graduate degree in chemistry. Perhaps because of the Jewish quotas in eastern Europe, she applied to an Italian university, where rules were more elastic. "She learned Italian," my mother told me without elaboration, "and enrolled in the University of Pisa."

Within weeks Zosia had mastered the language and fallen in love with Italy. With her university friends she sat at outdoor cafés in dusty piazzas and threw back brisk cups of espresso. The night before her exams she cracked her books and breezed through graduate school. She pocketed her degree in the spring of 1934.

"That's why Zosia is such a good cook, and I'm not," my mother says in defense of her own cooking. "Zosia is a chemist; she understands how ingredients mix."

Determined to stay in Italy, Zosia applied for a work permit. Months went by, but she received no response from the government.

"You have to go in person," her friends told her. "Go to Rome, apply in person. Otherwise you'll never get anywhere."

She took the train to Rome in the early summer of 1934, just as the city began to swell with heat; dozens of cats lay like ribbons of fur over ancient ruins; lush palm trees stabbed spikes of green into the baked blue sky. A city scattered with toppled pillars, enormous palazzos, marinated Italians bursting from streetcars and buses. History tumbled from every street corner and stuck to her heels as she walked down the sidewalk.

She found the Ministry of the Professions and the Arts and asked to speak with the Executive Director. "I'm a chemist," she announced, "from Poland. I would like to apply for a work permit."

She never imagined that her interview with the Executive Director that day would change the course of her life. She was brought up a marble staircase by a guard in a blue uniform and shown into a palatial room with high ceilings and enormous sun-soaked windows; from outside, the muffled sounds of the city drifted up: engines and street vendors, hawkers of underground papers, bicycle bells and car horns. Sunlight spilled through the windows, dropping puddles of gold on the marble floor, on the enormous Oriental carpet. Across the room, a heavy mahogany table, leather-bound chairs, the intricately carved crest of nobility resting on each polished corner.

Suddenly a coffee-skinned man stood with a flourish, dressed in a sparkling white uniform. Streams of medals and gold embroidery swam across his chest, and from his shoulders flowed a long white cape that brushed the backs of his polished shoes. He smiled and extended his arm; his face was warm and delicate; a small mustache fitted precisely over his miniature lips. Everything about him—the room, the air of aristocracy, the gentle way he guided her to a chair, the sweetness in his eyes—he seemed to have just stepped out of a fairy tale. She could not take her eyes off him, his sun-drenched skin against the white flowing cape, tailored white slacks, and a chest full of medals and Orders of Nobility. The world flowed through his fingers, sheathed in soft white gloves. Zosia sat where he indicated as he circled the desk and seated himself opposite her.

Zosia presented her graduate diploma in chemistry from the University of Pisa and explained that she wished to apply for a work permit so that she could remain in Italy. The Director smiled and nodded. He couldn't imagine anyone wanting to live anywhere else.

He was thirty-four years old, unmarried, a count, an attorney by training and profession. A cautious man, he was not given to outbursts of emotion, impulse, or whim, but within minutes of setting eyes on Zosia, he decided to marry her. He called in a colleague to attend to her request for a work permit. Then he asked her for a date.

"It was her blond hair and blue eyes that got him," my mother says with a smile. "He'd never seen anything like it before."

Zosia, it's true, was drop-dead gorgeous, with a graduate-school education and air of independence unlike any of the Italian women

82

the count had dated. He was, as they say, smitten, and he would remain so for the rest of his life.

He and Zosia saw each other every day during her stay in Rome, taking walks through the Villa Borghese, stopping for cappuccino and *cornetto* on via Veneto. Eventually Zosia's request for a work permit was granted, and she landed a job in Pisa with a pharmaceutical company. Over the next few months the count and Zosia wrote perfumed letters of desperate love. Finally he arranged for her to work at a pharmacy in Rome so that she could be closer to him.

At some point Zosia got scared. "She saw how serious Giulio was," my mother told me recently, "and realized she must break it off." Giulio was a blue-blooded count, bred on Communion and Confession, schooled in the most exclusive Jesuit schools, and born, as my mother says, in the wrong century. Besides, he was a government official, a devotee of Mussolini, a Fascist.

Zosia, on the other hand, was from the underbelly of a depressed land, a scavenger. How long could she hide this from him? She decided she had to leave Giulio; she packed her bags, moved south to Naples, and took a job in a pharmacy there.

"This is where Zosia underestimated him," my mother says. "You know how docile he is? How acquiescent? Well, that's true ninety-nine percent of the time. But once in a great while, when he digs his heels in, he can outlast

83

anyone. And Giulio refused to let go of her. He was absolutely determined. Every week he traveled to Naples to see her."

Gentle, soft-spoken, and impeccably dressed, Giulio is perhaps the only true lady in our family. It's hard for me to picture him winning a contest of wills with anyone, much less Zosia, who could probably have stared down Mussolini himself.

It was during this period, I imagine, that Zosia must have finally told Giulio everything, that she was Jewish and outlawed in Europe now. But the count, hopelessly in love, didn't care. He got her another job in Rome, where they could be together. There was always a way around problems, he believed; with time, a solution could be teased out.

"Eventually," my mother told me, "he wore down her will and got his way."

But if he married Zosia, Giulio knew he would lose his post in the government— his career, his status, and his family—none of which he was prepared to do. Instead, Mom told me recently, he decided to try to get Zosia a Catholic birth certificate. And so in August of 1935, when my mother was still in high school with her face buried in books, her feet in lace-up boots, and her arms looped through the arms of her schoolmates, Giulio accompanied Zosia east to her hometown of Lvov.

My mother remembers peeking out the kitchen window at her sister and her man walking toward their little apartment on Owacowa Street. His dark skin, dazzling black eyes, and double-breasted coat. He shivered visibly under layers of wool while the rest of the street was in shirtsleeves, windows thrown open to the summer sun. It was a Polish sun, all show but stingy with warmth.

Behind her, Mom heard her mother fussing with the tea on the stove, arranging cookies on a plate. Her father had a long-suffering face of paternal concern. Her mother flew around the apartment in a flurry of activity, her personal stamp of complaint, seizing control over the only things she had left to control: her younger daughter, the stove, her husband, the house.

"Hurry up, Moshe, get the table out in the other room. Quick! They're coming any minute!"

"I see them!" my mother called out.

"Get out of the window, Batya! Straighten your blouse, run a comb through your hair! Move it, move it!"

Zosia's parents were distraught to think that they would lose their daughter to a man with whom they could not communicate except with smiles, gestures, and shrugs, relying on Zosia as the dubious interpreter of their wishes and remonstrations. A man with such small feet and lovely hands. It didn't seem possible that their hurricane of a daughter could be happy with such a quiet, docile creature. That she would settle in such a distant land—oily little Italy—stripped of her home, her culture, her community.

The count sat wrapped in his three-piece wool

suit, his wool gabardine coat resting over his shoulders, a blanket over his thin legs. He smiled sweetly and sipped his tea with one tiny finger held out, lifting the cup to his lovely pink lips. Careful not to wet his neat mustache, he tilted the teacup ever so slightly and let a tiny bit of tea tumble into his mouth. He nodded, delighted, and smiled feverishly.

Giulio pretended to be Jewish for purposes of this home visit, and never let on that he was Roman Catholic. It would have been inconceivable to Zosia's parents that their daughter was dating a non-Jew. Even so, it was a shock for my grandparents to consider an Italian for a son-in-law.

Zosia and the count made inquiries, but as it turned out, her birth certificate could not be changed. The couple finally had to admit defeat and pack up for their return trip.

Perhaps Giulio went ahead, eager to return to the sun, blowing on his blue fingers, and smiling more avidly than ever. The train pulled out of Grodecka station, and Giulio would have closed his eyes, hugging his coat to him. Zosia zoomed through Lvov with her friends, whom she hadn't seen in years. Some were married, some were preparing to marry. They went to their old cafés and walked down their favorite streets. They sat in the park and talked about men, about marriage and children. And in muffled voices they spoke of other things, of armies and dictators, of political parties and acts of violence. In the university there was trouble. And in the villages, in the streets. Tempers were flaring, and the city was splitting apart. The Catholic Church fanned the fires, and Poland was in a broil. With Pilsudski ousted, everyone was scrambling for power, eager to trample everyone else. Zosia and her friends did not linger on these thoughts but glanced over them, like spots on the tablecloth from which one tactfully averts one's eyes.

She returned to Rome in September 1935. Rome languished in the long afternoons, golden rooftops baking after the midday meal; stores closed down, and eyelids grew heavy. Giulio made inquiries among close contacts in Rome, working on the puzzle of Zosia's birth. Laws were changing under Mussolini, and Zosia was losing rights daily. Time was of the essence.

Finally, a ray of light. A friend knew a sympathetic priest in Frascati, outside Rome. Giulio visited the priest and they struck a deal. The priest agreed to marry Zosia and Giulio, but only if Zosia converted and joined the Catholic Church. Then the priest agreed to falsify her birth certificate, bypass Mussolini, give her evidence of Catholic identity, and marry the couple.

When word would finally reach my grandparents in Lvov, they most likely pronounced their older daughter dead.

"Since they were Orthodox," the rabbi in Israel told me, "they could not have tolerated

87

their daughter's marriage to a Catholic. Absolutely impossible. They would have considered Zosia dead and severed all connections with her. They would have sat shiva for her and followed traditional Jewish customs for the dead. She no longer existed for them."

My mother evades this issue but points out that a year later, in 1937, my grandmother actually sent Mom to join her sister in Italy. Perhaps by then the violence in Lvov had reached such a pitch that my grandmother relented and decided to send her younger daughter away from the killings.

But all that would come later. Now, on a sultry day in August 1936, Giulio married Zosia in Frascati. Zosia's family was absent, and so, too, I suspect, was the count's. Although perhaps his younger brother Arturo came, I really don't know. No one speaks of this wedding; there are no photographs. Zosia was young and Giulio extended his hand, and they embarked upon the Secret together.

After honeymooning in Ospedale on the Italian Riviera, the newlyweds set up house in Rome, in a little apartment on via Giordani, in the northeast section of the city. Giulio continued to head the Ministry of Professions and Arts, and Zosia worked in the pharmacy. It seemed, for a time, that they were happy. Italy was growing stronger, and Rome was, after all, sunnier than anything Zosia had ever seen before. You can fall in love with light.

9

At the end of November 1936, my mother's high school held a dance for her senior class. Eighteen-year-olds in hand-sewn skirts and fresh-pressed blouses took turns waltzing each other across the pinewood floor, while others clustered in the corners. The room was packed with boys dancing with girls, and girls dancing with girls, boys stepping on girls, and girls kicking at ankles. Into the melee of swirling couples my father crashed with some friends of his from the university. They were older boys with rougher edges, uncuffed slacks, and borrowed ties. The University of Lvov was a war zone by then.

My father was a fourth-year medical student, and he'd learned to keep an eye out for Nationalist Party, or "Endek," attacks, training one ear on the professor's lecture and one on his razor-wielding classmates. He was tall, ostrich-legged, and broad-shouldered. A decathlete on the Olympic team, he almost had enough confidence to make up for the enormous chip on his shoulder. His looks, after all, didn't betray him. But underneath all that athletic prowess, all that height, those slate-blue eyes and aquiline features, underneath all that, he was just a penniless Jewish kid from the sticks. *Zhid.* The word stuck to him like a fly to paper.

From a corner in the room he watched my mother waltzing with her classmate, a heavyset girl with breasts that reminded him of the great pyramids. My mother, by contrast, was lithe and willowy, with dark almond eyes that made him suck in his breath. Abruptly he stepped between my mother and her partner.

"May I have this dance?" he asked formally, his voice dripping with sarcasm.

My mother tried to brush him off. "When I'm finished dancing with my friend," she said.

He didn't budge.

"It's okay, Batya," her friend murmured, and stepped aside. My mother blushed and her girlfriends tittered behind her. She was the school valedictorian and a renowned bookworm; boys didn't waste time on her.

My father grabbed her a little too roughly and swept her across the room, his chin thrust forward as if he meant to slice through the other couples with it. She bristled at the feel of his arm against her shoulder, and she kept tripping over his enormous feet. *Crocodiles,* she thought. Shoelaces knotted in three or four places, his soles worn thin as sheet music.

"How did you get in?" my mother asked him frostily. She knew that he was not on the list of invitees. She had been responsible for checking names at the door. He spun her around the room without answering.

"Where are you from?" she demanded, annoyed by the pressure of his hand against her back. It was the first time my mother had danced with a boy. This was no boy, but a man, in his early twenties, a foot taller than she, with a snide smile and cool indifference in his gray eyes.

"My name is Bruno," he said in sloppy Polish with a peasant twang. "I work in the butcher shop across the street. I was closing shop and saw this party— all the lights and all— so I figured, hell, why shouldn't I have some fun?"

That did it. My mother's eyes flashed, and she decided to humiliate him in Latin, a language that clearly established her superiority. "The beggar is still a bum," she told him.

My father smirked. Dropping his head close to her ear, he repeated the Latin phrase but corrected her grammar, using the proper declension of the noun.

My mother's cheeks went red. She began to wonder about this character. He was no butcher, that she knew.

"So you fell in love with Dad because he corrected your Latin grammar, is that it?"

My mother shrugs, embarrassed, and pushes her bifocals back up her nose. My father, lips pressed in a tight smile to keep from laughing, has a gleam in his eye. She looks across the kitchen table at him. "Well," she says, smiling.

They danced all evening, and at the end of the party he walked her home. "Where are you from, really?" she asked.

"I already told you."

"No, come on. Really."

They were at her door. "Can I see you tomorrow?" he asked.

My mother nodded.

"At Platz Mariacki, under the big clock. Four o'clock?"

"Okay." She slipped in the door and slowly walked up the stairs. Her mother was sitting in the kitchen waiting for her, sewing a seam on her husband's torn sleeve.

My mother stopped short. She looked at the white shirt, at the frayed ends of the sleeve, at her mother's swollen fingers pushing a needle and thread through the worn fabric. Her mother, sewing, had once been a bride.

My father had been raised on pickled herring, horseradish, and beetroot, sour cream dollops in good times, and a pumpernickel rye you could rub your hands on till you grew calluses. Unlike Mom's parents, Dad's father, Juliusz, was an assimilated Jew. But at his maternal grandmother's insistence, Dad learned Hebrew as a boy and went to shul in their little town of Monastyrzyska.

Galicia was the forgotten little mud pie of the Austrian Hungarian Empire, and its Jews were devoted to Kaiser Franz Josef for the simple reason that he did not persecute them. Hundreds of thousands of Jews, including both my grandfathers, fought in the First World War for Austria—which, ironically, would join forces with Hitler twenty years later and slaughter all of them.

My paternal grandfather, Juliusz, a career sergeant in the kaiser's army, was stationed all over central Europe during the war years. His wife, Helen, moved with him, picking up and putting down for a few months here, a few months there. My father was born in Budapest in March 1915, during a brief touchdown. Three months later the family was off again and running.

My father remembers nothing of Budapest, of course, except that he had an uncle there—his father's older brother Zigismund, a shopkeeper. Uncle Zigi sent Dad beautiful toys and gifts as a child, which his mother promptly shipped back to Budapest after she divorced her husband. My father almost never speaks of his parents or their divorce, although he once mentioned—without a trace of emotion in his voice—that his father used to beat his mother.

I know nothing else, except that my grandparents separated when Dad was seven or eight, and from then on my father lived under the iron-fisted rule of his mother and grandmother Erna.

"I hated my mother," Dad says. "But when I returned from the camps after the war, I found that she had been killed, and I felt sorry."

"So that's why you named me after her?" I ask.

"I decided to give her a second chance," he says with a tight-lipped smile.

As a youngster my father fell ill with TB, a common killer at the time. When all else failed, in a fit of panic his grandmother took him to a *tzaddik*, who looked the boy over, murmured an incantation, and sent him home with a blessing and instructions for his care. His mother and grandmother plied him with food and coddled him until he grew soft. Years went by and remarkably, with no further treatment, he eventually recovered from TB, although scars on his lungs still linger.

Dad told me this story last fall, in an excited whisper in the living room, while Mom was busy in the kitchen, out of earshot. His eyes gleamed with mischief. "You see?" he said with devilish delight. "I'm covered under both Gods. The blessings of the *tzaddik* as a boy, and the blessing of the Catholic Church as a man!"

And so he became a roly-poly boy, clumsy and overprotected, a soft child with big plans. When he was old enough for *Gymnasium*, his mother and grandmother picked up and moved to Buczacz so that he would be near the high school—the only *Gymnasium* in the district. Buczacz was a bucolic town on the eastern edge of Galicia, the county seat with a cobbled central square and onion-domed town hall. His family rented a tiny two-room apartment on the outskirts of town, along the bank of the soupy River Strypa in the poorest section of the village.

My father worked as a tutor after school and brought his meager earnings home to his mother and grandmother. The three of them lived on the court-ordered child support his father paid, supplemented by my father's tutoring wages. The family was knuckle-bone poor. My father owned one pair of pants, which his mother patched and mended year after year, adding pieces to the legs as he grew in great gulps.

She saved money for his schooling and scrimped on food and clothes to pay for his tuition and books. A high-school education had been an unattainable dream for his parents' generation, and my father eagerly set his sights on a university degree. He picked up books and soaked in all they had to offer, wringing them out and throwing them over his shoulder. He quickly shot to the top of his class, taking his professors by storm. His classmates came to him for help in every subject, from Ukrainian to calculus; his science professors deferred to his explication of Mendelian genetics and microbiology.

But his true love was music. He managed to save enough money to buy a cheap scratched-up violin and a bow that he glued together. He taught himself to play. Shipwrecked notes floated to him from other people's radios, wisps of melodies that he collected and memorized. He befriended a boy who received private violin lessons, and he invited himself over whenever the boy's teacher came. My father listened carefully to each lesson from behind closed doors, and afterward he ran home to try it for himself. When he was fifteen he found a local music teacher who agreed to take him on as her student.

His music teacher, a white-haired Ukrainian widow named Anya Karelewicz, would become a key figure in his life, although neither could have imagined it then. She became the only link that would enable him to find my mother in Rome twenty years later, after he escaped from the Gulag.

To earn extra money as a teenager, my father played the violin in the little movie theater in Buczacz. He was the background music for the silent films. The theater was in an old building, with oak floors and wooden foldout chairs bolted together into rows, lined up like ancient soldiers facing the screen. My father stood in the back of the room, to the left of the projection booth, and played the violin while the black-and-white reels spilled silent images onto the screen. Each evening he improvised a sound track for the drama flickering on the opposite wall. The movie theater was the only one in the county, and every Sunday evening the rows of seats were crammed full of eager Poles, Ukrainians, and Jews. They cracked sunflower seeds in their teeth and spat out the shells as they watched. My father's music was punctuated by the steady patter of sunflower shells hitting the floor.

When Lara and I went back to Buczacz, we found a toothless white-haired woman who remembered the silent films of the early thirties. She smiled, recalling the young man who had played the violin in the back of the room. We showed her pictures of my father and told her his name, but she didn't know him personally. "The lights were always out." She shrugged. She walked with us to the old building, up a narrow dirt road along the river. In the high-ceilinged movie house, Lara and I watched the rows of dark wooden chairs being dismantled, uprooted from the floor by shirtless workmen. The theater was being converted into a police station.

At his music teacher's urging my father practiced with another promising student, Katrina Czezynski, who accompanied him on the piano. Katrina was a full-throttle blonde of dramatic proportions—Polish, pink-cheeked, and voluptuous. Her boyfriend, Markus, a cocky aqua-eyed sprinter, escorted her to her lessons. "Her boyfriend was a very big deal," my father says dryly. "The regional track star, very popular, and dumb as a brick.

"Actually," my father adds thoughtfully, "Katrina was no mental giant either." He tosses me a half smile and a shrug. "I was interested in her other qualities," he admits.

My father and Katrina began practicing duets together, and soon my father fell in love. He likes to blame it on Chopin. Every few weeks he and Katrina gave a recital in the little music hall at the foot of Trenowska Street. Her boyfriend, Markus, dutifully attended and dozed off in the back row, wedged into a folding chair, his huge head drooping like a sunflower on a stalk. At the end of the evening he sprang up, smiled broadly, and walked Katrina home through the park.

My father nestled his violin and bow in the worn leather case and followed the couple outside. Under a sputtering streetlamp, he watched his beloved Katrina recede into the darkness, enveloped in the arm of her boyfriend. My father turned and walked home, quietly vowing to win Katrina for himself.

It was early summer. My father had a plan. He began to train in secret in the field behind his house. He ran wind sprints and leapt imaginary hurdles, pumping his arms and springing from his toes as he'd seen sprinters do at the local track meets. He practiced shot put with a rock. He improvised a discus with a flat piece of iron. Day after day he trained relentlessly, like a machine. Gradually he lost his pudginess and improved his strength and speed. When school began in the fall, he continued his training in secret.

At the end of the fall season the regional championship track meet was held at the stadium overlooking the town. To everyone's amusement, my father entered his name in the one-hundred-meter dash and took his place at the starting line. Katrina's boyfriend, the local champion, strutted back and forth across the track, shaking the ropes of his long arms and legs. My father dropped to one knee, sweat beading his upper lip. He had never used starting blocks before, and he fiddled with them a little before getting the hang of it. His feet felt awkward pressed against the metal. The other runners stretched and approached the blocks, then crouched into position.

"Take your mark!"

The gun went off.

"I shot out like a cannonball!" my father says, grinning from ear to ear, his dentures soaking in a glass by the kitchen sink. "I beat him!" He chuckles. "Of course no one could believe it! I'd never been on an athletic team in my life! That poor fellow didn't know what had happened!" My father's face is gleeful.

And sure enough, not only did he win the race, but he also won the girl. Katrina dumped Markus and started dating my father. "That should have tipped me off," he adds a little ruefully. "She would do the same to me a few years later."

When his mother, Helen, discovered that he was dating a Catholic girl, she slammed doors and crashed pots and pans. "You will break it off immediately!" she shouted. "I forbid you to see her again!"

"How can you do this to us?" his grandmother wailed. "Turning your back on your faith!"

My father dated Katrina on the sly. But Buczacz was a small town, and Kovik was a big boy. His mother did everything in her power to break up the romance.

"She enlisted spies," my father told me, still rankled sixty years later, "people all over town who reported back to my mother if I was seen with Katrina."

My father knew that Katrina was neither deep nor bright nor complicated. He loved her because she was Polish and beautiful and because she played the piano like an angel. He had won his spoils, and he wanted them badly.

While he was still seeing Katrina, my father made the Polish Olympic team as the second-best decathlete in the nation. ("Which isn't saying much," he admits. "Poland was a small country.") He was to compete in the 1936 Olympics in Berlin, but he had to choose between his studies and training for the Olympics. By then Hitler had already been in power for three years in Germany, and in Poland, anti-Semitism and social persecution were quietly condoned by the government.

My father opted for his academic studies. "I wouldn't have won anything, anyway," he says. "Jesse Owens was unbeatable. I wouldn't even have come close."

Despite strict quotas, my father was one of nine Jews throughout the country admitted to the prestigious Lvov medical school, fulfilling his mother's dream for him. "I enrolled at her insistence," my father says. "Me, I wanted to be a violinist."

The University of Lvov was a hotbed of violence at the time. In the 1930s two Jewish students were beaten and killed by their schoolmates in two separate incidents. Professors and students alike applauded the violence; the National Socialist "Endek" students swaggered through the halls, boasting of their deeds. Attending classes grew more and more dangerous; the remaining Jewish students were taunted, beaten, and slashed. My father forced himself to classes, determined to get his medical degree. By the time he met my mother at the age of twenty-two, his hair had grown white with rage.

The day after the dance, November 1936: a rain-soaked Sunday. Bells rang in muffled tones—the Benedictine church, the Church of Santa Maria, the Franciscan cathedral. Batya sat in a stuffed chair near the window and watched the umbrellas below stretched like wings of bats gliding down Owacowa Street. Her mother had finished mending Moshe's shirt, and now she darned a pair of black stockings. Batya stared at a book of poetry on her lap, but the words ran together and the letters swam across the page. She was studying for the Matura exam, but the Matura was a long way off, and her mind wandered. Back to the dance, to the tall man who had corrected her grammar and walked her home. His cocky smile as he leaned toward her, his cool eyes when she refused to kiss him. He was aloof and abrupt, and he had no manners, none whatsoever. Or he was trying to have no manners. Something about him was calculated, forced.

The clock in the kitchen ticked dully through the afternoon. She memorized three stanzas, then promptly forgot them. He had no right to interfere with her studies like this. She decided not to meet him at the appointed hour under the clock at Platz Mariacki; she would put a dent in that muscular ego of his. Let him learn a little humility.

Pleased with her decision, Batya settled into Mickiewicz, curled into the chair. The sky bit its fingernails now and spat them on the city: a rain full of rancor. In the distance she heard the city hall clock strike four. He would be standing under the clock, proud, erect, and soaked to the bone. Batya smiled. All the better, she thought, let him get drenched. Soak that smirk right off his face.

She would not be bulldozed into anything: This has always been my mother's first lesson to anyone who underestimates her stubborn resolve. *I am not the pushover that you think,* she was saying.

But neither was my father; he had a message for her as well. Standing alone under the clock at Platz Mariacki, my father waited in the pounding rain, his shoulders hunched, leaning against the building. Rivers of water ran over the cobblestones, sinking into his only pair of shoes. The air was chilly; winter was flexing its muscles, and in another few weeks this would be snow. He had arrived, as usual, a few minutes early. He had always been obsessed with punctuality. It represented character to him, discipline and integrity. He was always early for everything, one step ahead of fortune. Consequently he waited a lot.

The wind picked up and the rain lashed him. His shoulders were soaked; he was shivering. The clock struck four, and she was nowhere in sight. He began to plot his revenge. Fifteen minutes, then twenty. He straightened his shoulders and let the rain lash his face. A smile sneaked across it, and at four-thirty he walked home, a spring in his step.

She received his note the next day. *I'm sorry,* he wrote, *I was unable to make our date yesterday. I hope I didn't keep you waiting long.*

And so they became engaged in a strange and bitter struggle of wills, each trying to deprive the other of the satisfaction of supremacy. It was a close and loving battle, but it took a great deal of determination, and in moments of weakness and doubt each feared they had met their match.

10

In 1969, at the age of twelve, I went on my first date with Davy Harrison, a beautiful blond, blue-eyed boy in my class. He invited me to a Chicago concert at the outdoor amphitheater about twenty miles away. His older sister, Glenda, and her boyfriend, Ron, would be driving. Glenda was a glamorous junior at the high school—one year older than my sister—and she was known to be "fast." (My sister, the dream of every teacher she ever met, was so off the speed scale in my opinion that she was not only slow but a complete nerd.)

I have no idea why my mother agreed to this date. I may have let her believe that Chicago was not a rock-and-roll band but the Chicago Symphony Orchestra. My mother always approved of youngsters going to concerts together, as opposed to the more dangerous one-on-one "date." I am quite sure she did not know that Glenda's boyfriend, Ron, was in trouble with the law and that his license had been revoked. The '65 Chevy he drove may have been stolen, but I'm not sure about this. Another couple went with us, friends of Ron's. I think they were in their twenties.

In any event, to my amazement I found myself holding Davy Harrison's sweaty little palm as we weaved our way between sleeping bags of heaving couples on the lawn at the concert. A haze of marijuana floated over everything like a blue ghost. The stage was so far away as to be irrelevant, and the real performance was here on the grass, amid army blankets, sleeping bags, and picnic baskets of drugs.

In my chartreuse-and-pink paisley bell-bottoms and blue Nehru-collar blouse, I spent the evening terrified that somehow my sister would find out about this from Glenda Harrison at school. Armed with information of my debauchery, Lara would immediately report me to my mother. Then my mother would kill me.

We drove home at midnight. As we approached my neighborhood, Ron swung left and took the road out to the local airport.

"I gotta get home," I said. "My mother will kill me."

Glenda giggled in the front seat.

"Just a little detour," Ron said.

We parked on a deserted dirt road overlooking the runway. Ron killed the engine and lights.

"Really, you guys," I said. "I gotta get home."

Ron's friends got out of the car. "We'll take the trunk," they said. The car rocked as they climbed into the trunk.

"You guys can have the backseat," Glenda said. She slid closer to Ron and started necking.

Davy and I stared at each other. "I gotta get home," I whispered. He shrugged. His sister was in charge.

Cautiously, Davy and I started kissing. I didn't want to spoil Glenda's time. If she got angry with me, she'd tell my sister, and then my sister would tell my mother, and then I'd be dead. So I tried to go along with things.

Every fifteen minutes or so I sat up and interrupted the heavy breathing in the front seat.

"Glenda," I said. "Look, I hate to do this, but I'm really going to get killed. I really have to get home."

"Mmmnph."

Finally I interrupted them so often, Ron bolted up. "All right, all right!" he said. "Jesus!" He flipped on the engine and gunned the ignition. The couple in the trunk leapt out and came to the window, their clothes in disarray.

"Get in the car!" Ron told them.

We drove to my house. The whole time I made Glenda promise she wouldn't say a word to anyone at school who might tell my sister.

My mother had left the light on for me, but no one was awake. I was never questioned about the evening; my mother seemed satisfied with my report the next morning that I had enjoyed the concert. Lara never found out the details, so my mother never found out. Davy Harrison and I broke up a few weeks later.

At the age of twelve, I sensed that my romantic life would be completely different from my mother's.

Buds flew open in the gardens along the streets of Lvov, and a new green leapt into the arms of trees. May 1937: The benches of Mickiewicz Park blossomed here and there with young couples holding hands and whispering. Kovik tilted his head and caught a faint strain of a violin floating over the city. "Hear that?" he said, his eyes sparkling. Batya looked at him. He had the expression of a five-year-old who had stumbled upon a secret container of sweets.

"What?" she asked, puzzled.

"Shh! Listen!"

She heard the wind in the trees, a dog barking somewhere in the distance. She heard the wheels of a baby carriage squeaking on the path, and the soft step of a woman with a long braid of dark hair. Faint gurgling of water from the marble fountain at the corner of the park. On a distant street, boys kicked a rubber ball against a wall and chased it into an alley. Cats moved noiselessly around street corners, suspicious of feet, cautious of small hands and sly laughter.

"What?" Batya said, looking at the rapture on Kovik's face.

He sat perfectly still, head cocked, a smile of wonder, eyes lit. "Taa-deeeee," he sang softly, "taa-deeeee."

Batya closed her eyes, and the sun on her lids felt golden and warm. She smiled because she was next to Kovik, who was sweet but strange, because her classmates whispered behind her back, unable to understand how she could have snared such a dashing young man; she smiled because she herself could not understand it, could never have imagined herself sitting here in the park, splashed with sunlight, Kovik's enormous arm looped lazily over the back of the bench, brushing her shoulder. A breeze ruffled the leaves in the elms. She leaned against my father, his face lit up by a distant voice that she could not hear.

She passed the Matura with flying colors, and the summer was hers. But soon she would become trapped in a tug-of-war between her mother and sister. I'm not sure exactly when the family upheaval occurred, most likely in the early summer of 1937, after my mother passed her Matura exam. The increasing anti-Semitic violence at the University of Lvov may have frightened my grandmother enough to send her younger daughter away. Although I don't know the details, I do know that one day my grandmother announced that Batya would have to go to Rome to live with her sister, to study at the university there.

"I was terribly hurt and angry," Mom told me. "She made me leave! I didn't want to go!"

"But why?" I asked. "Why'd she do that?"

"She said I'd need a sister more than a mother and father."

This seemed to raise more questions than it answered, so I pressed my mother further.

"It was Mother's way of pushing me ahead," Mom said simply, "but I didn't realize it then."

As with many of my mother's stories, I realized that she wanted me to know something, but not too much. She refused to speak of it again, so I was left to puzzle the story out on my own. My grandmother, I realized, had made an offering of her younger daughter to her older: it was a gift, one of those twisted gifts of opportunity in a crazy world of absolutes. In our family, the one with power gets to give the most. She gets to give and give and give, and I know what it is to be the last born, to receive the gift of sacrifice, to spend a life swimming in a fishbowl of guilt, looking frantically for a way to break through the glass.

My mother told Kovik she would be leaving for university in Rome, but she did not tell him about the secret of Zosia's Catholic marriage. The religious tension underlining my mother's departure remained a family secret.

"I was hurt," my father told me later. "We were planning to get married when I finished medical school, and I had expected her to stick around for that." But he respected my mother's pursuit of a university education; it was something they had in common. For my father, though, studying was a weapon to wield against the world; for her, it was dessert.

That summer he took long walks with Batya and occasionally tried to steal a kiss; she would wriggle free. "Dad was the kissy type," Mom says.

Mom was not. She permitted him to hold her hand or walk arm in arm as they followed the river, talking about the future, a life together.

One evening, my father told me, they were sitting together on a bench in Mickiewicz Park, his arm draped over her shoulder. It was late summer, a warm night settling in, and a sliver of moon rising over the treetops. Bushes rustled behind them, and suddenly a gang of young men appeared, flashing a light in my parents' faces. "Yids!" the men snarled. "Let's teach 'em a lesson!" They circled my parents.

"You're dirtying up the park!" one shouted.

"Filthy Yids! Get the fuck outa here! Go to Palestine!"

The leader looked closer at my father, holding the flashlight six inches from his eyes. "Wait a sec, I don't think this one's a kike."

The others studied my father closely.

"Hey, Jumbo, you a Yid?"

"She's gonna find out soon enough!" another hooted.

They burst into laughter and moved slowly on.

"I was furious!" my father told me. "And

humiliated. I couldn't stand up to them, they were five or six big fellows, they would have finished me off. So the next day, I went to my sports club and told my friends about it. 'Let's form a patrol,' I suggested. 'Let's make a Jewish Patrol to protect our parks, so that we can sit in public without getting harassed or beaten up.'

"But none of them wanted to. I couldn't get a single Jew to patrol the parks. So then I went to the Ukrainians. 'Today it's us,' I said, 'but tomorrow it will be you. Join with us and let's defend ourselves!'

"And some of them were interested. But they had to check with their leader, who vetoed it." My father shook his head. "The Ukrainians were fighters," he said. "But the Jews weren't. And that's what I hated most about being Jewish—Jews wouldn't fight back."

I wonder what my father thinks now of the Israeli army. He never speaks of Israel, as if it were a forbidden topic.

Zosia wrote her sister with instructions for enrolling in the University of Rome. It wasn't worth paying for the fall semester, she said, since Batya could study hard and complete a whole year of university in the spring semester. And it wasn't worth studying Italian; she would pick it up quickly while she was there.

So during the rainy fall of 1937 in Lvov, my mother lived at home and studied English with a private tutor. She read Dickens and Shakespeare, conjugated verbs and tripped along the pebbly road of pronunciation. For years she had been building up her arsenal of languages to unleash someday on an unsuspecting world. She studied herself westward, out of Poland and into the sunny countries of Spain, France, and Italy. America sparkled in the back of her mind like an exotic jewel. She pictured cities of glass and steel, enormous buildings that stretched higher than the eye could see, broad-faced Americans with unbuttoned collars sitting on verandas in the sun, eating steaks and watermelon. She memorized words for these images but never imagined she would actually see them.

February 1938 she left for Rome. Zosia was waiting for her at the station, in a leafy-green coat that made Mom think of broccoli. Milk-chocolate leather boots stretched over Zosia's calves, a gold band on her finger. She took my mother's suitcase and marched her through the crowds of businessmen and street vendors to an immense square. They took the bus to the northern corner of the city and walked from Piazza Boletti down a narrow street to the apartment building. Inside, it was cool and dark as a tomb, with a red narrow carpet snaking through the lobby. They rode the small elevator to the top floor, something my mother had never done before.

She walked into the apartment openmouthed, dazzled by the tall windows opening onto a little terrace: palm fronds and lemon trees, blood oranges in mid-February among flowering cyclamen and violets.

Giulio came home at midday to have dinner with them. He was wearing his black Fascist uniform, which, he pointed out with disappointment, did not set off his fine features and olive complexion as well as his white Order of San Sepulchre uniform. But as a government official he was expected to wear the black uniform, regardless of his fashion instincts.

He already adored my mother, whom he affectionately called *Cucca*. Cuckoo. Twenty years older than Batya, he walked with slightly stooped shoulders, manicured hands folded behind his back. He reminded her of her father with his quiet sweetness, and she felt, in some ways, as if she'd never left her parents.

My mother looped arms with Zosia and walked through the streets, marveling at the shapes and colors of cheeses, the smells of fresh bread and olives, grapes spilling over wooden crates and lemons larger than her hand. Cries of street vendors boasting their wares: bananas from Abruzzi, heads of broccoli, gleaming green columns of zucchini. People winked and shouted, pushed, pinched, and waved their hands good-naturedly. The streets spilled with colors and motion. Italy was a great skillet, and the city sizzled with life.

In her sister's apartment were pictures of the Madonna, a sweet-faced, gold-crowned woman who looked so sad and lonely. My mother looked at her for a long time but could not imagine what the Virgin Mary was doing in such a bright city, with colorful streets to explore, ancient buildings and palaces, arches for emperors, and Latin words etched into marble columns. What was the Madonna doing here, listless and mournful on the dark wall of Zosia's apartment?

Perhaps, my mother thought, the Madonna was a cover, a symbol, a shield. My mother was learning about makeup, about painting one's face. Zosia, who had always known so much about fashion, about presenting oneself in public, understood the importance of disguise. A surface is an intricate city; Zosia knew how to dress her streets and fill her walls. My mother was beginning a course of study that would save her life.

"Architecture," Giulio suggested. "It's the wave of the future. Urban planning, construction, cities, and buildings. There are no women in it yet, and you'll launch yourself into a splendid career."

So she enrolled in the School of Architecture at the University of Rome: a class of 150 architecture students, two women. "Giulio would walk me to and from classes each day," my mother says, laughing. "To protect me from the men, you see—he was always very conscientious about these things." Her eyes twinkle mischievously. "It was so like Giulio— although he was no bigger than I, he insisted on escorting me to school."

My mother bought used textbooks, drafting paper, and pencils. She sat in the cavernous lecture hall, listening to the lectures in the lilting language that stretched from the professor's mouth like taffy. It was Latin made simple, Latin made edible. It was easy to soak in while sleeping, while sipping soup, while tucking her blouse into her only skirt. Italian slipped effortlessly into her mind and spilled easily from her mouth.

Architecture was another matter. Her hand was awkward and her drawing cramped. She admired buildings but could not imagine them; she could walk through them but could not create them. And the numbers, the physics, the engineering were torture. She wanted to lie in a room and recite lines of poetry etched in the walls of her memory; she wanted to walk through gardens and learn of historic meetings and long lost wars. But creating a building and planning a city were beyond her. She looked for places to hide, nooks and crannies, a shelf for a book, a corner in the pantry in which to curl up and read, or to daydream, and to wait for Zosia and Giulio to come home.

She dutifully finished her year in one semester, as planned. But architecture, she knew, did not sing to her. It was too immense, too bulky, and too full of hard lines and permanent facts. A wall would always have to be a wall and could never be a roof. She could not live in a world like that, ruled by such absolutes, such responsibilities. She preferred the elasticity of words, the rubber of languages, the chance to be both wall and roof, both support and protection. At the end of the spring she returned to Poland.

My mother stepped off the train at the Grodecka station in Lvov. She sported a flashy Roman hairstyle, the latest rage: a Mozart cut with curls bubbling around her ears and a tiny pigtail down the back. Her friends had never seen such a thing, and they laughed at the sight of her. If Rome had opened her horizons, Lvov put her back in her place. Ashamed, Batya wore hats until her hair grew long enough to camouflage Roman high fashion.

She enrolled in the Institute of International Trade and studied economics, which made more sense to her than architecture. My father, delighted that she was back in town, strolled down the Wale Hetmanskie with her, bought her *napoleonki* at Zalewsky's bakery, and assured her that her hair was growing out quite nicely.

The year passed quickly amid growing political tensions. It was less than twenty years since the last war, and a generation was still staggering through the streets, armless, deaf, or on crutches. My grandparents had spent most of their lives running and hiding—first from the Tsarist pogroms and the Cossacks, then from World War I, next from the Russian war, and now from the Polish Nationalists. There seemed no escape from the waves of violence that swept through Poland every few years.

One day, at the end of an anatomy lecture at my father's university, a Polish "Endek" student jumped up and called out to his comrades. They began to chase the nine Jewish medical students out into the courtyard. My father tried to blend in with the crowd, he told me, hoping his Polish looks might save him. "Get the big one!" cried one of the Polish students as he neared the door. The room went wild and chased him. Outside, he saw that the courtyard gates had been closed and an army of students stood waiting, with razors tied to the ends of long poles. "Get the big one!" they shouted, and rushed him. The courtyard was filled with the screams of his eight Jewish classmates, as blood spurted, razors slashing them as they scrambled for cover.

My father paused for a moment, he said, then turned directly toward the advancing mob. He put his head down, sprang onto the balls of his feet, and barreled straight toward his attackers. My father was a large man, and the sight of him coming at them full speed must have caught them by surprise. Before they could grab him he had plowed through them all, leapt over the wall, and sprinted home. The "Endek" students gave chase, but my father was the second-fastest decathlete in Poland at the time, and he tore through the streets with a wild fear. He bounded up the steps of his building to his tiny room on Zulinskiego Street; leaning against the windowsill to catch his breath, he looked down at the street. Below him on the sidewalk, a handful of winded students rounded the corner, pulled up short, and finally turned back.

My father was the only one of his Jewish classmates who was not mutilated that day.

The student pogrom had been tacitly endorsed by the university and by the government, so no action was taken against the attackers. The following day my father went to classes as usual. He stood alone in the back of the room and heard nothing of the lecture. His face was hot, and he could not concentrate on the droning voice of the professor, nor the squeaking chairs of the students, nor the sound of chalk on the board. He could hear only the fire in his ears, the rage of his pounding heart, and the vow that he would get back at all of them.

At the end of the summer of 1939, Zosia came to visit. She and Giulio had been vacationing on the Adriatic near the border of Yugoslavia. Giulio had returned to Rome, but Zosia decided to continue east to Lvov to see her family.

What was she doing, traveling across the sitting duck of Poland in August of '39, on the eve of destruction? Europe was tiptoeing across a razor blade, holding its breath. War, the possibility of war, was on everyone's lips. A year had passed since Kristallnacht. Mussolini watched Hitler with skepticism. Chamberlain shifted uneasily in his seat.

Zosia was trying to save them, I think, to bring them back with her. It had been over two years since she had seen them, and her sense of loss must have been unbearable. She had thrown her family away, her heritage, and now I think she was returning to collect them.

Uncle must have sensed what was coming.

His brother, Arturo, whispered in Mussolini's ear and sipped sherry at his table. Uncle must have known that Zosia's family was lost. How could he let her go back? She must have insisted, knowing that she was her family's only hope. She could never have lived with the guilt if she hadn't gone back.

But she was too late. The bombs fell while she was still unpacking her bags in her childhood room she shared with Batya. All her power and energy would now be needed just to keep their necks out of the noose. Each month, each year, the rope would grow tighter around their necks. Zosia would blast through, but she was not left with much of a life after that. She managed to yank out a few friends, her sister, whomever she could. But it was not enough, after all, and her rage and grief were so great that she would eventually banish herself from her own memory.

11

Sisters are big in our family. Marriage is not. The most passionate couple in the family has always been my mother and Zosia; whenever they're together they seem to drink each other up. I can see them walking slowly on the beach at Torviannica nearly forty years ago: arm in arm, heads bent together in rapt attention, gesturing now and then with a free hand to emphasize a point. Or sitting on canvas beach chairs, my aunt in her freckled skin, curvaceous black bathing suit, and seaweed-green sunglasses. Leaning toward her, my mother is bony and more angular, the straps of her bathing suit pushed off her suntanned shoulders. Their heads nod and smile, and a ribbon of Italian words streams endlessly from their mouths.

My father always hated the sun; he suffered that summer of 1960 at Zosia's little beach house outside Rome under layers of suntan lotion, straw hats, and button-down shirts. He would pack a chess board under his arm early in the morning and walk the long white sandy beach in search of a game. It would be late evening when he returned, and he would sink into a thick book, oblivious to the world around him.

Left to our own devices, my six-year-old sister (twice my age at the time) and I spent our days shoveling sand castles or marching along the Roman beach for miles, hunting for seashells and jellyfish, and failing to live up to our mother and aunt's model of ideal sisters. I sulked and whined, refused to walk farther; Lara called me a crybaby and threatened to leave me alone on the beach a million miles from home, where I would be eaten alive by sea monsters and strange Italians. Miserably, I would trail twenty feet behind her, plotting revenge.

"You're just like your mother," everyone used to tell me, since I was careful not to display this behavior in public. I had my mother's dark eyes and Mediterranean complexion, her skinny build, her tendency to sleep late, be quiet, and require little attention. I was famous for keeping myself entertained without supervision. Lara, on the other hand, was energetic, rambunctious, and restless. She required an audience, a slave (me), a list of activities and adventures. She was decidedly high-maintenance, not unlike Zosia.

Lara and I were opposites in every way until we grew up, left home, and discovered that we were more alike than we'd thought. Sisters only get to be opposites within the family; separated by the world, they become practically identical. Perhaps this is behind my mother and aunt's great intimacy. Perhaps even my sister and I could achieve that closeness if an ocean separated us.

But more than simple geography had forged my mother's relationship with her sister. Their bond was sealed with a fifty-year vow to keep secret their true identity. So a funny thing happened when Lara and I tried to uncover the secret: We found ourselves drawn together by a similar glue. Like my mother and aunt's, ours was a bond of mutual need. Lara and I became tied together, mast and sail, on a voyage of discovery. We telephoned each other two, three, four times a day with memories of our parents' stories, names of survivors, versions of our past. We shot adrenaline back and forth; things clicked, fell into place.

Still, toppling a family structure is daunting. "You will kill Zosia!" my mother warned Lara when she wanted to tell Zosia we knew the truth. "You must never speak a word of this again!" Death and exile were the threatened consequences. History had demolished our family; why should my sister and I set out to destroy what little was left?

With the stakes framed at such extremes, my sister and I struggled with our consciences. In our phone conversations Lara insisted upon open confrontation with our parents and Zosia. I argued for restraint. Lara was the steam engine, I was the brakes. Later we would swap roles. Neither of us really knew what we were doing. We were on fire; all our talk and theories went out the window. In the end, a burning house follows only the laws of physics. We were consumed by our need to know.

"It was the middle of the night," my mother told us. "I woke up and the sky was bright as day, bombs whistling and airplanes roaring overhead. The city was on fire, people screaming, complete chaos. We crouched on the bed, my parents, Zosia, and I huddled together. That was the beginning of the war, September 1939."

The radio buzzed with news from Warsaw, confused reports from a disintegrating Polish government. Thousands of Polish soldiers rushed west to fight the invading German army, while the Polish government slipped out the back door and raced for neutral Rumania. Warsaw teetered and fell to the Germans in a matter of hours. Poles tore off their uniforms, jumped into wooden wagons, pulled on peasant's shirts, while Germans careened across the country. In Lvov, food disappeared overnight. Vandalism and looting, a sense of carnival, a sense of doom. Soldiers from the collapsing front rushed through the city, heading south for the mountains. Two weeks evaporated into a gasp of alarm, and then— just as Lvov braced itself for the German invasion from the west—the sound of Soviet boots crunched in from the east.

Gray coats with red sickles, broad-faced men with a taste for onions and women. The fleeing Polish army ran smack into the Soviets, and the eastern half of Poland—including Lvov—fell suddenly under Soviet command.

My mother sat in the cellar on Zamarstynowska Street and waited for the air raids to end. It was her first war; she was new at this. Her parents and Zosia, on the other hand, dusted themselves off and donned their discarded faces from the previous war; they now seemed hard and dry, with new lips sewn under new noses. My mother had not yet found a shell of her own, but the first night of bombings she began to grow one, stitch by stitch, a thick skin that would be hard to shed. A wall is built, brick by brick. Batya would be an architect, after all.

Two weeks later my father showed up in Lvov, an impossible loaf of bread tucked under his arm. He whistled the tune he always did as he rounded the corner of my mother's building. She raced down the stairs and flew into his arms.

The family sat down to eat the bread fresh from Buczacz. I have heard a lot about that loaf of bread. My mother remembers it as if it happened yesterday, as if it is still happening: that dazzling loaf of bread, and my father whistling his signal song from around the corner.

They sat in the kitchen, pulling up an extra chair for my father. Behind them on the shelf, my grandfather's big black radio scratched out songs. Russian songs. Without even trying, they had become Soviet citizens.

The River Strypa is lazy, small, and slow, milky green in summer, and rusty in the fall. It winds around the little town of Buczacz; too tired to enter the main square, it snuggles the outskirts of the town, dipping under three small bridges, which it wears like bracelets over its narrow body. For five days my father had watched the Russian tanks pound across the bridge over the River Strypa next to his mother's home, an endless gray stream of metal and men.

The Russian soldiers were young like my father, restless, with sparkling eyes and grand smiles of rotting teeth. They were in love with *things*. They gobbled up watches, shoes, belts, dresses, stockings, paper, glue, nails, string. Consumers run amok, they cleaned out entire stores. A loud bunch, good-humored and unruly, they paid what they could and took the rest, and within days the town was empty.

My father had come by train to Lvov and told my mother's family what he had seen, while they divided his loaf of bread. It was the first time he had ever laid eyes on Zosia, Mom's older sister from Rome. I don't think he knew anything about her secret conversion at the time.

He was anxious to finish his last exam and collect his medical degree, but the medical school was closed. Dozens of professors had disappeared overnight, scooped up with their families and shipped to Siberia. The Soviets didn't trust Westerners who knew too much; an education was a dangerous thing.

After scouting the city, my father returned to Batya's house. My grandmother took his jacket, and noticing the frayed collar and cuffs, she carefully folded it and laid it over the back of a chair so as not to embarrass him. She had always liked my father. Although penniless, he was clever, hard-working, and ambitious. "She encouraged my relationship with Mom," Dad once told me, then smiled sheepishly. "But Mom's father didn't. He thought I wasn't religious enough."

My grandmother set out a jar of her raspberry jam and a few remaining slices of bread. "Are you hungry?" she asked, placing a spoon next to the jam.

"Oh, no, thank you," my father said. He sat in the kitchen chair she indicated, and fidgeted, trying to find room for his legs under the table. "I can't believe it!" he said. "One exam shy of a medical degree!" He scraped his chair backward in order to cross his legs, then immediately uncrossed them. He was not built for waiting, and he didn't know what to do with himself now that the university was closed.

"Just be patient," my grandmother said quietly. "It's war. Let things calm down a bit." She moved toward the stove. "Tea?" she asked.

"Just one exam," my father said. "One lousy exam. I can't wait until things calm down." He rubbed his forehead with both hands, elbows propped on the table.

My grandmother leaned toward him and touched his shoulder. "You can take your meals here," she offered. "Eat with us. Join our table."

"But I have no money—"

"I'm asking you to eat with us," she said, smiling. "I don't want payment. You'll be with us, that's enough." She thought for a minute. "As for a room to stay in...let me ask our friend, Mr. Blumenthal. He has a large apartment. I'm sure he'll agree."

That was the beginning, then, the bang of the gun on September 1, 1939. Everything went into the washing machine, an ethnic cleansing the likes of which had never been seen before. A new detergent, modern technology. Clean, tidy housewives with their hair tucked neatly in buns. So much dirt to clean, so much muck that kept bubbling up underfoot. My family was the thin rim of black under their nails. They scrubbed and scrubbed, but we are still here.

The wealthy sections of Lvov were the first to be emptied. One family after another disappeared east. The rest of the city learned quickly; deportations during the night were on everyone's lips by dawn. No one needed radios, they could sniff the air.

People turned their coats inside out and wore the tattered lining outside to hide the quality of the fabric. Furs, silver, and linens were hidden in attics, and people wore scraps of mended rags. They took off their rings and watches, bracelets and earrings. They lowered their gaze. Overnight, Lvov turned into a city of waifs, of hunched-over hoboes without a penny to their name.

The Soviets were not fooled. NKVD agents lived on tips and rewarded denouncers, and a new occupation was born: It was lucrative to offer information, to talk. For turning in a neighbor you were awarded the neighbor's property. Trainloads of aristocrats and intellectuals disappeared east every night. Soviet officers brought their wives and settled into the comfortable homes of exiled Polish landowners and businessmen. The Russians were cleaning Lvov of its ruling class.

"You see, space was wealth, and families with too much space were suspect, even if their clothes were tattered and their fingers cold," my mother told me. "So people doubled up on housing, forfeited their apartments, and moved in with friends or strangers. That's why Dad was able to move in with our friends the Blumenthals. Their apartment was too large by Soviet standards, and they would have been forced to share it with others. So they were only too happy to have Dad stay with them."

Commerce ground to a halt, and my grandfather Moshe had to end his business. The black market sprang up overnight. Stiff competition for eggs, milk, bread, and vegetables. Salt disappeared altogether. My grandmother made kasha and found vegetables once in a while. Long lines formed on the streets. One got in line and then asked what it was for. "Bread," someone might say, and the word was passed back. You waited an hour, two, sometimes four. When you got to the counter they might have a loaf left, or they might be out. You went down the street until you saw another line, and you stepped in the back. "Plums," they said, and so you waited. Maybe you were lucky, and after an hour you came home with a kilo of plums. You had hoped for eggs, but you would have settled for bread, and now that you had plums you would go home and cook plums instead.

Once, when I was a teenager, Lara and I split the cost of a book of photography by Roman Vishniac as a Christmas gift for my mother. Vishniac's son was a survivor of Russian labor camps and a friend of my parents', so we figured my mother would like to have the book. Besides, the pictures had all been taken in Polish cities and towns in 1939, just before the war broke out.

But when I leafed through the book before wrapping it, I had misgivings. Its title was *A Vanished World,* and the photographs were all of bearded, black-coated Orthodox Jews on their way to synagogue. Jewish boys in yarmulkes wore curly locks that dangled below their ears like corkscrews.

"I don't know," I said to Lara. "Do you really think Mom will like this?" It all seemed so foreign to me.

Lara shrugged. "It's pictures of Poland," she said. "And she'll want to have a book by Vishniac. I don't think it matters if it's not exactly the people she knew."

The next morning my mother took the book from under the Christmas tree and unwrapped it. She slowly turned a few pages. Then suddenly, to my amazement, she burst into tears. "This is my home!" she cried. "These were my people, our neighbors!"

Lara and I exchanged glances. "I guess she likes it," I whispered.

Soon after the Russian occupation in 1939, my mother told me, my grandmother packed two small suitcases with all the valuables of the house: linen tablecloths and silverware, some jewelry and things for my mother's trousseau.

Their washwoman came to boil the sheets every two weeks, and my grandmother pulled her aside. "Listen," she whispered. "I've packed these two suitcases with linens and silver.

Would you take them with you? Keep them in your house till after the war. The Russians won't think of looking for them there."

The woman nodded. She was a loyal friend and lived in an even poorer section than my family; no one would think of searching her apartment. She carried the two suitcases home with her.

But someone must have seen her leave Owacowa Street with the two suitcases. Or someone must have seen her arrive at her own apartment with suitcases. Her neighbors whispered, "What is she doing with suitcases? She has nothing, where has she gotten two suitcases from?"

NKVD soldiers pounded on my grandparents' door. "Police! Open up!" My mother released the latch and three NKVD soldiers burst into the small room of their apartment, boots clacking on the wood floor. They smelled of long days in close quarters. One of them kept wiping his nose on his sleeve. The officer in charge was young, with arrogant gray eyes in a bony face. He stood with his legs spread, one hand on his pistol belt. He threw down the suitcases on the floor. "Recognize these? Know what this means?" He flashed a self-satisfied smile, revealing two black teeth. "This will cost you a lot," he said, drawing the words out slowly. "You've been conspiring to steal from the State! This is State property you've taken and hidden!"

My grandfather Moshe stood in the center of the room, speechless. My grandmother leveled her gaze on the officer and spoke calmly. "I've stolen nothing," she said. "These were linens and things for my younger daughter's trousseau." She pointed to my mother, who stood in a corner, terrified, unable to look in the soldiers' faces. "I didn't know any better," my grandmother said. "You see we are poor, we have nothing. I bought that over a lifetime of work, hard work with our own hands. I didn't know any better. I meant no harm. Take the suitcases. Let me make you some tea. Surely you are hungry."

The officer scowled and turned to Moshe. "Come," he said, "you're under arrest. You'll learn what it means to steal from the State." He grabbed my grandfather roughly by the arm. Moshe did not resist but moved quietly, a blank expression on his face.

My grandmother lurched forward. "Wait!" she said. "Please, it's all a misunderstanding!"

"Move!" the officer snapped.

In the other room, Zosia had been sitting on the bed, listening. She had sat quietly, staring at the wall and thinking of Giulio. He would be worried, folding his hands and walking back and forth across the apartment on via Giordani. The radio would be on. The news would not make any sense, and the reports would be conflicting and contradictory. He would grab his cap, straighten his uniform, dust the shoulders, and fly out of the apartment, down the street to Piazza Vescovia with its elegant shops, and flag down a taxi.

He would rush to military headquarters, to his brother in the Special Guard, and find out what could be done.

Zosia heard the voices in the next room. She had heard the suitcases thump to the floor, spilling their contents. She heard her mother's words, and she could picture her father's face. His soft eyes and long, dark lashes looking lost. With a faint sigh of resignation he would walk out the door, and she feared she would never see him again.

Zosia slipped the gold band off her finger and put it in her pocket. She put on lipstick and a pair of high heels. She tucked her blouse in and straightened her skirt, brushed her hair and puckered her lips.

"Hello," she said breezily as she stepped into the living room, gazing serenely at the NKVD officer who gripped her father by the arm. She smiled at him, calculating her chances. His eyes grazed over her, her hips, her breasts, her legs. The soldiers stood rooted to the spot like mannequins, mesmerized by her magical appearance—the impossibility of such red lips and blue eyes in this little room in Lvov. She seemed to have just stepped out of a storybook.

She focused her attention on the chief officer's face, his knobby cheekbones and thin neck, ears that tilted at a reckless angle. She gazed at him with such sparkling blue eyes, such rapt interest, such a mysterious smile— as if he were Odysseus, as if he were a hero who had come to sweep her off her feet. The officer felt his face flush, his muscles swell, and his shoulders broaden. He smiled proudly and nodded at her.

October 1939. Uncle sat in his fifth-floor study, looking out the window to a line of sheets flapping under the open gaze of the Roman sun. He was writing a letter to Zosia in his careful handwriting. He wrote her every day, numbering each letter, so that she could tell how many had been lost or confiscated in between. Stuffed into sacks, opened by censors, and passed along or thrown out, his letters would be used as toilet paper, or to clean a gun barrel, or to wipe a nose. A few of them slipped through. He was careful to fill each page from top to bottom, front and back, so that the Russians would not be tempted to use the paper for their own writing, for scribbling messages in the margins, or calculating figures in the spaces between sentences. The envelopes, he knew, would be stolen, so he wrote her address on the letter itself as well.

His letters were read by Fascists and Communists, by decoders and spies, postal clerks, censors, and border guards. He wrote for the whole world, long passionate letters declaring his never-ending love for Zosia; he wrote poems to her, he courted her anew. He told her how much he missed her, how everything reminded him of her, how he went from street to street looking for her; he told her how he lived and what he ate, he gave her news from Rome and Berlin.

He wrote every day for over two years. A thousand letters, of which she received only a few. She wrote him when she could, in short sentences that said little. I doubt she mentioned that she had saved her father from deportation by dating the NKVD officer. The family, she said, was all right. She was working as a pharmacist in a nice part of town. Batya had completed her studies in economics in a matter of months. The Russians had put her to work as a translator in their central office near the railroad station on Grodecka Street. Father, Zosia wrote, was growing despondent, sitting at home, waiting for his daughters to return from work. Sarah cooked and cleaned and stood in lines for food, a scrap of bread, a few grams of flour or lard, some substitute tea, some lye. Batya's fiancé came over three times a day and took his meals with them. He was a good man, intelligent and clever, Zosia wrote. He was waiting to take his final exam, but the medical school was still closed.

Frost blew into town as winter approached. It was the long-distance greeting from Siberia, reminding people in Lvov that it waited for them, longed for them, and bid them visit.

Batya and Zosia grew elastic. They stretched to fit the contours of a new occupying force. On Saturday nights Zosia powdered her face, pressed her eyelashes, trimmed her nails, and painted her lips. She put her hair up in waves and arranged it around her face. She selected stockings that would show off her legs, and high heels that gave more shape to her calves. She tightened the belt around her waist and unbuttoned the top two buttons of her blouse, throwing the collar casually open. She selected a face, an expression, a laugh, and an attitude that was appropriate for the job before her. At seven o'clock the NKVD officer came for her. She applied her smile, her laughing voice, her cheerful eyes, and ran out to meet him, leaving her father in his armchair in the living room, staring out the window at the thin streetlight that someone had forgotten to extinguish.

Working for the Russian government, my mother earned a pittance of a salary. Both her parents were out of work, so it was Zosia who really supported the family, bringing home bartered goods from other shopkeepers. "She'd come home with the most amazing delicacies," my mother said, "sugar and milk, and even pastries from Zalewsky's bakery!"

As a pharmacist at Platz Akademicka, Zosia made deals with other merchants. She promised to save various medicines for them if they saved supplies for her. Then, at an arranged time, they bought from each other at the official State prices, which were quite cheap.

"She worked the black market," my father said.

"No!" my mother corrected him, shaking her head with irritation. "She *outwitted* the black market." She shot my father a glare; he shrugged and kept quiet.

"You see, under the Soviets," my mother explained to me, "the problem was not the cost of goods, but their availability. Everything was scooped up by the black market, so nothing was left in the stores. The black market was not only terribly expensive, but also dangerous—it meant instant deportation to Siberia."

So Zosia became an operator, running her own exchange market, choosing her contacts carefully. Zosia kept her head. It was a very good head, better than most. She nearly saved her family with it.

My father woke at dawn, as always. The bed was too short for him, but he was used to that by now. His feet hung over the end. Gray light grazed the window, skimmed the edge of the chair, and fell over his ankles. He was careful not to wake the Blumenthals in the other room. He dropped his feet quietly to the floor and sat up, rubbing his eyes. The house was silent. Outside, a hint of horse manure, faint but fresh. The city lay meekly in the palm of the Russians' hands. Kovik lifted his shirt from the chair and pulled it over his head, buttoning the top two buttons. He pulled on his pants, then tiptoed down the hall to wash his face.

He stepped into the street with a book under his arm and walked briskly to the park. It was cool, and the sun slowly climbed the branches of the trees. He sat opposite the university and began to read. The university was barricaded. Three soldiers stumbled down a street after a long night of reveling.

After a few hours Kovik walked across town to Batya's house and knocked lightly on the door. My grandmother opened it with a smile, her blue apron smudged black with coal, and a handkerchief bunched up in her sleeve. "Come in, Kovik, come in," she said. He bowed elegantly and kissed her hand, snapping his heels together with elaborate formality. She smiled. "Now, sit down, don't exaggerate." She pushed him toward the table, poured a cup of hot chicory mixed with milk, and cut him a slice of bread. "Get started," she said. "Let me drag Batya out here."

Moshe wandered into the kitchen, newspaper in hand, and nodded to Kovik. A lock of hair stuck out above Moshe's ear, and he patted it absentmindedly with his left hand, pressing it to his head. He poured himself a cup of the ersatz coffee and sat next to Kovik, scraping his chair across the wooden floor. "What do you hear at the university?" Moshe asked in a low voice. Although my grandfather was twice my father's age, his hair was still jet black, while Kovik's was already streaked with white.

My father shrugged. "Still no word. But things are settling down a bit." He lifted his cup, held it to his lips, and spoke through the steam that rose before his face. "They're still arresting people, but the deportations are slowing down, I think. I think there'll be a lull." He blew small ripples across his coffee cup. "Then they'll open up classes again."

This is what the word on the street was, although no one knew where the word on the street came from. It was never clear whether it could be trusted. News was whatever one wanted to believe, and Kovik wanted to believe that classes would resume.

Zosia suddenly appeared in the kitchen in her narrow black skirt and white blouse, a bright red scarf tied around her neck. "I'm late!" she said, dabbing her lipstick with a handkerchief. She pecked her father on the cheek, poured herself a small cup of watered-down milk, and threw it back before running out the door. She nearly collided with my mother, who was shuffling into the kitchen, yawning.

"Mmmm," my mother mumbled, and collapsed in a chair. My grandmother poured her a cup of warm milk with chicory and carved up slices of bread into a basket. "Eat," she commanded, to no one in particular, and slapped down a jar of her plum jam.

Kovik sneaked a grin at Batya, who was too sleepy to notice. Moshe sat stiffly across from them, mulling over the Yiddish paper. "Terrible," he mumbled, shaking his head. "Ach."

The papers were full of German anti-Jewish actions in western Poland. Jews continued to flee east to Russian-occupied Lvov, from Warsaw and Lodz, Krakow and Radom, spreading horror stories of German atrocities.

After breakfast my mother dressed quickly and rushed out the door to make it to the office by eight. Down the stairs, two at a time, and onto the street. She heard the screech of the streetcar, raced to the corner, and hopped aboard as it rounded Zamarstynowska, a block before the Krakowska stop.

How strange, she thought, to eat breakfast with her parents and Kovik and then run out to work. It was not what she had pictured her life would be. She remembered the first year she met him, when he lived on Zulinskiego Street, and he used to walk her to her school in the sleepy light of morning, when the church spires threw shadows on the cobblestones, and the houses around the Rynek glowed apricot against an early blue sky. He towered over her, carrying her books. She liked the way his arm swung by his hip and the easy way he held his head, the way the sun caught the silver in his hair and doused his face with pink light. She liked the way he imitated the accent of his professors, the way he rolled his *R*'s and laughed at his own jokes. She blushed when her friends saw her; they might wave or wink and run ahead, and then Batya's face would redden, and she would look down at her feet and see how big Kovik's were, and this made her blush even more.

"Come with me, you're under arrest!" A policeman suddenly grabbed her arm and pulled her off the streetcar. His face was unshaved, his jaw immense; it belonged on a fish, she thought.

She stumbled to the street and had to run

to keep up with him. He did not loosen his grip on her arm.

"What is it?" she asked in Russian. "I must get to work, I'll be late!"

He steered her across the street and down several blocks to the police station, where he pushed her into a room and locked the door.

A lightbulb dangled on a frayed cord from the ceiling. An hourglass, she thought, with sand in the bottom. In the middle of the room, a small rectangle of a table, worn and wooden, scarred with cigarette burns and coffee rings. Two folding chairs. Gray plaster walls, cracks skidding across them.

Footsteps and voices echoed in the corridor; then silence. My mother glanced at her watch. Her boss would be wondering where she was. She knew she could lose her job for being late to work. Or deported for failure to appear at all. With growing anxiety, she waited for the police to interrogate her.

"It was because I'd jumped on the streetcar half a block before the stop," my mother told me a few years ago. "So they arrested me and interrogated me, and by the time they let me go, my boss had already filed a report of my failure to appear at work.

"That was the real problem," my mother said. "Because when my boss tried to verify my story with the police, the NKVD refused to acknowledge I'd been arrested."

"So what happened?" I asked.

She shrugged. "Oh, nothing came of it in the end." My mother waved her hand, brushing off the incident as hardly worth mentioning. But for some reason I kept trying to picture the details for myself, in order to find my mother. After all these years I still don't know who she really is. The clues are there, I think, if I could just piece them together.

As a child I used to sit at the dinner table, staring at my plate of overbaked frozen potato fritters. Little nuggets of white potato paste, hardened like Elmer's glue, that my mother cooked straight out of the freezer. She also made boiled chicken or hardened hamburger patties that were small and round and tough as dried dog turds.

We always ate dinner at the kitchen counter, facing the windows that looked out over the rock garden. My father had rigged a bird feeder at the edge of the woods, to give us something to look at. In the middle of a mouthful of potatoes, he would suddenly point out the window and say *"Look, look, look!"* with such alarm that it was easy to imagine that tanks were rolling across our lawn. Instead, it would be a purple finch that had flown away or a cardinal preening on a branch. We kept a little Audubon paperback near the kitchen counter and consulted it upon each of my father's outbursts. It was his way of calling our attention to the beauty of the world.

Since my father was almost always at his office or making rounds at the hospital, the adventure of child-rearing usually fell to my mother. A trim five-feet-four and 114 pounds, she was deceptively strong and did not suffer fools. But she had a weakness for sleep, and it was in the early mornings that Lara and I hatched our most successful schemes.

Once, when I was seven or eight, a blizzard dumped three feet of snow in eastern Michigan, shutting every school in the county. I jumped onto my parents' bed early in the morning and begged my mother to take us skiing. She was snoring softly in her usual pose: facedown on her belly, with her hair frothing from her head like a Kewpie doll. My father had left an hour earlier for his hospital rounds; his pale brown-striped pajamas lay across his pillow, shapeless waifs of cotton from Kmart.

"Mommy," I said, bouncing on the bed, "wake up!"

Within minutes Lara and I had packed the car with our gear, and my mother stumbled after us, zipping her shirt into her black stretch ski pants.

As we turned onto the main road, our car fishtailed and sideswiped a snowbank, then spun drunkenly back onto the street. There was no traffic, although from time to time we passed the hoary hulk of an abandoned car that had skidded off the road and into a ditch.

I settled into the backseat and buried my nose in *The Call of the Wild* as my mother drove our car onto the Brandon Bridge, across a deep gorge carved by the Manistoo River. Suddenly I felt a giddy sense of weightlessness in the pit of my stomach. I glanced up. My mother was leaning forward, clutching the steering wheel tightly. Through the windshield, with its frantic wipers beating back and forth, I saw that we were high above the half-frozen river, traveling oddly sideways. I lurched up in my seat, keeping my finger in *The Call of the Wild* so as not to lose my place.

Our car was skidding with a sort of slow-motion inevitability toward the edge of the bridge, picking up speed as we went. I let out a pathetic little puff of air and waited, breathless. Time seemed to freeze, and for a moment the three of us sat suspended in the bubble of our car, detached from the world, as the sharp angles of guardrail and towering bridge supports grew larger in our side windows. The river seemed to be pulling us like a magnet, overpowering our will.

Lara's mouth popped open, a perfect pink *O*, the blood drained from her face. I felt a surge of satisfaction at her terror, almost forgetting my own.

"Hang on, children," my mother said evenly. "We're going over."

There was something exquisite about the tone of her voice—it was neither alarmed nor frantic but perfectly matter-of-fact, clear-headed, and informational. It was the tone of someone who has been to the brink countless times, someone who is at ease in emergency. It was a cool, composed warning of impending disaster.

We held our breaths as we hit the guardrail,

and the car lifted off the ground, spun around, and landed more or less in the middle of the road, pointed in the direction we had been traveling.

Lara clutched the dashboard with white-knuckled fists. My mother calmly drove across the bridge and then pulled over to get a look at the damage.

"You okay?" she asked, turning her head. Her voice was even, unemotional, a can-do mother without fear or sympathy. We nodded, speechless. My mother got out and circled the car. A headlight was smashed, a dent in the frame, nothing more than that, and we continued north to ski country.

It's this image of my mother I try to reconcile with her stories during the war. Is she now who she was then? Is anybody ever just one person?

12

After some months my father finally took his last exam in the fall of 1939 and was awarded his medical degree, but he never actually saw the diploma, because it was placed in the hands of the Russian police. As a Soviet citizen his medical expertise now belonged to the State. Within a few weeks he was informed that he would be transferred a few hundred kilometers east of Lvov, where he would work in the hospital in Tarnopol.

I don't know how he said good-bye to my

mother; my parents never speak of his departure. But my father did tell me that before he left, my grandmother pulled him aside and asked him a favor. "Kovik," she said, "if anything should happen to us, look after Batya, will you?"

He nodded. "Of course."

My grandmother kissed him good-bye. He walked down the stairs, and my grandmother closed the door softly behind him. He never saw her again.

My mother took the tram every morning to work and brought back her meager paycheck. Her Russian was quite good now. She was getting used to this war, getting used to separation. She had not heard from Kovik. She had not heard from Lucia, who left a year before for the Gulag with her family. Or Mathilda. Or Brocjak. Or Stefania. Or half a dozen others with whom she used to play on the corner.

She tried to think of Kovik, but her feelings were very far away. She was calm. Things were like that. People came apart during war. Everyone was on hold. People went to work and thought of food. They looked at the ground and looked at their hands and walked home in the dark and tried not to think too much about tomorrow. It's easy to lose feelings. You can get used to it after a while. You can grow calm, or numb, everything quiet inside. You can get used to anything.

How did it end, the affair with the rotten NKVD officer? Zosia dated him for months,

144

playing the coquette, keeping him soft and pliable in her hands, like a lump of dough. He changed his report to his superiors about the two suitcases of linens and silver, and the danger of the family's deportation to Siberia was over. Zosia no longer felt the imperative of her relationship with the man, and she became more irritable and less flattering. He grew tired of wrestling with her for his fun and decided, finally, she was more trouble than she was worth. In this way she engineered the end of the affair: She succeeded in getting him to dump her.

By then the war was an ever-present rumble in one's stomach. Food was scarce. One day leaked into another, and food was stretched to cover the week. One by one, shirts were sold, traded for food, for wood or coal, a few potatoes. Substitutes sprang up: substitute tea, substitute coffee, tobacco, sausage, and sugar.

Another winter came, rain turned to snow and froze to people's shoes, which frayed and popped open. They stuffed them with rags and walked gingerly, with cramped toes. Pipes froze, and the buildings inhaled icy air. Streetlights stood against buildings like dark skeletons. The streets funneled the wind from one end to the other.

And then one day, spring came like a kiss. No one trusted it at first, no one believed that spring would come with a war going on. The days lengthened, and people began to smile, for no reason, just because the air was warm and the sun was good.

•

To me, a suburban child in the 1960s, a food line meant waiting at the supermarket checkout counter, eye to eye with a wall of tantalizing, brightly colored candy bars. I thought of food shopping as an action sport. Arms extended, running full-tilt through the supermarket, I'd push the shiny steel grocery carriage ahead of me; then I'd hop onto the little metal wheel guards and careen down the aisles until I was yanked off by my mother. If my parents mentioned the scarcity of food during the war, it meant no Pop Tarts.

It wasn't until my twenties that I tried to imagine what my parents had actually gone through. I didn't know the details yet, but I knew that starvation and physical hardship figured prominently, and I wanted to see if I could measure up.

Once, in February 1982, after a week in the Mahoosic Range, I started the five-mile hike back to my car along a beautiful cascading brook. I stuffed my mountaineering skis through the side pockets of the backpack, roped the snowshoes to the outside, and lumbered through the woods like a giant tepee. My sleeping bag and tent were stacked over my head, and a ski pole dangled from each wrist. I had not eaten more than a few crackers over the past few days, and my head felt light and pleasantly detached. I was vaguely aware that I was trying to prove something, but I couldn't have said what.

Suddenly, my foot slipped on an icy ledge.

For a graceless moment I fought to regain my balance, flailing arms and ski poles like a windup toy. Then I crashed face-first down the embankment and into the brook—skis, snowshoes, and crampons strapped to my back in a burlesque of baggage. The ice water took my breath away. Panicked, I tore at my hip belt and shoulder straps, wriggled out from under the backpack, and shot up for air. Pushing it in front of me, I kicked my way to the edge of the stream. The ground felt unsteady under my feet, and I stood doubled over and shaking, hugging my pack as if holding on to my life.

An image of my parents suddenly leapt into my mind. Could I have survived what they had been through? Exactly what *had* they been through? Nothing I could ever do would be enough, I thought. And my admiration soared and my spirits sank and my sense of self-worth could have been rubbed away under the heel of one shoe.

In June 1941, just before the Germans invaded Lvov, my father was hustled off in a boxcar to the Gulag, where he would spend the next six years in labor camps—"I was a guest of Stalin's," he says dryly.

The Gulag saved his life, oddly enough. "If I'd been left for the Germans, I would have come to a bloody end," he says. He didn't have the stamina to go into hiding, like so many of his friends—holed up in an attic or burrowed underground for months at a time. Nor could he have assumed a false name and identity and marched defiantly through the streets, acting and laughing his way through the war. He was not made of such supple stuff. No, he would have run for the woods. "I would have joined the partisans," he says. "I wanted to fight." He would have met, he readily admits, with a quick and violent end.

But as luck would have it (a strange word, the wrong word, but there it is), as luck would have it the Soviets scooped him up and sent him off to Siberia; he was sentenced to life in hard-labor camps as a "Socially Dangerous Element." Because, of course, he had not managed to keep his opinions to himself, my brash father with his mouth like a zipper that flew open with a zing. He had already been spouting off what he thought of the great Soviet ideal.

It's not clear exactly what happened. But nothing is ever exactly clear. History is a card table full of illusions, and we must sort through and pick the ones we wish to believe.

And so I choose this one: In early June 1941 he was sitting at a makeshift table in the camp outside the hospital at Tarnopol, sucking down a watery soup with fish bones and potato peels, for which he had paid half a week's salary. He had already sold his sweater, shirt, and wool pants for food and rent money. His salary as a doctor barely covered the rent for his little garret, a tiny eight-by-ten room with a ceiling that leaked when it rained and froze when the wind came up from the northwest. He chewed the fish bones carefully, so as not to pierce the roof of his mouth, but gave up finally and spat them out.

"This great Soviet Mecca," he said bitterly to the older doctor sitting across from him. The old man was also a Pole, trained in the West; he had practiced in a Lvov hospital, where the Soviet tentacles had not reached him until then.

"It's crazy," the old doctor agreed. "I have a friend in Chortkov, a gifted surgeon; he's down to fifty kilos. He can't even earn enough to eat. You ask me, the whole system is for bloodsuckers!"

"When the war is over," my father nodded, in a low voice, "I will return to Poland and write about this. I will tell the world what the Soviet ideal is really all about! One day I will get my revenge."

A week later my father was traveling east, plunging across the tundra, over frost-covered lichen whipped by arctic winds. It was a persuasive lesson in betrayal, and my father would never again make the mistake of trusting another living soul for the rest of his life. He wore a T-shirt and his one remaining pair of pants, a pair of thin socks, and the shoes that he had worn as a student, stitched over a dozen times by the shoemaker in Buczacz. In the cold that seeped through the slats of the wooden boxcar, the leather cracked, and his toes went from blue to black. He wiggled them and rubbed them with his hands, blowing on his fingers from time to time, thinking of the old Polish doctor. I should have known, my father told himself, remembering the tattered coat of the older man. No one had a coat anymore; he should have known.

The old doctor would be sitting at the table now, eating the hard-boiled egg that his information had won.

Bad news travels quickly. In Buczacz, Kovik's mother knew her son had been deported. She woke to hear bombs in the distance and knew that he was gone. Her son had passed her on the eastbound railway tracks that crossed the sluggish River Strypa a week before. She had not awakened then, in the middle of the night, when his boxcar creaked across the bridge in town. It was a sound that she was used to. But now, at the end of June, she awoke with a start and strained her ears. The bombs were falling, and she knew her son was gone.

She made inquiries. The Red Army was flying through the streets, coats flapping. Their jeeps and tanks and trucks rumbled crazily across the bridge behind her house; soldiers were running, men in torn boots and foolish civilian shoes, faces wild and bewildered. Their rifles banged against their backs, and their fingers were chewed raw. Among them were flocks of young Poles, Jews running east to escape the tanks of Hitler's army. They had been given a token pistol or rifle, a red star to wear on their torn shirts, a belt to hold up their pants. They were yanked from their wives, their mothers, and children; they ran into Russia, which pulled back its skirts and drew them in.

My father wore no red sickle or star and carried no pistol. He rubbed his feet and thought of my mother, of her dark eyes, her childlike smile. How she tilted her head and shrugged her shoulders when he teased her. She had square shoulders and a strong head, and she was fun to tease, because it changed the lines of her body, because it made her laugh, and because it made him feel clever. She was all bones and angles, small-hipped and flat-chested, but maybe it was the war. Maybe it was her age, the geometry of youth. He wondered when she would hear that he had been arrested, how she would hear it, what she would do. He had promised her mother he would take care of her.

It is Sunday, and my parents are at home, still sleeping. In another hour or two Dad will wake, creep out of bed, dress, and step into the early light of the living room. He will pick up his book and read until eight, when he will hear the drapes rustling open in the bedroom. Mom will rub the sleep from her eyes, scuff into the kitchen, and put the kettle on the stove. She'll take out two cups, two saucers, two plates, and measure out the instant coffee. She heats the milk and pulls out the coffee cake from the tin. She cuts two slices, one large and one small, and sets them on the plates. The kettle whistles, my father closes his book. Mom pours the coffee, and Dad pulls up a seat. They face the rock garden and admire the snow. They watch the birds and worry about the squirrels. They are hidden in the woods in a beautiful house, amid long shadows of pine trees and oaks.

A long road trails behind them. It lies to the east, across an ocean, across another continent. I've circled the globe, looking for home. They are sitting at the kitchen counter in the middle of the woods, watching the squirrels steal seeds from the birds. The snow sticks and melts and the sun pours butter over everything. In another few hours they'll get into the car and drive to church.

They are in their seventies. My father feels cheated, betrayed, but he's not sure who is to blame. He is left, after all, with this house and this garden, these trees and their shadows, the snow in the winter and the grass in the summer. His wife, who still laughs, but not at his jokes. His children, who have grown and left, and understand little, or nothing, or less. He had so much potential. He could have been a biologist, a chemist, or a physicist. He could have found a cure for cancer. He could have repaired hearts, flown a spaceship, written a symphony. The trees brush the blue sky and whistle softly. So much potential, so many trees, so much snow and sky and time. The hands on the clock never grow wiser. He sips his coffee and eats his coffee cake. The crumbs tumble down his shirt, but he is too tired to notice. In the evening, if the temperature drops, he'll light a fire and read the paper. His wife will heat their dinner. His daughters are living on different streets in different states. He had so much potential, but time took care of that. He sits in the living room, opens his book, and falls asleep.

June 21, 1941. My mother was at Russian headquarters at the railroad station on Grodecka Street, translating a battery order onto a form. Her office hummed with self-importance, papers rustled, and the sun gleamed through the windows.

Suddenly the windows exploded. Shattered glass flew everywhere. My mother fell to the floor and scrambled under her desk. Across the street, the train station exploded in flames. Airplane engines roared overhead, a thin whistle as the bombs fell, then the burst of impact, bricks flying like pebbles. People in the streets scurried for cover, amid shrieks and bursting glass. The roof of my mother's office building collapsed, and the east wall blew open to blue sky.

There had been no time to run—no sirens, no warning, no place to go. Batya clutched the legs of her desk. It was a good desk, solid wood, worn and polished from years of use. Glass and bricks skidded across it.

A colleague of hers, Jiri Ryrcz, burst into the room and ran to her. "Come on!" he yelled. "We've got to get out!" He yanked her by the arm and pulled her toward the door. "Run!" She couldn't hear and couldn't think. Her legs were moving, leaping over piles of rubble, burning beams, splintered wood. She ran through waves of knee-deep glass, following Jiri as he darted ahead of her. They reached the street and fled northeast, to Krakowska. The Red Army had assembled a battle line of sorts, tanks lined up in the streets, soldiers cowering in doorways and alleys. Across from the Soviet tanks was a line of German tanks, pushing the Russians back.

Jiri crouched in a doorway, and my mother caught up with him, breathless. Jiri seized her by the wrist. "German tanks!" he shouted over the chatter of machine guns. "Look—there!" He pointed and ducked as a grenade exploded a few meters from them. "We can't get through now, while they're fighting. Let's go back, we can stay at my apartment till it's safe."

Jiri lived in the southwestern part of town, not far from the railway station, which lay in ruins. The Germans had already overrun the area and were pushing the Russians east, one street at a time.

"No," my mother said. "My parents—I have to get home."

The doorway in which they crouched was covered with shattered bricks. "Okay, look," he said quickly. "I'll get you across the front line, then you run home along side streets."

She shook her head. "You go home, Jiri. There's no need for you to cross the line, it's foolish." Dust coated his curly black hair, and she resisted the urge to brush it off. "Go on, I'll be fine."

He squeezed her hand. "Be careful."

She watched him run back across the rubble to his apartment. Tanks slowly rolled into position on the next block. Her face was bathed in sweat, and for a moment she thought it must be raining. But the sky was a beautiful scorching blue, and small marshmallow clouds puffed like a picture in a child's book. A burst of gunfire erupted between two rows of tanks, and German soldiers scurried along the sides of the buildings, opening fire with machine guns and ducking into doorways. A Soviet tank burst into flames, and Russian soldiers were flung into the air like bits of confetti. The streets rattled with bullets. My mother inched forward, then sprinted to another doorway a few meters away. She had stopped thinking and had become a quiver of senses. Soldiers lay groaning in the street, and blood soaked the walls of Janowska Street, dripping down the sidewalk toward her.

Her legs uncocked, and she flew forward again, sideswiping a German tank and running through the no-man's land between the lines. She heard shouts and gunfire, but she kept running. Her feet did not seem to touch the ground. The city disappeared, and she was flying past Soviet tanks, past fallen soldiers, bags of supplies, and belts of ammunition. She kept running until the sounds of explosions and gunfire were behind her. She rounded the corner of Krakowska, where she had jumped the tram last winter. It seemed years ago now. She raced down Owacowa and up the stairs to the second floor.

"So I ran across the front line to my parents, on the other side of town," my mother told Lara and me recently at the shopping-mall food court.

"What do you mean, you ran across the front line?" I blurted out. She made it sound like a stroll through a field of blueberries. "Between the tanks? You ran between the tanks?"

"Yes, of course," my mother said, annoyed by the interruption. She drew a line with her hand on the table. "Here was the street," she said, "and here were the German tanks. Over here, the Russians." She pointed to imaginary tanks on the counter. "I simply zigzagged my way from one tank to another and ran across."

My jaw dropped.

"I didn't have a choice!" my mother exclaimed, irritated by my reaction. She was impatient, almost offended, by my lack of comprehension of these matters. This was war; she wanted to get home to prevent her parents from worrying, so she had to cross the front line. No point in blowing it up into a major accomplishment. She simply crossed the front line; she was lucky and made it across unharmed.

When she reached the apartment her parents threw their arms around her with relief. But Zosia was still missing—they had not heard from her since she had left for work that morning.

"There was no way to reach her," my mother said. "The phone lines were down, and my parents wouldn't let me go back out in the streets, so we waited."

Evening fell. As the minutes ticked by, they grew more anxious. They listened to the radio, but there was too much interference, and the bulletins were sketchy. Their neighbors whispered back and forth, and words flew across the city. "The Germans have taken the city," people said. "It's over for us, we're finished."

The night passed slowly. My mother and her parents lay awake and watched the house go dark. The family had lost its leader.

The sun rose the next morning on quiet streets. My grandmother made a pot of chicory and the family sipped in silence. My mother wanted to go to the pharmacy to find Zosia, but her mother wouldn't let her out of the apartment. Instead, they heard that a neighbor, Gorzinsky, was heading into town to buy food. As a Pole, it was safer for him to move about in the streets, and he promised to stop in at the pharmacy on Akademicka to see if Zosia was safe.

"Sure enough," my mother told me, "a little while later he returned, with Zosia on his arm."

Zosia looked shaken and pale, but she was all right. When she saw my mother, Zosia gave a cry of shock and threw her arms around my mother's neck.

"I didn't believe him!" Zosia said when she was finally able to speak. "He told me you were all right, but I didn't believe him. We heard the Grodecka railroad station was bombed— yesterday, on the radio—and I must have fainted. I don't know what happened. I stayed at the pharmacy. This morning I was walking home when I bumped into Gorzinsky now, on the street. He said you were fine, but I didn't believe him."

Gorzinsky sat down for a cup of tea and jam. My grandmother gave him four potatoes, which he refused at first, but she pushed them into his coat pocket.

13

This is the part of the story where the men sit helpless on the outskirts of Europe: my father behind barbed wire in the Gulag, and Uncle in an office in Rome. They frame the two sisters, who have fallen into the hands of warring tribes. Theirs is a solitary despair. They have never met each other, my father and Uncle, and they are opposites in every way: my father with his tall athleticism, his cold fury, and clenched fist; and Uncle with his slight dark body, his sad smile, delicate hands, and curved shoulders.

Uncle made inquiries through diplomatic channels. He wrote letters and met with officials in an effort to find his wife, slide her across borders, and bring her back into the sun. A few of Zosia's letters had squeaked through to him, but they were months old and brief. He had exhausted his political connections, to no avail.

In desperation Uncle did an unlikely thing:

He consulted a palm reader. He found her tiny apartment on the third floor of a tenement building on a forgotten alley in Trastevere. A plump middle-aged woman answered the door. Her fleshy arms jiggled when she shook his hand. She led him into a dim room that smelled of lemons and rosemary and sat him down at a small round table.

"I've lost contact with my wife," he said, pulling out the photograph of Zosia that he carried in his wallet. "I must know if she's all right. Can you find her? Will I see her again?"

The woman examined the photograph, then the man before her, with his fine fingers and neat dress. He was a government official, a man of consequence.

She consulted her cards, closed her eyes, and rolled her head. She murmured something incomprehensible and seemed to fall into a trance. Uncle waited, worried.

She spread a map on the small table. Leaning forward as if she were playing the piano, she slid her fingers across the map in opposite directions. Her eyes closed and she mumbled an incantation that Uncle could not understand. Her body swayed rhythmically, and her head bobbed, spilling thick black hair over the continent of Europe. Her voice rose and then fell, like a ship riding an enormous wave. Uncle stared, transfixed, clutching the arms of his chair.

Her eyelids fluttered, and her face went blank. She stopped mumbling and lowered her head to the map. Her hands were still, and she seemed to be listening intently for something.

Uncle had stopped breathing, his eyes wide. Outside, in the street, a motor started and died.

"Here," the woman said at last, opening her eyes and pointing to a place on the map. "Here." She leaned forward and examined the name of the town under her finger. "Br-zu-cho-vice," she pronounced with difficulty. "You know this place?" She turned to Uncle.

He leaned over the map to see where she pointed. It was a small town northeast of Lvov. "No," he said, "but it's close to her hometown."

"She is there," the woman said, "your wife is there. Have no fear, she's fine. She will come back to you. Don't worry."

Uncle sprang to his feet and kissed her hand. "Signora!" he choked out. "Signora, I can't thank you enough!"

She smiled calmly and patted his hand. "Sit," she said, "please." She looked at him with a probing gaze and lowered her voice. "But tell me," she said quietly, "why did you come to me? You, too, have the gift. You could have done this yourself." Uncle stared at her, perplexed.

"I see that you have the gift. You don't need me. You could have done this yourself."

"What do you mean?"

She smiled at him kindly. "You are one of us," she said. "You should listen for it. You'll see. You need to develop your gift."

Uncle left the apartment enormously relieved. His legs, however, felt weak, and he wobbled a bit as he walked down the stairs and stepped onto the street.

Uncle bought two books on parapsychology. He pored over them, absorbing every word. He bought a pendulum from a nearby dealer, and then a charm. He read Nostradamus. He studied everything he could get his hands on about parapsychology and the occult. He began to get impressions of things far away. He felt he had reached Zosia. He felt he could understand things that happened in distant lands. The more he could see, the more worried he became. Zosia would come back to him, he repeated over and over. But in his heart was the weight of a new sense of dread.

When I was a child, Uncle showed me how the pendulum worked. He placed my right hand on the dining table, palm up. Then he took the little pendulum from his pocket. He held the string between his thumb and third finger, letting the pendulum dangle an inch above my upturned wrist. I could see thin blue veins that slipped just under the skin. Uncle went silent, and I held my breath. Almost imperceptibly at first, the pendulum moved very slowly in a tight circle. Gradually, the circle grew wider, moving above my wrist in a clockwise direction. I looked at Uncle's fingers and at his hand—motionless. He sat like a statue and smiled when he saw the wonder in my eyes. "You see," he said sweetly, "you are good. It means you are good."

"How can you tell?" I asked.

"It goes clockwise. It means you are sweet." His eyes smiled, his mustache curved up.

"Watch," he said. He went into the kitchen and brought back a lemon. He placed it on the table and dangled the pendulum over it. After a moment or two the pendulum swung in a circle around the lemon. "See?" Uncle pointed with his other hand. "It's swinging counterclockwise. It's not sweet, it's not good."

I nodded, full of awe at Uncle's magical powers. Zosia came into the room to replace a book on the shelf. "Oh, what rubbish!" she scolded Uncle. "Don't stuff her head with all sorts of foolish ideas!"

Uncle looked hurt.

"He twists the string with his fingers," Zosia told me with exasperation. "Don't be fooled by that nonsense. He maneuvers it with his fingers!"

"No, I don't!" Uncle cried, jumping to his feet. "I don't! The pendulum is a conductor, and it transfers energy. It doesn't work for everyone. I have the gift."

Zosia threw up her hands in disgust and left the room.

Uncle turned to me. He smiled an apologetic little smile and shrugged his shoulders. "She doesn't believe in this," he said. "But watch. I'll show you."

With small steps he went into his study and returned with a large cardboard box, which he carefully set on the table. He opened it and removed a huge contraption, a tripod from which hung a large black pendulum. He set the contraption up and placed my wrist on the table under it. "Here," he said, "now you'll see. With this pendulum I don't even touch the string. But the results will be the same. Watch."

Uncle placed his hand over the top of the tripod, and we waited in silence. The pendulum dangled an inch above my wrist. It took a little longer, but sure enough, the pendulum swung in a steady clockwise circle. "See?" he said. He looked into my face to see whether he had won me back. I wasn't sure. Zosia's reaction had made a deep impression on me. Uncle was a funny little man, and we didn't speak the same language, so I wasn't sure whether to believe him or not. I was accustomed to trusting Zosia. She knew everything.

"We'll try again with the lemon," he said, and placed the lemon under the tripod. After a moment, the pendulum swung counterclockwise.

"Yes," I said lukewarmly.

"You try it," he said. "Let's see whether you have the gift."

I put my hand on top of the tripod. I wanted to have the gift too. I knitted my eyebrows and squeezed. "No, no force," Uncle said quietly, touching my hand. "Just put your hand over it gently, like this."

I rested my hand on the tripod. We waited a long, long time and nothing happened. "It doesn't work," I said with disappointment.

"Just wait."

We waited another minute or two. Then I noticed a very faint movement of the pendulum. I leaned closer. It circled, ever so slightly, in a small counterclockwise arc. The circle grew and grew. I was elated. Even Uncle seemed surprised and somewhat gratified.

"You too!" he exclaimed. "You, too, have the gift!"

Petlura Day, June 21, 1941. My mother first told me the story when I was six or seven, curled up on the brick floor in front of the fireplace in the living room. My head was in her lap, and she was playing with a few strands of my hair. Lara, who was ten, was sitting in the chair, drumming her fingers on her leg and staring at the fire. Our cheeks were pink because we had been outside in the snow for hours, building an igloo, packing the walls, and reinforcing them with water that froze on contact. We had slid down the hill by the maple tree on our flying saucer, spinning and skidding across the icy driveway.

My mother brought us a plate of linzer torte and we spilled crumbs of almonds and powdered sugar down the front of our woolly blue robes. I put my head in my mother's lap, and she traced my ear with her thumb.

"Of course," she said, "I used to play in the snow like you as a girl. We had a lot of snow and I always got too cold, and my ears would freeze. Especially my left ear, I always had trouble with that one." She rubbed my ears and I smiled. "And I skied, yes, as a girl." And then her voice drifted off and her eyes grew vague, and we knew she had left us and disappeared back to a time before we were born. We were silent. The fire burned. The wood was dry and it crackled, shooting sparks up the chimney. Outside, we could hear the wind in the trees, their branches bending against the purpling sky.

The past was always like this, an empty space in our lives, a gap in our conversations, into which our mother tumbled from time to time, quietly, without warning.

"I had a pair of leather ski boots," my mother continued, "with hard square toes and thick soles. They were stiff and warm, and hard to lace up because the leather was so thick. I had to wear three pairs of socks with them, because my mother didn't want me to ever outgrow them. They cost a fortune!"

"Square toes?" I asked dubiously.

"Yes, they fit into the bindings that way. In those days, ski boots were like that."

I giggled. "Square toes!"

My mother went quiet again. A warning. There was something about those ski boots, I knew, that was dangerous. I held my breath. Lara knew too. We stayed quiet and waited to see what would happen. Maybe an accident. Maybe she fell on the slope. The longer the silence, the greater the danger. I wanted to fill the space with words, but I was curious to know about those ski boots, so I stayed quiet.

"Oh well," my mother sighed, and smiled. "Are you girls hungry yet? Dinner will be a while."

"No," we said. "What happened to the ski boots?"

"Oh, they were taken," my mother said nonchalantly. It was that tone she used to cover the danger, and we knew we were close. It was right there.

"When?"

"A long time ago."

"Did you get another pair?"

"No," she smiled. The smile meant we were moving away from the danger, we were missing the point.

"How did it happen?"

"How did what happen?"

"The ski boots, how were they taken? Who took them?"

"Oh, bandits," she shrugged. "It was during the war." She made it sound like something very foolish, very insignificant.

"How did they take them?"

"What do you mean? They just came in and took them!"

"In your house, you mean?"

"Of course!" She shook her head as if we were being silly for not understanding. "There were a few days after the Russians left and before the Germans came, and there was no law or order. So the local bandits just helped themselves to everything! They just broke into people's houses and took whatever they wanted."

That was the end of the story. We could tell by the tone in her voice that she was finished. We knew there was more to it, because we still

166

didn't understand it, and we knew we were not meant to understand it.

The next time I heard the story was eleven years later, in 1975. I was a freshman in college and I had to write a paper on psychological reactions to trauma. During spring break I came home, casting about for a suitable topic, and as usual, my mother came to the rescue. She was very good at schoolwork; she had a knack for understanding what people wanted to know.

So she told me to write my paper about Zosia and her, about two sisters' different reactions to a traumatic event.

"It was during the war," she began. This meant I was to be careful and remain quiet.

"Between the Russian and German occupations. There were no laws in place, no one to maintain order in the city. And so the local population took advantage of the situation, and for a few days they went on a rampage, looting and raping women right in the streets.

"So my father took Zosia and me into a big courtyard, and I remember my father taking my head and putting it in his lap, covering my face with his hands, so that I wouldn't be seen. I was a young girl of twenty; they would have raped me too. But Father hid my head."

"What about Zosia?" I asked.

My mother paused, just a split second, and then scoffed at the idea. "Oh, Zosia was fine," she said, waving her hand impatiently. "They wouldn't touch Zosia, she was a married woman!" My mother lifted her hand and pointed to her ring. "She had a wedding band on her finger!"

Was I supposed to believe this? Before I could say anything, my mother rushed on with her story.

"I was terribly shaken by what I saw that day," my mother continued. "And I remember it so clearly, every detail, as if it happened yesterday. Whereas Zosia, who was sitting right there next to me, Zosia doesn't remember a thing of that day. She has completely forgotten, as if it never happened. Total amnesia."

"Really," I said, amazed.

"Different people react differently to stress," my mother said. "This is a perfect example. Here we are, two sisters sitting next to each other, exposed to the same horrible event, and one of us cannot forget it, and one of us cannot remember it. It's interesting, don't you think? Write your paper about that."

I nodded.

"Actually," my mother added, less enthusiastically, "actually, I remember something else about that day." She lowered her voice and looked away from me. "I lost my period after that day," she said. "I stopped menstruating."

I waited for her to say more, but she remained silent. "For how long?" I asked.

She looked at me for what seemed a long time. "Nine months," she said, nodding slowly.

I didn't dare ask my mother any more questions, but I wondered about those nine months. Had my mother been raped? Did I have a brother or sister somewhere? My mother's stories always left holes that I couldn't fill.

14

While my mother was sitting in the courtyard in Lvov, my father found himself huddled against the wall of an eastbound boxcar, hugging his knees. His shoulders knocked against the prisoners on either side of him. The sun rose and fell; days clicked by like knitting needles. Squeaking wheels on steel rails, and the smell of steam on brittle air. Men toppled to the floor like oaks; the bucket of piss overflowed and froze in the cracks. Gusts of wind battered the wooden cars. My father slept sitting up, head on his knees. His legs tingled, then went numb. His mouth was stone dry, his tongue a lizard; rubbing his head in his hands, he heard the growl of his empty belly.

Another week slipped through the slats, then the train stopped. It sat in an open field for days. Russian guards brought a bucket of soup, a fresh bucket for excrement. The fish broth was salty, and thirst racked his brain. The doors shut; the train moved again. Hours later it stopped on a side rail and waited another two days. The boxcar smelled acrid, of bruised bodies and urine. Thirteen men were dead, frozen into hard knots of driftwood. The doors opened; the corpses were taken out like bundles of kindling and left by the side of the tracks. The men were given water, a slice of black bread. My father was dizzy. He held the bread to his mouth, but his legs wobbled and he collapsed. The sun danced over him and the moment was golden, and then it was gone. He was losing his way on the edge of a field, and then he was back in the boxcar, the doors were closing, and the train was moving. He leaned against his neighbor, opened his mouth, and passed out.

My father awoke in a prison cell, he told me, twelve feet by twenty. There were thirty-five men in the cell. Concrete floor, no windows. In the corner opposite the door was the shit bucket, and around it, the newest prisoners were clustered, forests of faces and blank, staring eyes. Men who had been in the cell the longest had the patch of floor farthest from the bucket. This was how you measured your status in prison—the value of your real estate, your distance from the shit pail.

My father lived there for months, as cycles of prisoners came and went. He lost weight, and his bones stuck out. He slept in a crouched position, back against the wall, arms crossed over his knees, head on his arms. This way he could protect his belongings from his cellmates—a T-shirt, a soup spoon carved of wood, and an extra pair of socks.

Fights erupted often and were broken up by the other inmates to prevent interference from the prison guards. Periodically, the guards emptied the cell, strip-searched the prisoners, and rifled through their belongings, confiscating homemade tools, paper, buttons, or pieces of string. When the inmates were returned to the cell, they would spend the rest of the day weeding through the pile of rags on the floor to retrieve their meager possessions.

To fend off boredom, my father and two or three other prisoners began a chess club. They painstakingly saved bits of their bread rations over a few days, fashioned them into chessmen, and improvised a game board. They played on the sly, with one prisoner keeping an eye out for the guards (chess and card games were strictly forbidden). During one of the random cell searches, the guards ransacked their belongings, leaving the tiny chess pieces scattered across the floor. My father rushed back to the cell, but he was too late. By the time he got there the other prisoners had already gobbled up the chessmen, swallowing the hardened bits of stale bread.

"Proof," my father told me with a smile, "that man does not live by chess alone."

A few weeks later the guards staged another search, and my father was one of the last prisoners to return to the cell. When he sifted through the pile of rags for his belongings, he discovered that his spare T-shirt was missing; it had apparently been stolen by one of the inmates who had gotten back to the cell before him.

Furious, my father stood and scanned the prisoners, staring into each man's eyes. "Who took my shirt?" he demanded. No one spoke. A dark-haired Uzbekistani glared defiantly back at him. *So he's the one,* my father thought. *I'll get him.*

"I will give you until tomorrow morning to return my shirt," my father announced to everyone in the cell, "no questions asked. Otherwise, I warn you. I have the Evil Eye, and you will be sorry."

The men laughed and turned their backs on him. My father forced himself to stay calm and concocted a plan to punish the thief. He squatted on his heels and settled for the night in his corner of floor between two other prisoners. He was hoping the men's superstitions would work in his favor. But in the morning his shirt was still missing.

"Very well," my father announced to his cellmates. "I see you have not returned my shirt. I've warned you, I have the Evil Eye, and I know who you are. You will be sorry."

Loud guffaws.

Now, my father thought, it would be a battle of wits. He dropped to his haunches and stared intently at the Uzbekistani across from him. Minutes melted into hours. My father neither spoke nor shifted his gaze all day. Only after all the other men had fallen asleep did he let himself drift off. The next morning, before anyone else was awake, my father resumed his vigil, so that the first thing the man saw when he woke up were my father's eyes fastened on him.

Did my father allow himself a moment of

doubt? He had committed himself to revenge, and now he was consumed by it.

Finally, after a day or two, the Uzbekistani began to be visibly disturbed. He mumbled to his friends and exchanged glances with others in the cell. He turned away from my father and laughed nervously, dismissing my father as mad, but hours later, when he turned back, he saw my father still staring at him like a vulture.

Toward the end of the third day the man suddenly jumped to his feet and leapt at my father, punching wildly. My father had been waiting for this, he told me. He sprang up and, with a sharp kick, flung the man back across the room. The ruckus brought the guards to the door, but my father waved them away, assuring them that everything was all right. Then he immediately dropped to a crouch and continued to stare.

The air in the cell crackled; all the men were tense now, jumpy. A few tried to reason with my father. "Let it go," they said, "forget about it. Leave the man alone, stop staring at him." But my father neither looked at them nor spoke to them. He sensed that he was gaining the upper hand now; he smelled blood.

From then on, my father told me, he forced himself to remain awake all night, afraid the man and his friends would attack him in his sleep. Each morning the Uzbekistani woke to find my father's eyes drilled on him.

The tension in the cell became unbearable. Groups of men whispered among themselves.

The Uzbekistani had trouble sleeping and eating. He kept looking around nervously, and each time he saw my father's eyes he cringed.

Finally, on the fourth day, the man leapt to his feet and grabbed my father's T-shirt from inside his pants. "Here!" he shrieked, tearing it to shreds. "Here's your fucking T-shirt, you son of a bitch! Here! You can have it!"

He flung the bits of fabric at my father, who remained impassive. "I don't care about the T-shirt," my father said, his voice wooden. "But you must learn that you cannot steal from your fellow man; we are all in the same boat; you must treat us with respect."

The man scowled and returned to his spot. "Go to hell," he said, dropping to the floor among his friends.

Still my father continued to stare at the man with unblinking intensity. What was he after? Everyone in the cell shifted restlessly, trying to put the incident out of their minds. But the Uzbekistani grew more and more uneasy as the hours dripped by. He tried to turn his back to my father, but he felt my father's eyes burning through his skin. He was coming undone.

At last the man cracked. He began shouting incomprehensibly and tearing his hair out in clumps. He started banging his head against the wall until blood oozed from his nose and mouth. His friends tried to hold him down, but he was wild, raving. Finally the guards came and carried him off. He was never seen again.

When I was five or six my mother caught me stealing coins from her purse. She and my sister had a long, humiliating talk with me, and I tearfully agreed to forgo my allowance for two weeks as punishment. My father never learned of the incident. He rarely meted out justice in our family; I was my mother's charge. But on those occasions when my father did catch me doing something wrong, his eyes were sharp, punishing, murderous.

It wasn't until a few years ago that my father told me the story of how he had destroyed a man with his eyes. A milk-white terror seized me, and I couldn't erase the image from my mind, those eyes of my father boring holes through his prey. Even today I still think about that Uzbekistani, one of my father's early pupils of ethics; I wonder whether the man recovered, whether such lessons are ever survived.

My father remained in the holding cell, languishing through several cycles of prisoners. His case was held up; his papers had not been forwarded from headquarters, perhaps because he had given the Soviets a false name. He sat in the cell for a year among the changing tides of prisoners and convicts, until one day the commanding officer caught on to him. He was called into the interrogation room by his true name. "Kovik Buchman! You've been playing games with us, I see."

The interrogator looked him up and down.

My father could barely stand without losing balance. He swayed to the left.

"We have found your papers, Buchman! What did you think you would accomplish by that little game?"

My father shrugged. The effort made him stagger forward.

"You're a fool!" the officer said.

My father concentrated on standing still, on making no sudden movements, on accustoming his eyes to the light in the room, on breathing evenly and holding his head up.

"Sign here," the commander said.

My father lifted the pen and scrawled a signature on his confession. He signed the wrong name.

The commander examined it. "Cut the bullshit!" he said. "What I need is your signature, Buchman! Do you need my help? Shall I guide your hand? Sign it!"

"I can't," my father said politely. "It's not true."

My father woke up on the floor. His mouth was on the concrete and next to his mouth was his tooth and a small puddle of blood. He sat up and blinked. The office was dark. He believed that he was alone. He looked around but saw nothing.

He heard papers rustling far away. The sound came closer, and then he saw hands, rustling papers on the desk. It was the commanding officer with a cigar in his mouth. The room grew lighter. My father rubbed his eyes. His mouth was sore.

Eventually my father would lose all his teeth; the ones that weren't knocked out rotted in his mouth. Years of watery soup and saw-dust-filled bread left his bones brittle. His teeth dried up and crumbled. His ankles ballooned out, and then his stomach swelled. Bit by bit, he turned into air.

After a year in the cell he was sentenced without a trial. Tired of waiting for him to convict himself, they expedited his case at last and sent him to a camp in northern Siberia. He entered the arctic institution of higher learning. He learned how to wrap his feet in rags. He learned how to make a needle out of a fish bone. He learned to keep an eye out for illegal tools: a scrap of paper, a piece of wire, a bit of metal. He learned to hide his handmade needle so it wouldn't be confiscated in the body searches. He played chess from midnight until dawn when sleep refused to visit him, and he learned to mark chips on a board, to recognize homemade chess pieces as kings and knights and rooks. He learned that the Gulag is full of chess masters, and he learned to kill his opponents on the chess board. He learned to wait and keep his eyes on the latch of the door. He learned to count the days, the swings of the ax, the angle of the sun, the time of the year. He learned to keep his mouth shut. He learned to avoid the stool pigeons in each cell, each room, each occupation in the Gulag. He learned to avoid the whores, the women on the make, the criminal prisoners. He learned to mistrust the other politicals, especially the ones who seemed most friendly. He learned to rely solely on himself, on his own wits, his own hands, his own feet. Occasionally he did a favor, but only when his back was covered. He managed a few favors, and a few favors came back to him. And only then was he able to survive in the Gulag. There is a delicate market in the camps. Favors pass back and forth. Careful gestures, tiny, apparently inconsequential—lives hanging in the balance.

15

My father often told me that surviving the Gulag was easier than raising children. When it came to puling, migraine-baiting, nerve-fraying torture, Lara and I had Stalin beat by a landslide.

"Daddy, Daddy!" I'd shriek at the top of my six-year-old lungs. "Lara stole my pen!"

"Did not!" "Did too!" "Liar!" "Daaaaddy!!"

"I'm on the phone!" he boomed. My mother whisked us away from the telephone stand.

"Mommy, my pen!"

"Ach, *Bosze, Bosze*," my mother cried, pressing her temples with both fists. "I should have died with my parents!"

"Make her give it back!" I wailed.

My father slammed down the receiver. "For this I starved six years in the Gulag?"

In 1965, when I was eight years old, my father finally enrolled us in family therapy. We all knew there was something very wrong, but none of us knew exactly what it was. We had a sinking feeling that it had something to do with the children. I spent as much time as I could out of the house, pretending I belonged to another family—almost any other family. At home I locked myself in my room for hours. My mother started sleeping in Lara's room to calm her night fears. It wasn't clear what these fears were, but Lara said she had to "check." Every night she flicked the lights on and off, on and off. Then she dropped to her knees and checked under the bed. Then behind the curtain, under the desk, and back to the lights. Her checking routine became so lengthy, so elaborate and time-consuming, that after a while no one got any sleep at all.

Family therapy was a brawling, breathless free-for-all, witnessed by Dr. Grokle and her sidekick, Social Working Miss Jameson at the Child Guidance Center. Friday afternoons vanished under their steady, provocatively psychological gaze. Feeling the pressure of a professional audience, our family cranked out the performance of our lives. We exhibited a flair for dysfunction; we were on fire with it.

I used to study Dr. Grokle, who always looked like she needed to brush her hair out. It was long and wrapped in a high bun like a wasp's nest, and it was starting to turn gray. And Miss Jameson, with her bovine hips, the amplified swish of her nylons when she crossed and recrossed her legs. I remember sitting next to her, seeing the solidity of those legs barely contained in a loud green or blue dress, which never quite covered enough. She seemed to spend the entire session trying to rearrange her legs within the tiny opening of that dress. It occupied my mind. I would stare at the profusion of dark hair on her legs, pressed to her skin under the nylons like filaments of kelp trapped under an invisible net. It was the greatness of those legs, the roundness of the hips, that held me riveted in those sessions. They were a great mystery, a presence of such magnitude and power that I fell into a profound silence before them.

In the meantime, my parents and sister fought and cried, raved and sobbed, launching a spectacle for the doctor each week. But no one breathed a word about the past, preferring to soak in the poison of the present.

Our family has always respected the power of secrets.

In June 1992, armed with our newfound knowledge, Lara and I spent hours on the phone, discussing strategy. "We have to get Mom and Dad to tell us more about what happened to them during the war," Lara said. "Why they hid it all from us. From everyone."

I trusted her judgment as a psychiatrist, but I felt uneasy with our plan to question our mother for more details. I was afraid of confronting our parents. I wasn't sure we had the right to find out about them.

"It's not just about *them*!" Lara said. "It's about *us*! About who *we* are!" The anger in her voice alarmed me. During our frequent childhood fights she used to chase me around the house, shouting, "I'll *kill* you!" in much the same tone. Once, when we were raking leaves, she had pushed me over the cliff behind our house in a metal garbage can. One minute I had been stomping leaves into the can, and the next minute I was barreling down the cliff, ricocheting off trees. "It was an accident," my sister said.

"They've left us out of a whole world!" she was saying now. "Don't you feel ripped off?"

I shifted uneasily at the kitchen counter and curled the phone cord through my fingers.

"What about all this Jewish stuff," she said. "Do you know the first thing about Judaism? Have you tried to go to services?"

I nodded weakly.

"Well?"

"I'm not very religious," I said. "Even if I'd been raised Jewish, I probably wouldn't be very religious." I shrugged. "But I know what you're saying, I do wish I knew more."

"Okay," Lara said. "So first we'll go home on the Fourth of July, and I'll bring a tape recorder, and we'll see what happens. Leave it to me. I'll talk to Mom. If you feel like it, jump in and ask questions too."

I shook my head slowly. "I don't know," I

said. "That last time we talked with them in May—that made me crazy-anxious. You're going to have to bring up the stuff about how Mom's parents died—I can't do that." I still felt guilty for blurting out in May that my mother's parents had been gassed in Belzec. I felt queasy every time I thought of her sitting at the dining table with her hands outstretched, demanding to know how her parents had been killed.

"Okay," Lara said. "I'll do the talking."

We were quiet for a moment. A baseball flew across my backyard, chased by the neighbor's kids in Red Sox T-shirts.

"What about all this other stuff?" I finally asked.

"What other stuff?"

"You know, childhood stuff. All those fights we used to have."

I could picture my sister pursing her lips. "I don't know about you," she said, "but things are definitely starting to make more sense to me."

"Such as?"

"Mom and Dad are trauma victims," Lara said, as if this explained everything. "Their ability to cope with ordinary, garden-variety anger is totally out of whack. No wonder it was so confusing when we were kids. Remember how Mom used to collapse to her knees and pound her hands on the floor? Or clutch her head and start sobbing? *'Bosze, Bosze, Bosze!'* And then she'd lose her breath, and I thought she'd die or something. I used to think I'd killed her, just because I'd had a fight with you or because I refused to practice the piano or something. It was nuts!"

I used to think of Lara as a monster when I was little, but now I was starting to view my relationship with my sister in a new light. She had gone from being my archenemy to my soul mate, strangely mimicking my mother's relationship with Zosia. Maybe, I thought, sisters in our family were like that. Four women divided into two teams: whichever pair of sisters had the stronger bond would win.

"All right," my mother said, "I'll tell you." Her voice was shaky, but she was prepared to talk.

Lara, my mother, and I were sitting at a booth in the Melrose shopping mall. July 4, 1992— half a century after the event she was describing, and half a world away. It was late morning, and teenagers in polyester uniforms and paper hats heated the oil for the fries and switched on the heat lamps. They ran dishrags over the stainless-steel surfaces and filled the cash register with rolls of coins. The heat from the grill rolled upward in waves and flushed their faces pink. They slouched against the counters, waiting for customers. But no one was coming to the shopping mall. It would be an easy day at the food court; Independence Day pays time and a half.

"It was in the summer," my mother said, "about this time of year. Or maybe a little earlier, in June." She paused to think a moment.

"1941," I offered.

"1941. The Russians had fled. German tanks invaded the city. They bombed the railway station. Remember, I told you. How I ran back home, across the front line. The Germans took the city. For the next few days, or weeks, it was utter pandemonium. The Ukrainians cheered the arrival of the Germans." My mother's face relaxed almost imperceptibly, her eyes widening, and her mouth softening. "You see," she explained, "the Ukrainians had always hated the Russians and were glad to be rid of them. The Germans, on the other hand, had promised the Ukrainians their own independent nation. So the minute the Russians fled, the Ukrainians went on a wild rampage. They looted houses, rounded people up, and forced them into the streets. They broke into apartments and helped themselves to whatever they wanted. They raped women left and right." She lowered her eyes and seemed to be staring at a spot on the table between us. She spoke slowly and deliberately. She had rehearsed this in her mind over the last few weeks. How she would tell this. How she would finally reduce that day to words.

"The Germans looked the other way. They let it happen. They let the Ukrainians have a field day. You can't imagine—" She shook her head.

"We tried to run out—my parents and Zosia and I—but they caught us just as we were locking up the apartment. They forced their way in, taking Mother with them. Father rushed Zosia and me down the stairs and out of the building. They were beating people with clubs and pushing us down the street. They sealed all of us in a big courtyard. They grabbed women and raped them, right there in the streets, in the courtyard, in front of everyone. Like a pack of wild animals with the smell of blood. That is when—remember—my father took my head in his hands and hid me in his lap, so that they wouldn't see me. They were guarding the doors at the entrance and forcing more people into the courtyard. It was—it was my first real experience, my first real shock, maybe that's why I remember it all so well. Afterward"—she waved her hand dismissively—"afterward we got used to things like this. There were roundups every week. People died every day. We stopped seeing it, it stopped affecting us the same way. It was just the beginning, you see—"

She shook her head again, trying to return to the strand of the story.

"The courtyard was filling with blood. The screams were terrible. There was no room to move, and the blows fell from all sides. This is when Zosia jumped up. She spotted a German SS officer overseeing the action near the entrance to the courtyard. She knew not to waste her time arguing with the Ukrainians. She marched over to the SS officer, drew herself up, and in her perfect German she said, 'Officer! How dare they treat me like this! I am an Aryan and an Italian citizen! My husband is a government official in Italy. This is an outrage! I demand to be released!'

"The officer was startled by her pure German. He addressed her politely and examined her documents. Sure enough, she had an Italian passport and an Italian name. Germany and Italy were allies then. The officer bowed and apologized for the mistake.

"You see, the Germans didn't know anything. They relied on the Ukrainians to pick us out and herd us up. The Ukrainians had lived next to us for generations; they knew us. They were our neighbors. Lvov was one third Jews, one third Poles, and one third Ukrainians. We all knew who was who. But the Germans didn't know a thing, they had never been this far east before.

"And so the officer escorted Zosia out of the courtyard and apologized again for the mistake.

"Zosia ran all the way home, quickly cleaned herself up (she was covered with blood), put on a new dress, earrings, and makeup, and ran back to the courtyard.

"SS officers were stationed at the entrance. 'My sister is in there!' she cried. 'They've made a mistake! They took my sister!' She showed the officers her documents and explained that she and her sister were Aryans; that she was an Italian citizen, and so on. They let her into the courtyard and accompanied her to find her sister.

"I was huddled next to my father, with my head in his lap. He held both his arms over me

186

so I wouldn't be seen. Suddenly we heard Zosia's voice calling, 'Cucca! Cucca!' above the din. I looked up but couldn't see her. Everything was spinning.

"'Answer her in Italian!' Father whispered to me. 'Go on, answer her!'

"And then—I will never forget this—then Father pushed me away from him, as if he didn't know me, and he looked away. As if we were strangers. I was—I don't know—that look on his face, as if I didn't exist. And so I raised my hand and waved it over my head and shouted, *'Sono qui! Zosia,* sono qui!'

"Zosia worked her way through the mob to me, and I stood up to greet her. She was with two SS men. 'Zosia!' I cried. And then I fainted.

"Which made things even worse," my mother said. "Because the SS men had to carry me out of the courtyard, and I still didn't come to. And so they insisted on carrying me home. Zosia tried to avoid that; she knew that when they saw where we lived, they would get suspicious. But it couldn't be helped. The officers insisted, and I was still unconscious, so Zosia led them to our home and thanked them.

"My mother was waiting for us at home. The apartment had been ransacked. They'd taken everything, including my ski boots. They even took the gift that Dad had given me for my birthday the year before—you know—that little model head made out of construction paper." My mother's eyes drifted past Lara's head and settled on something far from us, something in the distant past. She smiled.

I remembered stories of that little construction-paper model head my father had made for my mother when they were courting. My mother told us about it when we were children, while my father listened, grinning from ear to ear. The model was supposed to be my mother's head, full of all her knowledge. It had a Mozart hairdo the way my mother used to have, with a little pigtail in the back. If you lifted the pigtail the head opened up, and inside there were little drawers that you could open. Inside each drawer was a little piece of paper, representing all of her knowledge. One drawer was entitled *Math knowledge;* inside on the piece of paper was written *2 + 2 = 4 or 5 (?)*. Another drawer was entitled *Culinary knowledge,* and inside was a slip of paper that said *How to make napoleonki: Take 25 groschen and go to Zalewski's bakery on the corner of Wale Hetmanskie and Mickiewicz.*

"What happened to your father?" I asked my mother now.

"Yes," she said, "I'll tell you. It got late. Night fell. We were terribly worried, but Mother wouldn't let us go out of the house. We waited. Outside in the street the Ukrainians were still yelling and drinking. They were shooting people. We waited and waited. Finally, late at night, Father came home, exhausted, his pants torn, but he was all right. His shoes were missing. They had let him go finally, but he had walked home in his socks."

Maybe he traded them for his life, I thought. Maybe they were stolen from him, and later he escaped. I have trouble imagining the face of my grandfather, because I have no pictures, and my mother's descriptions are vague. "I look like him," she said. "He had soft dark hair. Dark eyes. And fingernails like mine. Look." But I can see only my mother; her father's face is fuzzy, it's meant to be. Yet this image of his feet I know by heart. I can see them clearly, shoeless and dusty, with thin black socks that once were almost elegant.

"Eventually," my mother continued, "they had to let everyone go. It had gotten so out of hand, so many people raped and shot and beaten, that the Germans finally put a stop to it. They saw that the Ukrainians had made too many mistakes, robbed and beaten too many Poles together with the Jews, and so they let all the prisoners out of the courtyard in the end." My mother shrugged.

She seemed satisfied with this conclusion, although I wondered.

I wondered about everything now. The more I knew the more I wondered. If you open one door, a thousand other doors creak open. At least there were two of us, Lara and I, tiptoeing through this wobbly past, doused with the blood of relatives we only now were getting to know. Lara gave me the courage to look, the courage to face our parents and our past.

"Hey." Lara called me a few weeks later, in July. "Guess what? Remember that story

Mom told us about the roundup in the courtyard, when she fainted? Well, I found it in this
book. It was June 27, 1941, Petlura Day.
And guess what else? That courtyard—that was
the courtyard of Mom's grade school, the
Sobieskego School on Zamarstynowska Street.
In the heart of the Jewish section of Lvov."

And so the story takes shape, it unfolds
and then folds again and again. Little things
change its texture, but I will never find it
just the way it was. All the details swirl around,
and what is left is the look on her father's face—
remote, unrecognizable, and the sight of his
socks making their way home in the dark.

Years later I would learn more about the
pogrom in the courtyard that my mother had
described to Lara and me. The roundup had
been so brutal, I read, that the blood smeared
the second story of the buildings. Over two
thousand people were slaughtered. In the
U.S. Holocaust Museum, I found a one-and-
a-half-minute film clip of the Petlura Day
action, showing men and women being rounded
up into the courtyard, stripped and beaten,
jeered at, and shot en masse. The film was taken
by a German SS officer. I sat glued to the screen,
replaying the grisly bit of archival footage
over and over again, slowing it down so I
could see it frame by frame, searching the
desperate crowd for my mother's face, for
Zosia's. They seemed to be everywhere: All
the women in the film looked like my mother,

dark-haired and wild-eyed, falling to the pavement, splattered with blood.

16

Summer 1978. A bottle of red wine leaned against two rocks at our feet. Pale sockless toes, hungry for light. It had rained the past two days and now the sun rose like an emperor, beaming over a shocked blue sky. The campsite was deserted—a chipmunk-chewed wood cabin sat at the edge of a mountain lake like a fallen stack of firewood. Gentle waves lapped the shore, and trees whispered to each other in strange tongues.

Lara took another slug of wine.

"Here's to us," she said, squinting in the sunlight.

I tilted the bottle back and gulped. "To us."

Lara grinned, a sixteen-ounce California-wine grin. Her shoulders were strong and tanned. We'd been hiking for two weeks, and tomorrow we would begin the long drive home.

"Let's swim to the rock," she said, pointing across the lake.

I shielded my eyes with my forearm. A huge granite boulder rose from the lake about half a mile from shore.

"Here," Lara said, corking the bottle and placing it under a bush. "We can finish this later. Let's swim out while the sun's hot."

We tore off our clothes and leapt into the water, shrieking with delight as the cold hit our naked bodies. Lara was already twenty feet ahead of me, graceful arms slicing the surface with each stroke as if braiding the lake.

The water was mesmerizing. Everything sparkled. By the time I reached the rock, Lara had circled it and found the best way up. Holding on to an outcrop, she let me climb on her shoulders and onto the ledge. Then I helped pull her up, scraping our knuckles and knees. There was enough room for both of us to lie down. The heat on my breasts and thighs felt intoxicating. I closed my eyes and drifted to sleep, rocked by the memory of waves.

After a while I sat up and dangled my feet in the water. "This is what Mom and Zosia have," I said suddenly.

Lara opened her eyes and blinked.

"Sisters," I said. "Mom always wanted you and me to be as close to each other as she and Zosia are."

Lara shifted onto her side. The rock was shiny and dark where her body had been. Her breasts glistened chalk-white, and two white stripes over her shoulders traced the shape of her tank top, like a negative exposure.

"The day before we left on this hiking trip," I said, "Zosia pulled me aside. 'Someday,' she told me, 'you'll come to appreciate what it means to have a sister. Remember, there is nothing so important in the world as the love of two sisters.'"

Lara's eyes widened.

"I'm starting to get it," I said. "I think you and I will be as close as they are."

July 1941: The Germans took over the nicest section of Lvov and spilled the locals onto the street. The Jews were packed into the Zamarstynowska district, cut off from the rest of the town by elevated train tracks. The crooked little streets of the poorest section were now crowded with all the Jews, rich and poor, Orthodox and atheist, who were forced to register and wear blue-starred armbands. The parameters of the ghetto were reduced periodically as the Jewish population was decimated—it was urban planning on a temporary scale.

One day, early in the German occupation, my mother told me, Zosia was walking along Krakowska Street with a friend of hers, a young man she knew in high school. A German soldier approached them, smoking a cigarette, his face bathed in July sunshine. Instinctively, Zosia stepped off the sidewalk into the street and continued walking, never raising her eyes. Her friend was not so quick to defer, and the bullet ripped through his forehead. He fell at Zosia's feet, eyebrows raised, his face a map of blood. Zosia kept walking, her feet obeying an unspoken order. Her eyes remained fixed on the cobblestones in front of her. She passed the German without looking up. The faint smell of his cigarette, familiar, acrid. He replaced his revolver in his belt, and his boots receded down the sidewalk behind her. Neither Zosia nor the soldier had broken their gait; between them, Zosia's friend lay at the moment of his mistake, his face flowing into the stones of the street that he should have stepped down to.

Zosia had hidden her Italian passport during the Soviet occupation—it would have been damaging evidence of her aristocratic marriage. But now, under the Germans, she carried it with her, and found herself reincarnated as an Italian countess. Still, papers went only so far. Her identity as a Catholic countess could buckle at any moment; she might still be recognized as a *Zhid* in her hometown. The streets were full of informers; people were eager to turn Jews in, and children ran through the streets denouncing them for a candy. If Zosia's true identity was exposed, then Uncle and his family in Italy would also be arrested as traitors, violators of the racial laws.

To play it safe, my mother told me, Zosia moved from her family's home on Owacowa Street, which would become part of the Jewish ghetto, and rented an apartment across town on Senatorska Street, in the Aryan section. She made connections with the Underground and began running goods and information between cities. With her bleached blond hair and blue eyes, her Italian papers and royal name, it didn't matter that her passport had expired under the Russians. She was not German, perhaps, but her German was flawless, and her instincts were sharp.

On Akademicka one day, Zosia heard the unmistakable lilting sound of Italian spoken behind her. She turned and saw a few Italian officers ambling down the street in their fascist uniforms. She stopped and introduced herself. The men were delighted to find someone who spoke Italian, and they reminisced about Italy while Zosia showed them around the city.

The following day Zosia slipped into the ghetto. She crept up the steps and knocked on the door of her parents' house—their signal knock. My mother opened the door.

"Good news!" Zosia whispered, unable to contain her excitement. "Italian officers are stationed in town. Near Platz Akademicka. I told them about my kid sister, and they want to meet you. You could work in their office, do their bookkeeping, whatever they need."

"But—"

"Meet us tomorrow at the Intourist Café," Zosia said, "at one o'clock."

"What did you tell them?"

"That you're my sister, my Polish sister. And remember," Zosia added, "take that thing off when you cross into the Aryan section."

My mother glanced down. It seemed to her that the armband on her sleeve glowed in the darkened apartment. She felt that the star would continue to shine on her arm even if she took the band off. She was a marked woman.

Zosia presented her expired Italian passport at German headquarters in Lvov and applied for an exit visa to return to her husband in Italy. But the Germans wanted to prevent word of the massacres in Lvov and the East from leaking back to western Europe. So despite her inquiries and Uncle's diplomatic efforts in Rome, her request was held up in Berlin.

Zosia went from office to office at German headquarters. Her eyes gleamed, and she laughed with delight at the Germans' jokes. She was always so good at playing games, my Zosia. She can finesse anything from closed hands to stern faces. The Germans, she quickly saw, were so many little bricks in a wall of bureaucracy. She began to chisel away at them, one chink at a time, hoping that eventually she would make a hole just large enough for her to slip through with her family.

In the meantime she managed to smuggle food to her parents, who sat inside day and night. War was nothing new to them, but this was a new war, and they were not as fluid as they used to be. They gave themselves over to their older daughter, who had become an operator. Her parents knew it was a gift she had, or she was the gift, and they grew used to her miracles: She found eggs when no one even had bread; she brought home milk and flour and jam when the streets were empty and people starving. She moved through clandestine channels, running risks and favors for the Underground.

It was during this time that Zosia developed a close friendship with a jeweler named Floda, a Jewish émigré from Vienna. He dealt in gems and food on the black market, and Zosia ran deliveries for him. She could take more risks, with her Italian papers and her Aryan looks. She traveled to nearby cities and towns, meeting his contacts, smuggling goods back and forth to the ghetto, bringing word from relatives, news from one city to another. She slipped through guards at the train stations and talked her way through tight spots. She had this knack, this instinct, a confidence and charm that enabled her to glide past regulations.

Despite her acrobatics, however, the family barely survived, bartering their clothing for food, until they had almost nothing left. "We each had only one overcoat," my mother told me, "which we wore day in and day out for years. The material began to wear out, so eventually we turned the coats inside out and wore them with the inner fabric exposed. But after a while even this fabric was completely worn out; we were reduced to rags. And then— you know what happened? We discovered the third side. It was like magic! We turned the coat inside out again, and found that the third side was really quite new by comparison!"

Under the Nazis the story gets choppy, the details clipped. There is a loss of sequence— images fly together, then explode apart. In one glimpse they are wearing armbands. A moment before, they were not. You can fill in the gaps with books, a little historical mortar between bricks of memory.

The Germans had a plan, but my mother's story has no plan. Images tumble from windows of memory without introduction, the face of a friend, a heel of bread, a hand on one's forehead. Now it is summer, and now it is winter, a jumble of images folding over and over each other like a woman washing her hands.

17

June 1992: I waded through a sofa-sized box of documents, attorney files, police reports, and billing records. A lawyer had delivered them to my office on a dolly, to prove he'd spent 52.75 hours working on various criminal cases one Saturday the previous May. My job was to prosecute him for overbilling the state, and I had a backlog of seventy cases like his. As the Miss Manners of public defenders, I had become a speed bump on the highway to attorney wealth.

After reading a few pages of hand-scribbled documents, I found myself mulling over my parents' stories, moving around the pieces I'd gathered so far. Maybe it was because of my job—forcing lawyers to keep records, to cough up all the smarmy little details of their practices—or maybe it was simply my birthright to guilt, but the more I learned about my parents' past, the more uncomfortable I started to feel about my own. I had my own secret that I'd been keeping from my parents for years, afraid of their reaction. They had suffered enough, I'd told myself, why burden them further?

But now that we'd pressured Mom and Dad to tell us about themselves, it seemed dishonest of me to hide my own identity from them. And so that evening, a few weeks before meeting my mother on the Fourth of July, I asked Lara whether I should tell my parents that I was a lesbian.

"Maybe not right away," Lara cautioned. "I mean, they have a lot on their plates right now; you don't want to complicate things."

But being a lesbian *was* complicated, I thought. My little descriptive noun, a mere attribute, like left-handedness. But to my parents, I figured, it would be triple-bypass material; announcing I was a lesbian would mean I was a screeching failure—possibly dangerous, definitely deranged.

"Look," Lara said. "You've hidden this from them for, what, five years? Six? So maybe you can wait a little longer. I mean, it's not like they're suspicious or anything. Besides," she added, "you're not in a relationship now, right? So what's the big rush?"

Lara knew I was still getting over the loss of my lover, who had died of breast cancer a year earlier. My parents had known only that she was my closest friend. They never asked about my personal life. Neither Lara nor I were married; neither of us had children, and despite our family's closeness, my parents had never inquired about significant others or plans for children.

"Doesn't it seem strange?" I said. "I mean, Mom and Dad practically know what we eat for breakfast, what brand of underwear we wear, but they don't even know if we're dating anyone!" I remembered Russell Collins, the earnest intern who used to follow Lara around in med school like a puppy dog. She actually brought him home to my parents once, but they pretended not to notice there was a man in the house.

Lara laughed halfheartedly. "Maybe they're too threatened by it," she said. "For us to have a lover—husband, partner, whatever—might mean our bond to them is somehow compromised."

It's true, I thought, our family was unusually clingy. Ever since I was a kid my mother had resented my lack of filial devotion. She had raised children the way a tree grows bark: for support and insulation. But I had a streak of selfishness the size of the Mississippi and an almost fanatic wish to be off with my friends.

"You know," I said, "I wonder whether the reason I haven't come out to Mom and Dad in all these years is because of the model of secrecy they've set—it's sort of the standard of behavior in the family."

In the background I heard strains of a violin concerto. Lara had inherited my father's taste for music. Her library was full of Beethoven and Brahms; mine was full of Pearl Jam and Jimi Hendrix.

"Right, the Bocard Doctrine of Protecting Loved Ones from Bad News," Lara said. "Remember when Uncle was hit by a car? And Zosia didn't even tell Mom about it for months?"

Four years earlier, in 1988, Uncle had lain in a coma for two months, while Zosia and my mother kept up their usual lively correspondence. Zosia never let on to her sister that Uncle had been hit, much less that he was comatose and on his deathbed. My mother finally found out in the spring, from Zosia's son, Renzo.

"Yeah," I said. "Or that time when Mom had lower back surgery, and you wanted to call Zosia to come to the States and take care of her?"

"God, that was crazy," Lara said. "Mom nearly took my head off! She forbade me to let Zosia even know she had a back problem! I don't think Zosia *ever* found out about that."

"Well, sooner or later," I said, "I'm going to have to come out to Mom and Dad about being gay. It just doesn't feel right, running around trying to find out who they are, without coming clean about who I am."

"You're right," Lara agreed. "You should, when you're ready." She laughed. "Just don't do it when I'm around."

Sometime in late 1941 Zosia introduced her sister to the Italian officers stationed in Lvov, and my mother was an instant hit, especially with the chief transportation engineer, Luigi Cotulli—a soft-spoken man in his mid-thirties, with dark chocolate eyes, a sharp Adam's apple, and an easy smile. My mother spoke nearly fluent Italian after her stint at the University of Rome, and she had two years of experience as a translator for the Russians. Luigi hired my mother on the spot.

Within a few weeks she had made herself indispensable, organizing the bookkeeping, translating documents, and answering correspondence. This is when my mother began to play her role as Maria, the Catholic sister-in-law of an Italian count, and none of the Italians suspected otherwise.

The faces of my grandparents fade out during this time. My grandfather must have stayed home—for years he stayed home? He had stopped working when the Russians came, and he wasn't about to start now, under the Germans. "He was old," Mom says, brushing the question off in her familiar way.

Not that old, I figure. He would have been something like fifty, maybe fifty-five, by the time he was killed in 1943. His wife would have been younger—late forties under the Russians, maybe almost fifty by the time the Germans came.

The truth is, my grandparents were doomed by their accents; they could never pass for Polish. But Zosia and my mother molded themselves like clay. Their survival would depend on the creative shapes they could twist into, the speed with which they shifted, and how well they played their roles. Hollywood had nothing on them. They were acting for their lives. To what extent did they become who they pretended to be?

In the mornings my mother gulped down a cup of hot chicory and the crust of bread her mother had prepared for her. She pecked her father on the cheek and slipped out the door into Owacowa Street. She was still her parents' daughter, still the good girl with the white-and-blue armband of a dying race.

She stepped cautiously across Zamarstynowska Street and into a side street. In the shadow of a doorway she slipped the armband off her sleeve, tucked it into her pocket, and walked out of the ghetto. Her gait changed, her eyes, her face. In an instant she turned into Maria, a Polish girl, the sister of an Italian countess.

She held her chin up and smiled a self-satisfied smile. Her arms swung freely by her sides, and there was a slight bounce in her step. This was her second life, a life she worked hard to maintain before the shrewd eyes of daylight, under the gaze of informers and extortionists, Ukrainians and Poles, Nazis and scavengers. She turned in a convincing performance, day after day. She met Zosia at appointed hours and passed news to her from home. She smuggled food back to her parents, sugar that Zosia had bought, bread and potatoes. During the day my mother shopped for the Italian officers, buying them food at the Julius Meinl on Akademicka, where everything was available: fresh cheeses and smoked meats, herring and fruit, chocolate, coffee, wines, and liqueur. She used their official documents, and purchased whatever they ordered. She found ways to smuggle a bit of this back to her parents at night.

At the end of the day Maria's work for the Italian officers was finished. She strutted back across the city, head high, a confident young woman feeling proud of the gazes of young soldiers on the street. Quietly she slipped into a side street and ducked into an alley. The armband slid back up her sleeve, and she crossed the border into the Jewish ghetto. She ran the last few blocks home, so as not to be late for curfew.

This was the beginning of something that seemed to come naturally to my mother: every day she slipped between two personalities, two identities, with the flick of a wrist. The armband went on, and she was her parents' daughter, stepping over skeletons in the street. The armband came off, and she was her sister's sister, shopping in exclusive stores.

In her role as Maria, the plight of the Jews bounced off her armor, that breezy exterior she slipped over her skin without even noticing. Maria could walk down a street and not see the blood on the pavement or the young man being kicked in the main square, his teeth knocked out against the curb.

My mother, I'm now starting to realize, has never forgiven herself for her armor. Even after the war she would continue to lift it upon her shoulders when it no longer served any purpose. She believed she could not live without it; whatever was inside had long ago died. Only the armor remained, and she would clank with it down the streets of America fifty years later, into grocery stores and bridge parties, but inside she knew she was hollow. Her soul had slid out of her and was lying somewhere on the pavement, mixed with the shattered teeth and blood of the boy who had fallen, of a dozen boys, on a dozen streets, in a dozen countries.

She cannot imagine a number as big as six million.

Her armor is hot in the summer and freezing in the winter, and its joints are rusty now, and creak. But it props her up and helps her forget everything she lost of the young woman she once was, Batya, who slid out through the cracks and never made it back.

Early in 1942 my father's mother, Helen, somehow sent word to my mother asking her to come to Buczacz. It was too risky for my mother to make the trip, so Zosia, with her Italian papers, went instead. On a sunny morning she boarded the eastbound train and made the four-hour journey to Buczacz. In her Italian pumps, she walked from the little station along the River Strypa until she reached the tumbledown building bordered by a small yard with chickens pecking at the ground. Zosia climbed the stairs and knocked on the door of the second-floor entry.

My grandmother welcomed Zosia into her little two-room apartment and offered tea, which she had gone to great pains to procure for

Zosia's visit. When they were seated on wooden chairs at the rickety kitchen table, my grandmother handed Zosia a sack of gold coins. The cloth was smooth as butter, and coins bulged like the bones of a sea creature.

"Take this," she said to Zosia. "Give it to your sister, Batya, to hold for Kovik." She smiled, the skin around her eyes splintering into a scattershot of lines. From the little lace-curtained window, sunlight floated across the table, making patterns on the wood.

Zosia dabbed her lips with a napkin. She found herself staring at my grandmother's upper lip, the beginnings of a blond mustache sneaking around the edges. Her gray hair was pulled tight in a bun at the back of her head, which reminded Zosia of the sea gulls she had seen at Ostia. My grandmother had that same sharp-eyed look, fierce, unrelenting.

"He doesn't even know about this money," my grandmother said. It had been almost a year since the Russians had arrested my father, and no one had heard anything about him since. But my grandmother was certain he would survive and return after the war.

"I've been saving this money," my grandmother explained, "a little at a time, for years, since he was a child. It was to be for his medical practice, to purchase an office and equipment, to get him started."

Zosia smiled weakly, pained at the futility of foresight. Her hands fiddled with the latch of her purse, clicking it open and shut, open and shut.

"I can't keep it here," my grandmother said. "They raid every day." She squinted through the sunlight at Zosia. "There's not much time left."

Zosia shifted uncomfortably. The scratchy weave of the cane-bottomed chair bristled through her gabardine skirt, and she suddenly had the urge to stand up and walk around.

"Batya must save herself," my grandmother said, as if issuing an order. "She must escape and survive for Kovik's sake. When the war is over and he returns, they'll have something to start a new life."

Zosia was silent. Would there ever be a new life? Would her sister survive? Would any of them? She stared at the sack of coins Helen Rosenbaum held out to her. Fifty gold coins—a small fortune—bearing the stamp of the Russian tsar. "Take them," my grandmother insisted. "Have Batya keep them for Kovik when he returns."

It was the first and last time that Zosia ever saw my grandmother Helen Rosenbaum. She wrapped the sack of coins in newspaper and placed them in her bag.

"Good luck," my grandmother said, kissing her on both cheeks.

Zosia smuggled the gold coins back to Lvov and passed them on to my mother, who hid them in her parents' apartment.

My father, in the meantime, knew nothing of the existence of the gold coins. Marooned in the Gulag, cut off from the world, he watched the sun spin around the planet, as if he were in a different galaxy. He found it oddly comforting, he told me later, to expect nothing from anyone. He received no food parcels, no letters, no word. His family and friends heard nothing from him or about him. He was lost in a world of ice.

March 1942. In the faint purple light of dawn, the Blue Shirts—Ukrainian militia—surrounded the Lvov ghetto, sealing off the streets. They burst through doors, fired shots, swung truncheons, and rounded up thousands of Jews for transport to extermination camps.

In narrow hallways, desperate deals: jewels traded for another day of life, watches and silver changing hands at the last minute. The streets filled with women running, holding children in their arms, and old men hobbling. Everywhere boots and shouts, the sound of clubs and gunfire. Afterward, silence. The cattle cars pounded for days, heading north to Belzec.

Where was my mother when they kicked down the door? Was she dressed in her skirt and blouse, serving the Italian officers coffee? Was she meeting Zosia and telling her stories? Where were her parents when the blue uniforms ran down Owacowa Street? Did they hide in a closet, under beds, in a cellar? Did they have friends with whom they stayed, or friends who warned them?

It was Zosia who warned them, I think, Zosia and her friend Floda, the jeweler. Or my mother's friend Jiri, who now worked as a truck driver for the Germans on false papers. A network of whispers—these few tightrope walkers tiptoed across the city and warned their friends of the approach of death. A word of notice was sometimes enough to outlast the day. And luck could flip like your heart, turning somersaults for no reason.

Zosia was the magician, the tightrope walker, and my mother was her student. My mother soared through the air with the greatest of ease, her heart in her throat.

For months, my mother told me, Zosia had been trying to find a way to return to Italy, first through the German administration, and then through the Italians.

A point would come later when an Italian officer would close the door and tell her with a tremor in his voice that she should stop waiting for a visa from Berlin; that such a visa would never come; she should get out as soon as she could, the sooner the better. "Do whatever you have to—forget the visa—but go quickly," the officer warned her, mopping his brow with a cloth. "There's going to be a massacre here."

She rushed across town to German headquarters, flanked by a flotilla of Italian officers. Storming past the German guards at the door, she demanded the return of her expired passport. Her high heels clicked across the polished wood floor. "I can't be bothered with this nonsense!" she announced. "I demand that you return my documents immediately!"

The room fell silent. A Hauptführer rose to his feet, brushing crumbs from his jacket. "Madam," he said officiously, "I'm afraid that's impossible. We've forwarded them to Berlin." He rounded his desk and walked toward her with a premeditated toe-heel, toe-heel drumbeat. For a moment it seemed he intended to sweep her up in his arms and spin her around the room. Behind him, on his desk, lay a child's drawing—a big black dog next to a flower-sprouting mountain chalet. A name was scrawled at the bottom in blue crayon.

"Then see to it that you get them back!" Zosia snapped, using her .16-gauge glare. You could almost see the steam rise from her shoulders, and through the mist, that piercing one-two punch of her eyes. Stronger men have run for cover in the face of those eyes.

The Hauptführer stopped in his tracks, squeaky black boots stuck to the floor as if nails were driven through them. He swung one hand up through his thinning yellow hair and patted the back of his head absentmindedly, as if congratulating himself.

A puzzled smile crept across his lips, and he bowed his head uncertainly. "I beg your pardon?" he said.

"I demand the return of my papers!" Zosia said. Around her, Italian officers stood rigid as a row of matches, their chins jutting out, shoulders back. "You will have my papers for me by the end of the week," Zosia announced. She turned on her heel and marched out, followed by her green flock of Italian officers.

Perhaps it was the combination of Uncle's pressure on Berlin and Zosia's demands from Lvov, or perhaps it was pure dumb luck, but the Germans did finally return her expired passport, and she snatched it and ran. I don't know when this happened exactly, March or April '42. By the end of April she was gone. How did she get to Italy on her expired passport with no visa? Mom says she just took a train and talked her way across borders. Uncle, in the meantime, was pulling every diplomatic string he could find in Rome. But who knows. It's one of those details that Mom simply brushes off.

I can't explain it, and I won't stop trying. I will fill this vacuum with words until I recognize them as memory.

18

In 1968, when Lara was fourteen, she stopped eating. Slouched over the kitchen counter, refusing dinner, she blew small ripples across the surface of her teacup. My mother offered her a special portion of lean steak and steamed green beans, rising colorfully from their plateau of white china like an undiscovered island. My father's hand clutched his fork and trembled. "I starved for six years in the Gulag," he said, "for what? For this?" He gulped his meal in three shovelfuls and bolted for the door. We heard the rumble of his Chrysler, then the rustling of leaves as he whizzed down the driveway and off to the office for evening patients.

The house exhaled, and my mother pleaded with my sister to eat a morsel of food. But Lara had become convinced she was too fat, and she could not be persuaded otherwise. My mother wrapped her dinner in cellophane and placed it in the refrigerator.

A high-school freshman, Lara had become an earnest, welterweight nail-biting redhead. Painfully shy, she lacked my flair for arrogance and bullshit. Instead of capturing friends by storm (my modus operandi), she focused instead on things within her control: her figure and her hair. She started setting her alarm clock an hour earlier every morning in order to plug in her Clairol Heat n' Curl set. Before dawn she would roll her thick wavy hair in moist plastic curlers and wait for it to dry. Then she wore out the bathroom mirror searching her face for imperfections.

In the meantime I spent my afternoons playing tackle football with Mark Jackson, Billy Reed, and other boys in the playground behind the grade school. I proudly came home with bleeding elbows, scraped knees, and grass-stained clothes. It's no wonder that my parents concluded that Lara and I were bent on opposite, bizarre, American-induced courses of self-destruction.

That winter, in an effort to engender old-world family values in us, my parents took us on a ski vacation in northern Michigan. Our first day on the slopes, a blizzard swept across the region; gale-force winds ripped chair lifts from their cables, shutting down the mountain. My father inched our car along wind-whipped roads back to the little inn at which we were staying.

It was dusk when Lara and I headed out into the blizzard, layered with wool and thermal underwear, and marched across the wide fields behind the inn. The wind was fierce, and the snow drifted up to our thighs. We took turns breaking trail, hiking in our heavy winter boots. Our tracks disappeared behind us. The snow turned purple, a deep, dark contemplative color. Behind us, far in the distance, the faint flicker of light from the inn. After a while even that was lost in the swirling snow.

We continued, breathing hard, not speaking. Ice froze to my eyelashes and blowing snow stung my face. I imagined that we were in the Gulag, two sisters making their nighttime escape across the frozen wasteland, whipped by blizzards and gale-force winds, driven by a single thought: to press on, to move forward, to survive.

We began to stumble and fall more often. It took longer for us to get up; our legs were numb. We sat, heaving, sheltered for the moment from the storm that blasted over our heads. Lara shouted something, but I couldn't understand her above the wind. She leaned against me and yelled again, cupping her mittened hand around her mouth. I could feel her breath warm on my face.

"What?" I shouted. I put my mouth close to her ear. "Want to go back?" My mouth felt funny. The words came out wrong, frozen. I pointed in the direction we had come.

Lara shook her head. "No!" she shouted.

I let her lead on. Sitting had been a mistake. I had been sweating, and now I started to freeze. My legs were stiff. It was hard to stand up.

We walked for another hour, maybe more. We moved slowly, laboriously. The thrill of escaping from the Gulag had worn off. It was bitter cold, and I was tired and hungry and whipped. Siberia was not much fun. And the worst part was, we weren't even close to Siberia. We hadn't gone more than a few miles in northern Michigan.

By the time we made it back to the inn, we were soaked and frozen solid, our clothes stiff as cardboard, little balls of ice clinging to our eyelashes. The warmth of the inn hit us like a furnace. Instantly we began to melt, and we stumbled up the stairs on numb feet, peeling off layers of dripping clothes. A hot shower brought us back to life, and we raced downstairs to our parents, who were waiting in the little dining room. It was only eight o'clock, but it seemed as if we had been gone for days.

The innkeeper had set up a little table for our family and brought us rolls and a hot turtle soup. The weight of the day felt warm and heavy on my eyelids, and my legs tingled. Gold light doused the dining room. The smell of food was intoxicating, and we all looked so lovely then, my mother and father and Lara, sitting at a crisp white linen table, with the glint of clean silverware and the sparkle of glasses, our cheeks a fiery red, and outside, the snow banked up against the window ledges. I will never forget that soup, a thin broth, very hot. And the steam rising from the plate, leaning my face over it, inhaling. I will never forget it because it was the first food that Lara had eaten in weeks. Tears filled my mother's eyes, a smile teetered across her face. That night, my mother would later tell me, I had saved my sister's life.

One generation evens the score for the previous one; guilt walks down the generations. My aunt had saved my mother's life, and now I was paying the debt of gratitude to my older sister. It was the continuation of the myth of our power over life and death, and our family would arrange itself around it, each according to his or her role in the reworking of six years of tragedy.

It must have been in April of '42 that Zosia went to the train station with a suitcase in one hand and her expired Italian passport in the other. She bought a ticket west. Through Warsaw or Budapest—I'm not sure. She hugged her sister good-bye, not knowing if she would see her again.

My mother turned and walked through the station, past throngs of people greeting friends and husbands, sons and soldiers. The rain had drifted off, and the sun nudged its way through the crowds, dropping a glove of light here and there. My mother stepped into the sun and closed her eyes. She had not cried in over two years. During the war, tears had fallen into disuse, like words, like sugar. You couldn't afford to give up tears for anyone.

She walked back across town, past shuttered stores on neglected streets, deserted office buildings sandwiched between officers' quarters. Square-helmeted German guards stood at the entrances to buildings, their rifle butts shining dully in the pale sun. My mother was tired of being Maria, parading through the streets as if she owned them. Maria was exhausting to live with, a stupid Polish girl with an inflated image of her own worth. As Maria she hid her star in her pocket and tossed her head, so that her hair shimmered over her shoulders, but it was Batya's sweat on her arms and Batya's pulse in her neck as she passed German soldiers on the street. Maria threw the soldiers a defiant smile and flounced her skirt as she walked by. But it was Batya who drew herself into the pit of her stomach and held her breath. In her hand she clutched the keys to Zosia's Senatorska Street apartment.

Zosia had made arrangements with her landlord for my mother to take over the ground-floor studio apartment, an anemic yellow-walled room with lace-curtained windows facing Senatorska Street. Pieces of green linoleum dislodged themselves from the floor and skittered across the room, as if seeking more favorable accommodations. My mother paid the upstairs landlord her first month's rent and moved a few skirts and dresses into the closet. They drooped hopelessly on wire hangers, waiting for her to breathe life into them each morning. The Italian officers' headquarters was just around the corner, and my mother was careful to appear to live in the studio apartment. She ate lunch every day at the little foldout table and left her chipped dishes in the basin, resisting her congenital urge to clean up after herself.

But each night she slipped back across town to her parents' apartment in Zamarstynow, bringing them scraps of food and news from the front. The Italian and German soldiers were coming back from the eastern front half frozen in trains of makeshift beds, she told them. The Russian winter froze their ears and stole fingers and toes. They shivered in the trains and longed for home. The German Wehrmacht was sputtering in the snow. In Lvov, people whispered hope.

But in June 1942 my mother's friend Jiri warned her that the Germans were planning another huge action in the Jewish section. Word leapt through the streets like an electrical charge. My mother made plans to smuggle her parents across town to her Senatorska Street room, to hide them during the roundup.

In the ghetto, people clawed their way underground. Families bought hiding places for children. On the eve of the action my mother and her parents removed their armbands and slipped through the streets unnoticed. Perhaps it was evening, the bruised plum of dusk, before curfew, as the streetlights were just coming on. My mother stepped from the rim of a streetlamp into the dark, forcing her feet to move leisurely. Perhaps she carried a bag with clean clothes. Did her father bring his prayer shawl?

I can't picture how my mother accomplished this, hustling her parents through the streets of her city, armbands in their pockets. Did she walk arm in arm with her mother, as if they were best friends from long ago? Or did she walk ahead, as if she didn't know them?

She hid her parents in her apartment in the Aryan section of the city, while she went to work each day, immersing herself in the khaki world of typewriters and Morse code, clacking heels of soldiers. Paperwork, pencilwork, the filigree of ink and requisition forms. She was all bustle and business, jumping from her chair to collect the mail, nimbly slipping the blade of a nicked butter knife under the tongue of an envelope and slicing it open, clean, like a fresh throat. She was a turbopowered office hand, dominatrix of paperwork. In her white socks and oxblood laceless shoes, she marched back and forth across the office, leaning over and popping open filing cabinets with one hand, kicking them closed behind her with the flick of her heel.

Her parents, in the meantime, lay on the narrow bed pushed up against the peeling yellow wall of her apartment. The first morning, my grandmother sank to her knees and scrubbed the floor tiles near the sink, while my grandfather looked on with a dazed expression. Across town, in the ghetto, the streets were bleeding people. Trains pounded day and night. My grandfather heard almost nothing anymore, holding on to the faint memory of his wife's voice and the occasional whistle of shells from his first world war. But my grandmother jumped at the slightest sound—footsteps on the stairs, voices in the hall. Her head jerked up, and her body quivered. She heard the scraping of chairs on the floor above them, the heavy footsteps of the landlord and his wife. And during those stillborn long summer days when the landlord was quiet, my grandparents listened to the empty churning of their stomachs, the song of inside.

At noon each day my mother brought them heels of bread and leftovers from her own rations, and they chewed them ravenously. Between bites and swallows they whispered news and guesses about Zosia and Floda, Jiri and others.

The action lasted one day, two days. It lasted a week, and then a second week. And then there was quiet.

When my mother brought her parents back to their Owacowa Street apartment, they found the doors broken open, the apartment ransacked. Thousands of their neighbors had been arrested, never to be heard from again.

When I was little my mother would sometimes stagger into the kitchen in the morning, rubbing her forehead with the heel of her hand. Puffy circles of flesh tugged at the bottoms of her eyes, and her face looked swollen.

"Ach," she said, "I had that dream again." She filled the kettle with water and set it on the burner.

"What dream?" I asked, spooning soggy Alpha-Bits from my cereal bowl. I always read the cereal box thoroughly, as if the advertisements might miraculously change from one day to the next.

"The same one," my mother said, unscrewing the lid from the instant coffee jar. "Always the same dream. I'm here at home, and the police come and want to take the house away from me."

"What do you mean?" I asked. "How would they take it away?"

"I get so desperate," my mother said, shaking her head. "I'm frantic and beg them to leave me the house, but they always take it." She rubbed her eyes again with both hands, as if trying to erase the image from her mind.

"But how do they take the house?" I asked. It seemed a logistical problem.

"Then I wake up. I'm in such a state of panic that I wake up, and it always takes me time to realize it was just a dream."

I couldn't imagine police coming to take our house away. Police had never so much as set foot on our property. The only time I actually saw a policeman up close was once on the highway, when a state trooper pulled my father over for speeding. My mother remained calm, opened the glove compartment, and handed over the car registration. My father, on the other hand, was shaking; sweat broke out on his face. His breath came out in gasps, and he had trouble speaking to the policeman except in strangled syllables. Afterward, we stayed parked on the shoulder of the road for several minutes, waiting for my father to calm down. Not until long after the trooper had left did my father cautiously nudge the car back into traffic. For the rest of the trip he kept the needle of the speedometer planted five miles below the speed limit.

After the June action ended, my mother spent more time at her apartment on Senatorska Street. But her landlord who lived upstairs had seen her parents in the apartment during the action and became suspicious. He knocked on her door one afternoon. "Who were those people who were here in your apartment?" he asked. He rubbed his nose with the back of his leathery hand. His face was pocked with tiny craters, as if it had stopped hundreds of pieces of shrapnel. When he leaned toward my mother, she could smell the herring he'd eaten for lunch.

"Oh, just some friends," my mother said. "Come in, won't you?" Her face radiated innocence.

His eyes searched her face, skimmed her cheekbones, and landed on her lips. "But they were here a long time," he said slowly. "They were here weeks!"

My mother shrugged him off. "Oh, I hadn't seen them in ages," she said. "Listen, would you like some tea?" She flashed him a smile and touched his elbow, pointing him to her one chair.

He shook his head warily. "Who were they?" he said.

My mother breezed past him and lit the stove, setting the kettle to boil. "Well, I'm going to have a cup, you may as well join me," she said cheerfully. She measured the remaining doubt in his eyes and saw that she had not erased it yet.

"But you know"—she winked, with a conspiratorial grin—"I almost wish they hadn't stayed so long!" She tilted her head, letting her dark hair bounce against her neck. "After a while it's tiring to be pleasant to people." She laughed. "Don't you think?"

The landlord took a cigarette from his coat pocket. He didn't realize that my mother was Jewish, but he suspected she was hiding Jews, and he didn't want to run such risks in his own home. "You watch yourself," he grumbled, striking a match, then slowly bringing it to the tip of his cigarette, as if performing a delicate operation. He snuffed it out between his thumb and forefinger.

"I knew then," my mother told me, "that I couldn't risk bringing my parents to my apartment anymore. He was on to them."

In the meantime, Zosia had made it back to Rome somehow (she has never told anyone how) and sent a message to my mother—probably through her friend Floda, the jeweler for whom she had smuggled money, jewels, and messages. He was now living on false papers in the Aryan section of Lvov.

"Change Kovik's Russian gold coins into German marks," Zosia warned. "Russian coins bearing the imprint of the tsar will be dangerous under the Germans. The coins must be changed immediately, before they're discovered."

Floda gave my mother a contact, a Jewish jeweler who could be trusted to make the exchange. I imagine my mother sitting at the arranged meeting place on a drizzly Sunday afternoon, a sidewalk café on Ulicka Bobrinska under a buxom red-and-white umbrella. Perhaps she noticed a small clean-shaven man with dark, watery eyes and frayed pin-striped pants looking uncertainly at the menu. He slowly turned and approached her table, then slipped soundlessly into the chair across from her. His eyes seemed to be focused on a point above her left ear, and he talked out of the side of his mouth, as if he had a toothpick in it. He picked at his right earlobe with his left hand, and she noticed that his thumbnail was missing. Everything about him seemed slightly off. "Okay," he said, nodding, "I can do it."

She gave him half the coins to exchange for German coins and told him she'd give him the rest to exchange once he'd completed the first transaction.

In a silky gesture, he slipped them into his pocket and returned his hand to his ear. "Give me a week," he said. "I'll meet you here same time next Sunday." He held up one finger as a farewell gesture and disappeared into the rain.

He never showed up. The Germans arrested him, and half of my grandmother Helen Rosenbaum's life savings went with him.

August 1942 came, and half the remaining Jewish population—fifteen thousand—were taken in two weeks. It started on the day of the Assumption, with the familiar sound of dogs barking and gunshots, women shrieking, soldiers shouting orders, policemen running. Thousands of people a day rushed through the streets under kicks and blows. My mother was caught off guard, unprepared for this action. In a panic she yanked her parents out of their Owacowa Street apartment and ran with them across town. How did she do this? What route did she pick? How did she avoid arrest and discovery?

"It was the middle of the action!" she says. "All around it was—I was frantic—I didn't know what to do! I couldn't bring them to my Senatorska Street apartment—my landlord suspected me already. I had no other choice!"

And so in desperation she rushed to the Italian headquarters and burst into Luigi's office with her parents. "Help us," she said breathlessly. "These are my parents. We're Jewish."

Luigi leapt to his feet. For a moment everyone froze, staring at each other in silence. My mother's secret, now shattered, hung in the air between them like a ripped curtain, through which Luigi caught a glimpse of my mother for the first time. A piece of paper drifted off Luigi's desk and floated aimlessly to the floor.

"In here," he said, hustling my mother and grandparents into a small back room. "Not a sound!"

The door closed behind them, and my family stood trembling in the dark. There had been no time to think things through, and now, while they huddled in the back room of the Italians' office, they agonized over my mother's decision. If Luigi was to wire Rome, Zosia and Uncle would be finished. The whole house of cards would topple.

Batya's mother held her hand. Her father had grown silent, his face blank as the moon. Hours drifted by. They could hear the Italian soldiers in the other room—talking, laughing, tapping requisition orders on the typewriter.

Fifty years later, on July 4, 1992, my mother told Lara and me about this while we sat at a table in the local shopping mall. My mother forced her lips into a wan smile. Buried in that smile was her own personal battle between memory and forgetfulness. Whatever crossed the line of her mouth would be given up forever to the world; whatever she managed to hold inside would remain safe.

"We didn't know what to do," Mom said. "But a few weeks earlier my mother had received a message from her sister in Busk, urging us to leave Lvov and go to Busk. It was still quiet in the countryside."

She looked away from me, and it seemed as if she were tunneling back in time, spiraling off, unreachable. I tried to hold her with my eyes, but she slipped past me.

It was too dangerous for them to remain in the back room of the Italian officers, so at the end of the day Luigi led them through the streets and up a flight of stairs to his own tiny two-room apartment.

"Stay inside, out of sight, away from the windows," he said. "Keep quiet. I'll be back tonight."

He brought them food and word from the streets. "They're emptying the city," he said, waiting for my mother to translate to her parents. "They have orders to make it *Judenrein*."

"We'll go to Busk," my grandmother said. "My sister is there, we can stay with her."

Luigi looked at Batya. She knew this look; she knew it was the end. "They're finishing everyone off," he whispered. "What good will it do to go to Busk?"

"My sister is there," my grandmother said calmly. "We'll go to Busk. Don't worry. It's a small town, there are woods. My sister knows people. We'll be fine. Don't run further risks. Please."

"Wait another few days," he said. "Let things quiet down here. You mustn't go outside yet."

They sat on the narrow bed, elbows on knees, and waited. Seconds dripped from one hand to the next. Sounds lifted from the streets and filled the little apartment. Sounds of children jumping rope in the backyard. Bicycle wheels on cobblestones. The woman downstairs locking the door and shuffling down the street, string bag in her hand. Late summer wind rustled the leaves in the trees. From across the city they heard the rumble of the trains, the shrieking of brakes, rust on the rails. Occasional shouts, faint, distant. A far-away thin gunshot, another, and then silence. The sound of the trams snapping electricity as they moved down Akademicka.

19

My mother was twenty-three years old when she hid with her parents in Luigi's apartment. When I was twenty-three in 1981, I was in my last year of law school. I was a quiet student, hardworking, with good grades, but my life had stopped making sense to me. Two months before graduating I suddenly dropped out of school and moved to Vermont, where I stumbled upon a job as a farmhand on a small dairy farm. I found myself oddly comforted by the ritual of waking at three-thirty each morning and milking thirty-five warm, hulking cows. Sixteen hours a day, seven days a week, I shoveled out shit gutters, harrowed alfalfa fields, and helped with the maple sugaring. I collapsed into bed each night, exhausted, and slept without a thought in my skull till morning, when I tugged on my boots and headed back to the barn. Miraculously, I stopped having the panic attacks that had besieged me in the city, and I stopped taking the drugs my psychiatrist had prescribed to me back in Boston. Defying parental and psychiatric advice, I availed myself of the Manure Cure, which seemed to work, at least for the time being.

Horrified, my parents assumed that my behavior was aimed at hurting them. They attributed my sudden infatuation with farm-work to irresponsibility and mental illness. This, they thought, was the result of their having spoiled me, of having given me everything I'd ever wanted as a child.

I myself could not say what was wrong with me, but I did know that milking cows and working outdoors helped. Perhaps I had simply been waiting my turn for a break-down; I'd never taken full advantage of the opportunity when our family had indulged in flamboyant dysfunction in the 1960s.

It would be years before I came to realize that my parents were right: I was unable to cope with the huge gap in our lives, and I despised myself for being spoiled, coddled, and protected by parents who had gone through so much and had sacrificed so much for me. I could not fulfill their dreams and expectations, and I did not deserve to.

"You sure you want us to tell you?" Lara asked my mother.

"Yes."

Mom was sitting across from us at the food court on July 4, 1992, waiting to hear how her parents had been killed. Her hands were folded, her face calm.

"Okay," Lara said. "This is what the testimony said. We had two different reports, one from a woman named Elsa Sonderling—she testified to what happened to your mother and Dad's mother. She obviously knew both families. And one report was from Mendel Goldberg—he testified about your father."

My mother nodded. Her cheekbones were smooth. Although the skin around her mouth sagged and her neck was creased in an intricate lacework of wrinkles, my mother looked to me very much the undaunted warrior she had always been—a no-nonsense woman of action and deception. "From both reports," Lara said, "it seems that your parents—and also Dad's mother—were taken by the Nazis to Belzec and were gassed there."

"Where?" my mother asked.

"Belzec."

My mother's thick eyebrows caterpillared toward each other, and she seemed to be concentrating on the word, as if it were a puzzle to be solved. She tried to pronounce it.

"Bel-zec," we told her, "B-e-l-z-e-c."

She shook her head slowly, gray roots showing through auburn hair over her unpierced ears. "I never heard of it," she said.

I wondered whether she and my father had discussed what Mom would say to Lara and me today.

"When were they killed?" Mom asked.

My sister shifted in her seat and drew a deep breath. "According to Mendel's testimony," she said, "your father was taken there May 23, 1943." Lara gazed straight into my mother's eyes. "Elsa Sonderling's report doesn't give a specific day, but it's also 1943. It seems likely that all three of them— both your parents and Dad's mother—were all killed at around the same time, in May of 1943."

My mother didn't flinch. She has a beautiful face, a seventy-five-year-old-child's face, open and unpredictable. "And how were they killed?" she asked quietly. "Gas?"

"Yes," I jumped in, trying—absurdly—to impress my mother with the detail of my studies. I was so nervous, I didn't even realize what I was saying. "But unlike Auschwitz, where they used Zyklon B, in Belzec they used carbon monoxide gas, they—"

Lara knocked my arm to get me to shut up.

"Belzec," my mother repeated with wonder. "No, I've never even heard of it." She was leaning forward slightly, but her voice was calm, and any trace of tension was swept aside.

"It was an extermination camp," Lara said. "It was just northwest of Lvov, about forty kilometers. All the Jews of Lvov and Galicia were killed there."

I piped up with some facts and figures, as if hoping for extra credit on a history quiz. My palms were sweating with anxiety. "Trainloads of people arrived," I said, "and were gassed immediately. It was in operation for a little over a year, and in that time six hundred thousand Jews were killed. Only two survived."

"Two survived," my mother said in amazement. She shook her head slowly. "I know nothing of it. After the war, when I was already in Italy, we heard—for the first time we heard about Auschwitz. And I always assumed that's where my parents ended up. I always had that terrible fear that they had suffered for months in Auschwitz before finally being killed."

She looked across the room to a family of shoppers in matching red-white-and-blue sweat suits. They were coming out of a store with a huge stuffed leopard in a Toys "R" Us bag. The daughter, a girl of five or six in bright red Nikes, was tugging at her mother's arm, but her mother was busy arguing with the older son, whose teeth were caged in shiny silver braces.

"No," Lara said authoritatively, "they were killed immediately upon arrival at Belzec. Everyone was. And then the Nazis destroyed the camp in 1943—they plowed it under and planted a forest to wipe out any trace of it."

My mother nodded, her eyes narrowing as if trying to read my sister's face for the fine print. "Belzec," she whispered. "No, we knew nothing of it."

A large man in a Michigan baseball cap lumbered toward our booth, examining the menu above the Taco Bell counter before moving out of hearing.

"But that's better, I think," my mother rationalized. "Better that they were killed instantly." She fell quiet. Was she saying this for our sake or her own?

"Jeez, Mom," I said, "that's—"

Lara kicked me under the table. "There's more," she said. "We have documents about many more of your relatives—aunts and uncles and cousins—"

"No!" My mother's voice snapped Lara's sentence in two. Her hands flew up as if to protect her face from a blow. "I don't want to know anything else," my mother said coldly, shaking her head. "I only wanted to know what happened to my mother and father. And to Dad's mother. That's all." She lowered her hands. The pink moons of her fingernails gleamed at the end of her fingers, spotted and scalded by years of digging weeds and burning dinners.

Lara nodded. "Okay," she said softly, "that's fine. That's okay, Mom. We have much more information, if you ever want to know."

My mother stared past her, deep in thought. Her face was relaxed now, and she did not appear too upset. She seemed to be arranging this information in her mind, as if she had just been dealt a few new cards to incorporate into a bridge hand. Perhaps she was trying to reassure herself that this was not such bad news—that at least her parents had died quickly. Or perhaps she wanted to let us think we'd discovered the whole truth, while in fact she held back more than we would ever know.

"Now look," my mother said, leaning forward and leveling her eyes at us, "I wanted to talk with Zosia about this, when you girls started all this business a few months ago. But now that she's staying with us for the summer, I realize it would be a mistake. She can't take it. You understand?"

"Okay," I murmured, wondering what would happen if Zosia found out.

"You mustn't mention a word of any of this to Zosia," my mother continued, "all right? She doesn't know that you girls know anything about it, and she would be utterly devastated. All right? Not a word."

We nodded. The tone in my mother's voice was ominous. There was something more, I thought, that we mustn't know about. Perhaps she was conceding this much information to protect her sister from us.

"I was wondering," I said slowly, "who was Elsa Sonderling? She must have known your mother as well as Dad's mom, because she filled out pages of testimony about both of them. Do you know who she was?"

My mother shook her head.

"Well, did anyone know both your families?" I asked. I plucked a white hair from my sweater and twirled it in my fingers. Christ, I thought, I'm going gray over this.

"I don't know," Mom said. "I never heard of her."

"The gold coins?" I suggested. "That's the only part of the story where there's contact between the two families, right? When Dad's mother sent you the gold coins. I bet that's the connection. Maybe Elsa Sonderling was involved in the exchange of the gold coins somehow."

Mom nodded unenthusiastically. "Maybe," she said. "I don't know."

That evening at dinner, Zosia cooked up a feast of *agnelotti* and *riso col pomadori*, with flaky *salatini*. After dinner we sipped weak tea and nibbled at Zosia's home-baked butter-crusted *apfelschnitten* for dessert.

"What was the name of your best friend, Zosia?" my mother asked her in Italian. "The one with whom you used to bake all of these Austrian desserts? Remember?"

"Elsa," Zosia said, pink-cheeked and smiling. "Elsa Sonderling."

I shot a glance at my mother, who winked back at me and took another bite of *apfelschnitten*. Her fluidity was a force of nature. I was amazed at how smoothly she offered me this tidbit, how obliquely, and it pained me to see that the secrets would continue to be kept, layers upon layers of secrets, thick lead shields against the truth.

"Whatever happened to her?" my mother asked, spearing an apple and popping it into her mouth.

"She moved to Israel," Zosia said. "She died several years ago."

I took a tiny sip of tea, staring over the rim of my cup at my mother, but she wouldn't meet my eyes. Instead, she was studying Zosia's face, the way her mouth twitched like a rabbit when she nibbled at a bit of pie.

"And her husband," my mother asked, as if she could not remember, "what was his name?"

Zosia twisted her lemon slice into her tea. "Floda," she said, swallowing a bit of crust. "He was a jeweler. They were refugees from Austria, near Vienna." Zosia's eyes twinkled. "Elsa's mother was a wonderful baker. I learned how to make all of these things from her."

My mother turned to Lara and me. "Did you understand?" she asked us softly in English. I felt my face flush.

"Mmm," I said, looking down at my plate. I chased a bit of apple across the china and tried to appear nonchalant. "What was her husband's name again?" I asked Zosia.

"Floda," Zosia said. "Actually, it was Adolf, but he didn't want to have Hitler's name, and so he changed his name to the reverse—*Adolf* backward is *Floda*."

I sipped my tea, fighting to retain an outward appearance of composure.

"And did Elsa pass on the tradition of baking all these Viennese sweets to her children?" I asked as casually as I could.

"No," Zosia said. "She didn't have any children."

Luigi continued to hide my mother's family in his apartment, day after day, week after week, waiting for the action to end. He was taking an enormous risk for them, and he had to be careful, toe the line between two roles: enemy soldier, starstruck savior.

Why did he risk his life? He must have loved my mother very much, I think. If I were Luigi, I would have loved her.

At the end of August the action ended, and the Jewish section of Lvov was sliced to ribbons. Of the 160,000 Jews who had lived on the crooked streets of Zamarstynow, only about 30,000 were left. Elsa and Floda Sonderling had already escaped to Hungary on false papers, with Zosia's help. My mother's friends had disappeared, except for Jiri, who was still driving trucks for the Germans in Lvov, posing as a Pole on false papers.

My mother finally emerged from Luigi's apartment in late August and walked to the Italian soldiers' headquarters with him; she resumed her duties as translator and bookkeeper, afraid that her absence from the office would raise suspicions. She felt less sure of herself now; she hung close to Luigi and had trouble laughing as she used to. Her face was thinner. Her eyes deep pools, her mouth less flexible. All the soldiers felt it, the weight of the action, the weight of the war, the sense of loss. It was a country of massacre. Their hands trembled when they read reports from the front.

Finally the day arrived when my family was to take a taxi to Busk. The morning dripped by, minutes leaking into hours, hands circling the face of the clock. A cold sun inched across the rooftops of neighboring apartment buildings. It was early September, and winter was waiting on white knuckles. My mother returned from the office at noon and brought her parents some bread and a container of leftover soup. While her parents ate, she folded her blouse into a leather bag.

"What are you doing?" my grandmother asked.

She added a toothbrush and small mirror.

"Now, look, Batya," my grandmother said, placing her spoon carefully on the small wooden table. "You're not coming with us."

My mother bit her lower lip. She had not slept in days, agonizing over this moment. She knew her parents would never make it without her. Their accents would give them away the minute they opened their mouths.

"We'll be with Checha Godja," my grandmother said. "Don't worry, we'll be fine." She rose from the table and walked toward her daughter in stocking feet, trying to keep her voice low. "Now, listen," she whispered, touching my mother's arm. "I mean it. I want you to escape, Batya. Do you hear me? You have to escape."

My mother stared at the floor. She felt the heat of her mother's gaze bearing down on her. She glanced across the room at her father, who sat like a lost schoolboy on the edge of the bed, his collar askew. "I'm going with you," she said.

My grandmother was silent a moment, then turned on her heel and walked to the window. She motioned my mother over. "Come here."

My mother inched forward.

"See him?"

A black-jacketed Nazi stood sullenly at the street corner, a rifle resting in his gloved hands. He squinted at an apartment building down the street and then picked at something on the side of his chin.

"If you come with us," my grandmother said, "I'm going down to him and turn myself in. Right now."

My mother stared at her in disbelief. "What...?"

Suddenly my grandmother marched across the room toward the door of the apartment. Her stride was forceful as a soldier's, but the pink of her heel poked through her threadbare stockings, and there was something forlorn and desperate about her.

My mother rushed after her. "No!" she cried. "Mom, you—"

Sarah spun around. "You're not coming with us! Understand? I'm still your mother, and you'll do as I say!"

My mother turned to her father for help, but his eyes were dark and full of sadness. Wisps of jet-black hair dangled over his forehead.

"Mom," my mother pleaded, "you can't—"

"Watch me."

My grandmother reached for the door handle, and my mother froze. Her jaw dropped, but nothing came out. "All right," she whispered. "All right, you win."

My grandmother dropped her hand and slowly turned to face her daughter. What she saw was a small girl, a girl who needed her mother. Summoning all her strength, she raised her hand to touch my mother's face, but Batya turned away from her.

My mother stared at the floor, rough seams coursing through oak boards. She had lost track of right and wrong; nothing made sense anymore, nothing would ever be right again. My grandmother stepped toward her and gathered her in her arms gently, as if my mother were made of glass.

They said nothing after that. The three of them sat together on Luigi's narrow bed and waited for the day to wear out. Moshe touched his daughter's head, stroked her hair, curling it around her ears. She had the tiniest ears known to man, small pink seashells. When she was seven she'd banged her left ear against the sharp edge of a brick building. Moshe had been walking her to school that morning, and a streetcar suddenly rounded the corner, coming straight for them. Moshe had yanked his daughter and flattened himself against the building just as the streetcar swept past them. He still remembered her shriek—a bone-chilling sound that seemed too immense to have come from his child. For years afterward, she would suffer from painful earaches, and he never forgave himself for the accident. Now he gazed at his daughter helplessly.

They chewed on a bit of bread and swallowed the leftover soup my mother had brought. They were careful not to heat it lest someone in the building smell it and discover them.

My grandmother glanced at the clock on the wall, then back at her daughter. Batya's face was empty; she had withdrawn to some far corner in herself. My grandparents finally stood and lifted their bags. My mother led them downstairs and into the street.

They followed narrow side streets and alleys, avoiding the sounds of children playing, the thwack of a soccer ball against a wall, engines rumbling. At the edge of the city a wiry, thin-lipped man in a pale blue cap sat waiting in a taxi. My grandmother embraced her daughter and whispered to her. "Don't worry about us now, we'll be fine. We'll be with Checha Godja—she'll take good care of us. And you—Batya, you must escape. Luigi will help you. You must do everything to survive."

But my mother did not hear her. She felt her mother's arms, the smell of her hair, the faint lilt of her voice, the breath on her cheek. That moment, that day, slipped off into a secret pocket of memory. She held her father for a long time. The man in the car looked straight ahead at the road. The smoke from his cigarette drifted from his hand. He squinted up at the clouds and twisted his cap. He didn't like these scenes. He took the money without a word.

Moshe let go of his daughter and turned away. My mother wanted to cry, but she had no tears, and no voice. Everything was very, very quiet. A dusty little street in a forgotten part of town, the middle of nowhere. She watched them climb into the car, their backs bent, their heads disappearing into the cab.

"I knew I would never see them again," my mother told us in the food court on the Fourth of July. "I felt I was handing them over to the German police." A single tear tumbled down her cheek. "I was handing them over to their deaths. And, you know," she added, shaking her head, "I never forgave my mother for that. I was just furious at her."

I stared with surprise at the simple honesty of her admission.

"I never understood how she could have done that to me," my mother said, her anger still razor-sharp. "All those years I hated her for it, for refusing to let me go with her."

My mother's hands played their usual tricks, looping together and then falling apart in her lap. She seemed suddenly ancient, wise, older than the world. Her face could have been sculpted of stone on a mountain temple. My mother has always seemed larger than life to me, now more than ever. "Until I had my own children," she said, looking me dead in the face with those dark, bittersweet dollops for eyes. "Until I had you girls. Then I finally understood. And now that I know, I forgive her. I would do the same for you." She sighed heavily, as if the realization had taken all the wind out of her.

The car left. Dust rose and the sun dropped below the horizon. My mother stood on the street until the sound of the engine faded. The sky was violet when she started walking home.

She no longer cared what happened. Her feet moved but her mind was numb. The streets ran together and blurred. She tried to remember who she was, or why she was walking. She was all alone, and the streets were strange. She had lost her way, and she began to walk faster. She didn't have a watch, but suddenly she sensed that it must be past curfew.

"What are you doing here?" a man's voice called out. "Jew!"

She sprang back to life. "Get your hands off me!" she said. "How dare you!"

A tall man in a brown overcoat had grabbed her by the wrist. His eyebrows like a plowed row of earth. "You're a Jew!" he said with increasing conviction. "How'd you slip away?"

"The nerve!" my mother stormed. "I'm as Polish as you, you swine!" She yanked her hand free of his.

"Oh, really?" he chuckled. "We'll see about that. What's your name?"

"How dare you!" she roared. "I work for the Italian officers! Just wait until they hear about this! You'll be sorry!"

My mother knew these lines by heart. She had perfected this tone of voice, the look on her face, the thrust of her chin. She had bluffed her way out of these situations before. Feigning outrage, feigning anger, she shouted her accusers down. Some slunk off into the shadows, perplexed, not wishing to run the risk they were wrong. Maria was convincing, a good act. There was no tremor in her voice, no panic in her eye. She was solid, sure, for the minute or two that mattered. She could transform herself into the wrongly accused.

But this time my mother was caught off guard. She had just handed her parents away, and she was not as flawless as usual. The man sensed this. He sensed a hesitation, a bewildered moment. Her disclaimers did not rattle him. Just like a Jew, you couldn't trust them. No, he wasn't going to let this one go.

"Come on," he said. "I'm taking you to the police. You can tell your story to them."

"Fine!" she said. "Let's go! I would be happy to give them a piece of my mind!" And with that she took the lead and marched toward the Italian military office.

"This way!" the man shouted.

"I told you already," she said, "I have work to finish up at Italian headquarters—I'm late as it is, and you're making me later. I'll be happy to go to the police, but I have to report first to my office or they'll think I've neglected my work. It will be worse for you if that's the case!"

The man shrugged. Confident of his catch, he let her lead him to the Italian military office.

My mother's heart was racing. It was late, and the officers might have left by then. There might be no one who would recognize her. She walked briskly, thinking of alternate plans.

At last they reached Italian headquarters. My mother barged in and walked straight into Luigi's office. "I'm sorry I'm late!" she announced. "I know I have reports to finish tonight, but this idiot held me up and insisted on following me here. He called me a Jew!"

Luigi picked up his cue without hesitation. "Christ," he muttered. "Get back to work! I'll straighten him out."

The Pole could not believe his eyes. She was a Jew, he was sure of it. And yet here she was, in the Italian officers' headquarters, and the commanding officer obviously knew her. She worked here. Her story, absurd as it was, was true. He couldn't understand it. He'd been so sure...

"Do you have a problem, buddy?" Luigi asked, drawing himself up.

The man looked from Luigi to the girl, who was already seated at a typewriter, fingers flying across the keys.

"Well?" Luigi asked impatiently.

The man stared at the girl. "No," he mumbled. "No, never mind."

By the beginning of September 1942, my mother did not go outside alone anymore; the streets were too dangerous. It was warm in the evenings, and the light was still soft, and the trees sang of summer, but she stayed in Luigi's room and held her head in her hands. During the day she did her paperwork, transcribed orders for shipments of Italian regiments moving east, and checked lists of casualties moving west again. She kept track of cartons of cigarettes, crates of dressing, boxes of bullets, helmets and canisters, canteens and belts. She translated, straightened files, dusted cabinets, made coffee, recycled envelopes, made phone calls, considered her options. Her options were shrinking. At night she walked home with Luigi, ate his food, held his hand, and tried to smile, but she did not remember whether a smile had anything to do with her anymore. He spoke gently to her, as if he were talking to a lost child. She trusted him, but there was so little of her left, she didn't know what it was that she trusted him with. The struggle to live seemed so pointless to her now. Her life could be tossed away with such ease, it weighed nothing.

Her friend Jiri came to see her after work one day. "Lvov is finished," he said. "We have to get you out. Are you listening? You have to escape. It's a matter of weeks now." He rubbed his left eye, which had started to twitch. "I'm working on getting you a place to stay in Budapest," he said. "It's safer there."

He fumbled in his pocket for a cigarette. "Damn this," he muttered. "Do you have anything to drink? Some vodka maybe?"

My mother shook her head.

"Maybe Luigi can help you," he said. "We'll work something out, okay? There's not much time."

Each morning my mother dropped her feet to the floor, tied her shoes, slipped on her skirt and blouse, and went to work. Every day she poured herself into her wooden role as Maria and hated herself for it. She grew increasingly despondent; she no longer slept, and no longer ate. She was not meant to live, she realized, and she was tired of fighting the inevitable. She had given her parents away, and now there was nothing left but to give herself away. She decided to turn herself in, to hand herself over to the Nazis.

Jiri started coming to see her more frequently. He was constantly chain-smoking German cigarettes now. His narrow face and bony jaw seemed to float on a haze of bluish smoke. He shook her by the shoulders. "Listen to me!" he whispered angrily. "We're working on a plan!"

Everyone had advice. Everyone had something urgent to tell her. But it was hard for her to listen. Those weeks were a blur, a dull pounding fear at the base of her spine. Even when Luigi did finally come up with a plan, my mother was sunk in a depression so profound, she wanted only to turn herself in to the Germans. She sat in the office and watched Luigi sign papers, review documents, evaluate travel passes. She filed papers listlessly and typed orders.

The plan went like this: Luigi had created official military documents and an identity card for my mother and told her to pose as an Italian soldier going on furlough to Budapest. Her new name would be Giuseppe Rossi, Private First Class. He gave her an Italian military uniform and boots, and she practiced saluting in front of the mirror, squaring her shoulders and snapping her hand to her forehead. But her heart wasn't in it. Although she longed to see her sister, she held little hope of actually getting out of Poland alive. She found herself going along with the scheme mainly because she didn't have the energy to object to it. Luigi planned her escape for early October, when Luigi himself would be getting a two-week furlough. He would accompany her to Budapest on his way to Italy.

She fingered her furlough papers and rolled her new name over her tongue: *Giuseppe Rossi*. She had to shed another skin now, and she was already so worn out. She had shed her parents, her past, her friends, her life. She had become Polish Catholic, crossed herself and said her prayers daily. Now she would change again. She would become Italian, a soldier, a man.

20

A few weeks after arriving in the Gulag, my father woke to find himself in the camp hospital with dysentery. The prisoner on the bunk next to him was writhing in pain, his face a pale, slippery color, as if the whites of his eyes had run down his cheeks. Fighting his own nausea and dizziness, my father crawled over to the man and touched his forehead, then moved his hands over his abdomen. The man howled, clutching his belly.

In the morning, the prison doctor, a prune-faced, red-haired woman in work boots, clomped into the room and leaned over the writhing prisoner. Her skirt brushed the edge of the bunk.

"Esteemed doctor," my father called from his bed, "the course of medication you're giving that man won't help."

The doctor stopped in her tracks and swung around. "And who are you?" she snapped.

"I'm a doctor from Lvov. That patient has appendicitis. He must be operated on immediately or you'll lose him."

The doctor almost smiled. "My dear *doctor*," she said sarcastically, "where do you propose that I get an anesthetic? And where do you propose that I get sterile instruments? Hmmm? And what do you propose I sew him up with?" She sneered. "We are not in a medical school in Lvov," she said. "To get materials for an operation, I must requisition the State. Do you know how many weeks it would take for the paperwork alone?" She crossed her arms over her monumental chest, a gesture that left her fingers clawing for a handle on the sleeves of her white lab coat. "Besides, you don't know what you're talking about! The man is suffering from alimentary dysentery, nothing more, nothing less. I am not going to make a federal case out of a stomachache for the benefit of your medical education!"

The man in the bed next to my father died. It was my father's first medical victory. The doctor grudgingly offered my father a position as a prisoner physician, and he leapt at the opportunity. It was a job offer that ultimately saved his life.

The work force of the Gulag was comprised of men at various stages of death. Sooner or later everyone starved; it was just a matter of time. The men in the ditches were the first to go, and the men carrying loads and lifting bricks were close behind. My father would starve a little slower because he worked indoors. It was his responsibility to present a healthy work force each morning of a set percentage of physically fit men.

Winters were the worst; men died faster, falling on frostbitten, blistered feet. Their fingers went numb and their noses froze. They staggered back to the camp in the dark, too tired to eat, too tired to sleep. They sat like lumps and died.

One subzero morning in January, my father told me, the camp hospital was full of inmates. They sat propped up on cots, on benches, or lying on the floor. My father examined them and approved one or two of the strongest men for work. The rest, he decided, needed to rest in the hospital.

His refusal to report the required number of inmates for work was tantamount to insubordination. The camp commander, a blunt-faced Russian with skin the color of boiled onions, exploded into a one-hundred-and-twenty-decibel rage, his face turning an alarming shade of red. "What is this?" he roared. "Ninety-seven men sick?" He threw the report in my father's face. "Four percent," the commander snapped. "Four percent. That's twelve men, period. The rest are going to work. Pick them."

My father stood with his hands behind his back. "I have," he said stubbornly.

The commander's left eyebrow jerked up. "You piece of shit," he said, "eighty-five of those men are going out to work. You are going to be the first one. You can pick the rest or do their work for them, I don't care."

"So I stepped outside to join the laborers," my father told me. In the meantime the civilian doctor selected the other prisoners for work, and within minutes she had presented the requisite work force of ninety-six percent of the prison population. Feet wrapped in rags, my father and the others were given a pair of torn felt boots, a patched jacket, and a shovel.

My father walked into the snow with the other prisoners, in columns of five abreast, flanked by black-belted Soviet guards and German shepherd guard dogs. The work site was a three-kilometer march through howling winds across a faceless frozen tundra. My father was dizzy and dehydrated before he even lifted the shovel. By midmorning he was stumbling.

Word had gotten around. The other workers knew about my father's defiance of the commander, and they helped him up and let him lean against them. They lifted his shovel for him and carried him back at the end of the day.

The next day was the same. My father staggered to the site and began to dig. He fell often. Silently, someone was there to pick him up. When the crew boss wasn't looking, they laid him in a corner and dug for him, finishing his quota. They lifted him gently and walked him back under the stars at the end of the day.

By the third day, my father said, he had adjusted somewhat. He was able to dig slowly, and although he was able to stay on his feet, he struggled with dizziness and exhaustion. By evening he was behind. The others in his crew made up for his work. No one said a word. My father looked at them helplessly. No one had ever loved him so much or been so kind. He was unspeakably grateful.

The men saved his life like this for months. Spring broke, and the weather lightened. The sun crept out and spread across the men's faces like yellow paint. The snow softened. Their feet got wet and their faces dripped with sweat. The work would go more quickly now. The commander pulled my father off the hard-labor force and returned him to hospital duty as a physician.

It must have been hard for my father to keep track of six years like this. Six years without a word from anyone, without news, without hope. He had the photo of his fiancée, a wrinkled photo of a dark-eyed girl with a childlike smile, a photo that had stopped making sense to him a long time ago. She belonged to a distant life, a life that seemed to have existed only in a dream. All the things he remembered made no sense anymore—the squares of Lvov, the clock at Platz Mariacki where he used to meet her, the feel of her hand on his arm, the look on her face as she bit into her *kremeschnitten,* whipped cream on her cheeks. The cheers of the crowds at the track meets. The sound of the volleyball spiking off the heel of his palm.

The only thing he cared about anymore was escaping from Soviet Russia and telling the world what he'd been through. He survived on pure rage, he said; his determination for revenge kept him alive.

One day a short stub of a worker showed up in the hospital with frozen and peeling feet. He was a scrappy streetwise Pole from Brzezany who had been a petty thief and black marketeer; when he discovered my father was from Lvov, he was overjoyed to have found a fellow countryman with whom he could speak Polish. My father treated the man's feet and did what he could to help him, giving him extra soup from his own ration and smuggling him a piece of potato or scrap of turnip now and then. My father managed to keep the Pole on the sick list for a few weeks, long enough for his feet to heal and for his strength to return. The Pole eventually recovered, returned to work, and survived his sentence.

Years later, in 1946, after my father's escape from the Gulag, the man would recognize my father in a food line in western Poland. My father was penniless and starving at the time, a fugitive on the run from the Russian police. The Pole would bring my father home with him, eager to return the favor after all the years. He eventually smuggled my father across the borders of Poland and Hungary and into Austria. He still had his criminal connections, and he would save my father's life. "If not for him," my father told me, "I would never have gotten out."

Actually, it's debatable whether my father has ever really gotten out of the Gulag, whether anyone does. "You will never leave here," the other prisoners had told him when he first arrived. They were right. The Gulag stays in a person. It pops out at unexpected moments, at the dinner table, or while sitting around the Christmas tree. Once, while my sister and I were tearing open our Christmas presents in front of the fireplace, my father opened a gift from a patient of his. He suddenly fell into one of his prehistoric stony silences—it seemed to suck all the oxygen from the room. Lara and I stared at him. Slowly, carefully, he removed two beautifully stitched belts of Florentine leather from a red-and-green mountain of wrapping paper. He gingerly held the belts between thumb and forefinger, as if they were made of precious silk. His eyes glazed over with a faraway look, and he seemed to be drifting away from us. "In the camps," he said faintly, "this would have been the greatest gift imaginable. Belts," he explained, "were confiscated in the camps—

to prevent prisoners from hanging themselves. Same went for buttons." He glanced quickly at me, a sudden urgency in his eyes. "You see, buttons," he said, "could be sharpened. Then you could slit your wrists."

He shook his head slowly. "And here," he continued, with a pained smile that made his face crinkle and his eyes wince, "here I've received the richest gift in the world, the ability to hang myself twice over."

Sometimes the Gulag intruded when we had company. One weekend I'd brought my college roommate home with me for a Fourth of July backyard barbecue. My mother fired up the grill and charred our burgers into hardened, juiceless eastern European hockey pucks. We layered our buns with tomatoes and onions, when I noticed my father had fallen into one of his sudden silences. He was staring at the sliced tomatoes on the serving tray as if they were an apparition from outer space.

"I remember one time," my father said with that hollow tone of his, "we were on a forced march across the tundra." My roommate's eyes went wide as she held her burger in two fists, an inch from her lips. "And we were starving, you know, we hadn't eaten anything to speak of in years." My father gazed up at me to make sure I was listening. I fidgeted, knowing that Gulag stories never ended well, and I didn't want my friend to be exposed to them. It was somehow humiliating, as if my father had suddenly stood up and begun urinating.

"And suddenly," my father said, his face lit up with wonder, "it was like a miracle—there appeared in the middle of that frozen tundra a bit of rotten tomato, stuck in the ground. You can't imagine what it was like to see something like that—" My roommate lowered her burger uncertainly and stared at my father, while I shifted uncomfortably on the picnic bench.

"And then the fellow in front of me—we were marching in columns of five— the fellow in front of me reached down and scooped it up in his hand and bit into it"—my father swept his hand to his mouth, imitating the man's gesture— "and just like that, point-blank, without warning, the guard shot him in the head."

My roommate coughed, and her burger dropped to her plate in a little striptease of ingredients—the lettuce fanned out and the tomato slithered off the bun, exposing an embarrassed little blackened burger.

"I had to step over him," my father continued. "I had to step over the man, pretending nothing had happened." He shook his head sadly. "And every prisoner behind me had to step over him too, as if nothing had happened—"

My mother interrupted suddenly, holding a brilliant yellow ear of corn in her tongs. "Want some corn?" she asked my roommate cheerfully.

My father's left arm is a souvenir from the camps, a token of his time there, a little gift from the Gulag. He almost never talks about it.

But as long as I can remember, my father always had one right arm and one wrong arm. The wrong one was shorter than the right one. It had a big bump that stuck out in the middle and a white track of stitches curving around the forearm and up to the elbow. A scrawny biceps above a thick, meaty extensor muscle, separated by a crazy knob for an elbow. My mother shortened the left sleeves of all his suits to match his arm. You couldn't really tell until he moved it. It bent at a crazy angle, and his hand flopped strangely when he lifted his arm. He could play the violin, but he didn't look like others who played the violin. And he could still do most things that needed getting done: chopping wood and hauling dirt, planting trees and building a rock garden, sawing wood and hammering nails. But it was always the wrong arm. It was the wrong arm to grab, the wrong arm to cling to. It was the wrong arm to get too close to.

When I was eight I found out how it had gotten that way. He didn't tell me. I found an article in the Irvington newspaper. It was an old article, from 1953, before I was born. The article was pasted in a scrapbook that lay in a cabinet under some old photo albums. Irvington was the tiny town in the snow belt of northern Michigan where my parents settled after my father passed his Michigan medical boards. It was his third medical degree, in his eighth language. The article was titled DOCTOR TELLS OF HIS ESCAPE FROM REDS.

I didn't know what "Reds" were. But I learned that my father's arm had been broken by prisoners trying to steal his clothes from him. This shocked me. I couldn't imagine anyone wanting to do that to him. It shocked me to think of my father—immense, powerful, and strong—a victim. And there was something else that bothered me—that they had tried to take his clothes away from him. It didn't occur to me that they wanted his clothes for themselves, for warmth. This was beyond my imagination as I sat in my parents' warm home, well-clothed. I could not picture anyone (much less my father) that cold. All I could imagine was that they had done something terribly embarrassing to him— they had tried to strip him naked, and he had fought back. There was something, I thought, dirty about this business. No wonder he had never told me about this. But why had he told the newspaper reporter?

It was too much news to keep to myself. I went to my mother with the article and asked her about it. She told me it was true, that the other prisoners had tried to take his clothes away and they broke his arm. "That's why it's so odd-looking," she said.

Other prisoners. So he was a prisoner? Yes. And he escaped? Yes. Did he get his clothes back? Yes. What happened to his arm?

After the war, when he got to Rome, he had an operation. They took out his elbow and made a new one. And he practiced bending it till it was almost good as new. Everyone was amazed at how well he had recovered. "Sheer determination," my mother said. "You know Dad! He kept exercising it and bending it, and lifting weights, until he recovered nearly all of his motion. He wanted to be able to play the violin again. The doctors said he'd never be able to, but you see, he showed them!"

That's your daddy. A tough cookie. An iron will. Hard as a goddamn rock.

A skinny child with gangly arms, big brown eyes, and a giant gap between my two front teeth, I was unequal to the task of being the heroine of the next generation. Far from stoic, I was the child who stubbed her toe on the concrete by the swimming pool and cried for her mother, the child who sneaked behind the house with her new plastic tommy gun and fired caps at imaginary Nazis but ran in terror at the sight of slugs or garter snakes.

My father obligingly built my sister and me a tree fort in the woods behind our house when I was seven so we could defend ourselves from our enemies.

"Who are your enemies?" my father asked me. No one had ever asked me that question before. It was a good question, and I had to think about it. "My enemies"—I shrugged— "you know, people who are out to get me."

My father smiled patiently. "Who are they?"

I was stunned to discover that I couldn't think of a single one. It seemed impossible that I should have no enemies. It seemed, at that moment, life-threatening not to have enemies. Or at least it would jeopardize the quality of my life not to have any. All of the things I most loved depended on the existence of enemies: tree forts and guns, war games and running through the woods as an Indian or as an infantryman. Enemies were always available in all my games of war. They were lurking in the bushes, surrounding the house, creeping under barbed wire across the stand of fir trees at the corner of the woods. Enemies could always be conjured up, to fulfill the requirements of life, to offer the opportunity for bravery, heroism, and superiority. Without enemies, I was nothing.

I brushed off my father's question. "Enemies," I said flatly. "Everyone has enemies." And I ran back into the woods to avoid further discussion of the matter.

I now realize that when he was my age, my father knew who his enemies were. They walked with their mothers and fathers to church each Sunday. Afterward they threw stones at him and called him *Yid.*

My father believed he could save me from his enemies.

When I was in college in 1975, my father told me more about his arm. One day in 1943 or 1944, he said, a gang of prisoners jumped him and tried to steal his clothes. They were all freezing. My father was a big man, but by then his bones were dry as kindling. His left arm snapped, his elbow shattered. He dragged himself to the hospital and requested an X ray.

The staff laughed at him. An X ray, that was a good one.

"Yes, an X ray," he said. "I need to see where the break is, so I can set it."

Naturally, his request was ignored, and he was sent back to work. Instead, my father decided to starve himself. He announced his strike, requested an X ray, and refused to eat until he was given one. He was bargaining on his position as an essential physician for the camp, he told me. It was a thin strand of hope, but by then he didn't mind dying.

The kitchen staff filled his bowl. He refused to eat. They cut his bread. He left it untouched. He lay in the corner of his bunk and waited. Pain shot through his arm, a good sign. As long as there was pain, it was not yet healed. Within the first few days the arm could still be set. After a week or ten days the calcification would be too great, and setting the arm would be impossible.

My father waited. He excelled at tests of will. He was perfectly capable of killing himself with it, and he set about the task with great determination.

Three days went by. He stood over the bucket and fainted. He lay on the mat and refused to touch the soup they brought him. His bread and soup were gobbled up by other prisoners.

After six days he had trouble lifting his head. His eyes glazed over. The room blurred. He could not distinguish faces. His arm stopped hurting. Time was running out on him.

By the eighth day he was unable to move. His thoughts were jumbled. He lay still and closed his eyes. There was nothing left of him but a faint memory of a battle of wits.

On the ninth day they relented. They lifted him off the floor and carried him into the X-ray room. They took a picture of his arm. He ate his ration of bread and looked at the X ray. The elbow was shattered, fragments poking out in different directions. A mound of bone had already formed a calcified bump around the fracture.

My father went to the barracks of the laborers and asked for their help. He picked five muscular men and told them what he wanted. And so they began. Three men held him down. He showed the others how to hold his arm and how to pull it. They placed their feet against his ribs and took his arm in their hands and pulled. The bones moved apart, and he fainted. They brought him to and began again. They could hear the splinters crunching.

Each time he regained consciousness, he felt his elbow with his other hand. "Again," he said dully, and held up his arm for the men to pull.

They worked on him for hours. Finally, he saw that there was no more that could be done. He thanked the men. He could not sleep. His left arm lay motionless, bent at a ninety-degree angle across his chest. He tied it in a sling and waited for morning.

He had set his arm as well as possible under the circumstances. In time the elbow hardened into a bony mass, locked in a ninety-degree angle. I don't know exactly how many years he was in the Gulag like that—two, maybe three years. The biggest danger was that he was defenseless now, one-armed, easy prey for future attacks by prisoners. He developed a mighty kick, which he practiced between hospital rounds. He jumped from one foot to another, kicking his right foot high in the air. He practiced with both legs until he felt safe. He had several opportunities to test his technique. After one or two assaults the other prisoners left him alone. His legs were still good. The prisoners went after weaker ones.

My father has always been fiercely proud of his willpower. "My word is like iron," he used to tell me, clenching his fist till the veins popped up in blue cords. "If I say something, I stick to it. You can always rely on my word."

Sometimes I wished my father were a little less reliable. Once, I remember, when I was home from college for Christmas, a heavy snow fell all night long. My father got up before dawn on Christmas Day and set himself the task of snowblowing the driveway. A few hours later I stood at the front door and shouted at him to come inside and open his presents with the rest of the family. When that failed, I finally trudged out in snow boots and overcoat and tapped him on the shoulder. He turned down the engine while I pleaded with him to come in and open presents with us. "We can finish the driveway afterward,"

I told him. The snow was still coming down heavily. "I'll be right in." He nodded, motioning me back into the house. "I'm almost finished." Two hours later he finally dragged himself inside and collapsed in a chair by the fireplace, his face a tangle of pain. He had succeeded in finishing the driveway as he had said he would. But for the last several hours he had been slipping and falling on the sheet of black ice that coated the pavement like candy. He had broken seven ribs by the time he was done.

21

Jiri walked to the tiny apartment before dusk. I imagine him taking the stairs two at a time, and my mother opening the door to his familiar knock. "Not long now," he said, shutting the door gently behind him. "You're getting out just in time." His eyes darted across the room to the window overlooking the street. "Remember. Keep your mouth shut. Luigi will keep an eye on you. When you get to Budapest, go to this address." He handed her a small folded piece of paper, smudged with engine grease. "Memorize this," he said, "then burn it. Ask for this man. He's one of our contacts, he'll be expecting you. You may have to spend some time there. He'll make all the arrangements. Understand?"

My mother nodded.

"Listen to me, Batya," he said, lowering his

voice. "Don't worry. Keep your eyes open and your mouth shut. You're a young kid going home on furlough, no one here knows shit. You'll be riding on a train with a bunch of Hungarians and Germans. They don't know a thing about Italians, okay? You'll fit right in, you're perfect." He winked, and his face broke out in a grin. "And now, soldier, you're going to feel the breeze on your ears!" With a flourish, he threw a towel around her neck and began cutting her hair.

"Jiri," she said as locks of dark hair fell around her shoulders and tumbled to the floor. "What will you do?"

He took a handful of her hair and cut it off, smiling. "Look at all this stuff," he said. "Do you think I missed my calling?"

He pulled her right ear forward gently and cut the hair close to her head. The sound of the scissors made her spine tingle. There was something so chillingly precise, so controlled about the way they sliced her hair, the way the hair fell lifeless to the floor.

"I'll wait to hear word from you after you get out. If you make it I'll let your parents know in Busk, and I'll send word to Kovik's mother in Buczacz. Then I'm leaving. It's too dangerous here now—there's no one left. I'll try to get to Warsaw, I think."

Her head felt naked, cold. His fingers were gentle, and she felt his breath on her neck as he cropped the hair close to her forehead.

"You're going to make a terrific little soldier," he laughed. "You are going to be one humdinger of an infantryman!"

"Leave me something," she said. "Leave me a little hair on top. Somewhere, leave me a little hair."

"*Befehl ist Befehl!*" he joked. "Sweetheart, you're going to get a regulation haircut, whether you like it or not."

She didn't like it. But she liked the way Jiri smiled, the way he ran his fingers through her crew cut, impressed with his work. "You're too proud of yourself," she told him.

"Why shouldn't I be? I'm still here, right?"

I don't know if he said this. I don't know Polish, or Yiddish, or whatever language they spoke to each other. I wasn't there. My mother didn't tell me. The way she told the story was like this: "And so I cut my hair short, dressed up as an Italian soldier, and marched out of Poland with the Italian army."

Jiri swept up her hair and tossed it in the garbage and handed her a mirror. She didn't look half bad—smooth-cheeked and doe-eyed, a meek Italian boy. She placed her soldier's cap on her head and saluted. The boy in the mirror looked serious.

"It's a good cut." Luigi winked. "Here's your furlough pass, Rossi. Try to get some sleep."

In the morning she put on her uniform and packed her knapsack. She wrapped the twenty-five gold coins with the stamp of the Russian tsar in a dark blue dress that she would change into when she reached Budapest. And she brought a blanket—the one item she had saved from her home. A burnished gold and black tiger-striped blanket, old and worn, mended countless times by her mother. She pocketed her papers and furlough pass, polished her boots, and marched to the train station with Luigi, grim with fear. She could tell he was nervous, though he tried to smile at her from time to time, wink, tell a joke.

Luigi boarded the train with her and settled her in a compartment with Hungarian soldiers. They were smoking and laughing, giddy to be heading home, away from the eastern front. She sat next to the window, opened it, and felt the chill morning air like a cool hand on her forehead. She saluted Luigi halfheartedly as he turned to find the officers' car.

The train started moving and the soldiers began a card game. They tried to get Giuseppe Rossi to play, but the Italian kid just stared out the window, clutching his jaw. He pretended to doze or watched the countryside skid by, pale yellow whisks of wheat, rutted roads, giant green onion-domed churches. Courtyards of rubble, red tile roofs ripped by mortar fragments and shelling.

The train compartment filled with smoke. My mother left the window open and inhaled the fresh autumn air. Potatoes and apples were being harvested in the fields among piles of burning leaves and lost bales of rotting hay. The train rattled over Poland, moving south and west.

Darkness dropped like a veil. The men

grew restless and walked around. Giuseppe leaned against the window of the compartment and closed his eyes.

It was late when they reached Budapest. The city was dark. My mother jumped down with the other soldiers and found Luigi waiting for her on the platform. They had memorized the directions to her contact and walked in silence. A full moon spattered white in the river beneath them. Their boots clomped across the bridge into Pest, where the streets narrowed.

They knocked on the door at 62 Lokjak Street. First a light, then footsteps. The door cracked open.

"Mr. Gromykow?" Luigi asked.

The figure behind the door jumped at the name.

"No," a woman's voice said frantically. "Leave immediately!"

"But he's expecting us," my mother said. "We've come from Lvov."

"He was arrested two days ago," the woman said quickly, glancing past their heads into the street. "You mustn't be seen here. Go!" She closed the door and locked it.

Stunned, they retraced their steps to the center of the city. The air was cold; the city seemed stiff with suspicion.

"We'll go to a hotel," Luigi said. "Tomorrow we'll see. Try to get some sleep."

In the morning the streets were blue, reflecting the river, the early morning sky. Soldiers everywhere in boots and overcoats.

Luigi took her into a *Konditorei,* and her eyes went wide at the sight of pastries in the glass case. It had been years since she had eaten anything like that. Luigi bought her a *kremeschnitten.* Thousands of layers of delicate flaky pastry— when she bit into it, she thought she would faint. Sugar and eggs and cream! She remembered Zalewsky's, walking with Kovik down the Wale Hetmanskie, under the green canopy of elm trees. They had bought *kremeschnitten* and licked the cream that squirted onto their lips, brushing the powdered sugar from their shirts.

In an instant she had devoured the *kremeschnitten.* She wiped her mouth and looked longingly at the remaining pastries in the glass case.

"Come on," Luigi said, smiling. "I'll buy you another one."

She wolfed it down in two bites. "Another?" she begged. The *kremeschnitten* tasted of the girl she had once been, of Kovik, of his eager blue eyes and his sparkling laugh. It tasted of home, of the streets she loved, the city she would never see again, her schoolmates and teachers. It tasted of childhood itself, of another world a hundred years ago, another life, when she had been a girl in Lvov.

She finished the third pastry but could not stop. She ate pastry after pastry, until she had finished all twelve *kremeschnitten* in the case. With an embarrassed smile, Luigi pushed her out of the bakery.

"You must have been sick as a dog!" I said to my mother when she told me this story.

"I was *scared* as a dog." She smiled, but in her smile was a stitched seam of pain. And it was this history of hers, hidden in the seam of that smile that rendered her permanently separate from me—unapproachable, unfathomable, and alone.

They walked to the hotel in silence and climbed the stairs to their room. Her feet were blistered from walking through the city in heavy black boots, and the straps of her knapsack bit into her shoulder. The room was small, neat, with lace curtains and a ceramic bowl on the washstand. Luigi touched her cheek. "Stay here," he said. "I'm going to see what I can do."

The sun inched along the windowsill, draping a rectangle of light along one corner of the room, then slowly dragging it across the wall as the day wore on. My mother lay on the bed, staring at the ceiling. She fingered the hotel regulations, written in thick black gothic lettering, and looked out the window at apartment buildings across the alley, letting her fingers slide over the wobbly glass windowpanes. She washed her face, trying to recognize the boy in the mirror who stared back at her with ancient dark eyes. She had not expected to be an Italian soldier for such a long time.

Luigi returned in the evening, quieter than usual. The next day he went out again. After a few days he finally told her it was useless. They would have to take the military train out of Budapest and head for Rome. It would be risky—they would be on an Italian train now, with Italian soldiers, and it would be harder for her to remain silent. Among Hungarians she had been relatively safe, but among Italians she wouldn't fool a soul.

"I'll talk to the guard on the mail carriage," Luigi suggested. "Maybe I can bribe him into letting you ride there. Don't talk to anyone."

They waited at the station. Italian soldiers on furlough milled around, smoking, laughing, anxious to go home. They wore their caps at a jaunty angle and poked fun at each other, boasting of their girlfriends back home. My mother hung back, with her knapsack of gold coins wrapped in a dress, covered with the tiger blanket. She took a sip of water from her canteen and held her jaw in her hand, feigning a toothache.

Luigi bribed the guard on the mail car, with a wink and some cash. He snuck my mother onto the car and sat her down among canvas sacks of letters. "Stay here," he whispered.

The Italian guard had a heart-shaped face with dark hair sprouting from his ears. He had short, thick legs and almost no neck, giving him the appearance of a low chest of drawers. He eyed her uneasily and smoked his cigarette down to ashes.

The train lurched out of the station and moved west, crossing into Yugoslavia. Luigi came back to check on her after a few hours. "Everything all right?" he whispered. She nodded. He smiled at the guard and slipped him a few cigarettes, then went back to the officers' car.

The train slowed several times as east-bound trains carrying supplies to the front whipped past them.

Luigi returned once again, but by then the guard was growing uncomfortable. "Listen, pal," he told Luigi, leaning toward him while keeping an eye on my mother, "the kid can't stay in here. We're getting close to the Italian border, and this car will be crawling with border officials. You got to get him out of here, understand?"

Luigi tried to humor him, then to plead with him, and finally to bribe him with more money, but the guard wouldn't budge. "I'm not taking any more chances," he said. "I can't afford a court-martial, buddy. I got a wife and three kids. Find yourself another sucker."

Luigi shrugged. "Let's go," he whispered to my mother.

They walked through the train to the soldiers' cars, where men were leaning out the windows, smoking, and playing cards. Luigi motioned my mother into a compartment with a free seat near the door. *"E libero?"* he asked the other soldiers. They jerked their heads up with alarm when they saw his officer's stripes, but he waved off any formality. *"Si, libero,"* they said. Batya slid into the seat. "His name's Rossi," Luigi said to the other soldiers. "He's got a bad toothache—let him get some sleep, okay?"

He left the compartment and went back to the officers' car.

"Where you heading, Rossi?"

My mother winced. "Roma," she mumbled, then clutched her jaw tighter, as if the word had caused her pain, and closed her eyes.

The men shrugged. "We're going to Bologna," one said, and winked. "Come with us, we'll show you a good time, kid." They laughed. Batya gave a pained smile, shaking her head.

"Don't let an army dentist do you, Rossi," one yelled. "Look what they did to me!" He grinned. The gap in his front teeth seemed wide enough to hold a boccie ball. "Son of a bitch yanked three teeth like he was clearing a mine field!"

Batya nodded weakly and closed her eyes, cupping her hand on her chin.

The train slowed before the western edge of Yugoslavia. Border guards clambered aboard and opened the compartments. *"Documenti!"* they commanded. Stern faces, machine guns over their shoulders. The soldiers went silent, and passed their identity cards and orders for inspection. My mother's hand shook slightly as she waited for the border guards to check her papers. It seemed to take forever. They looked up from the documents and examined each of the soldiers carefully. My mother could not meet their eyes. "Rossi!" they said. She raised her hand, and the guards eyed her coldly. They took the soldiers' documents and closed the compartment, moving quickly onto the next one. The door to the next compartment slid open, followed by the sharp command of the border guards, *"Documenti!"*

They sat at the Yugoslav border for hours. It was night. The men dozed. My mother shivered, although the air in the compartment was warm and stuffy. She closed her eyes and tried to think of Zosia, of her little apartment with the terrace overlooking via dei Giordani, of the lemon tree and azalea bush, and the palm trees lining the paths of the park in Villa Ada like giant green tongues. The train moved forward a few feet, then screeched to a stop. More border guards jumped on and snapped open the compartment door. "Lindrotti!" the guard snapped, and handed the soldier back his papers. "Fallacci!" The soldier reached for his papers. "Bocco." My mother held her breath. "Trevine!" If she was arrested here, she would not be able to stand up. "Corrello!" Her legs seemed to belong to someone else. In the pit of her stomach, a knot of dread. "Rossi!" She looked up. "Rossi!" Her hand moved hesitatingly forward, and her documents were slapped in her palm. The compartment door slid shut with a rush.

A strange feeling passed over her, like a warm glove sliding across her shoulders. She exhaled slowly.

After another half hour the train inched forward. It began to pick up speed, but then slowed again. Within minutes it was inching close to the Italian border station. She read the signs on the tracks: POSTUMIO GROTTO. She was north of Trieste, on the doorstep of Italy.

Italian border guards now boarded the

train, and boots filled the passageway. The compartment slid open again. *"Documenti!"* came the command. The soldiers handed their papers over again for inspection.

"Rossi!" one of the guards snapped. "This way!" He jabbed his head to the right, indicating she should follow him.

Her throat tightened. *"Cosa?"* she asked.

"This way!" he commanded. "Come with us."

The soldiers looked at her as she fumbled with her knapsack, lifted it to her shoulder, and followed the border guards off the train.

Her heart was banging so hard she couldn't hear the shouts of the soldiers on the train or the steam escaping as the brakes were released; she couldn't hear the pumping of the engine or the screech and rattle of the wheels over the tracks as the train slid slowly across the border into Italy.

On the platform, military police removed her knapsack and walked on either side of her, leading her to the station. Her head was pounding, and her feet moved as if in a dream. It's over, she thought. It will all be over soon.

Clusters of Italian officers and soldiers stood in the station, smoking. It was three in the morning. They led her down a dimly lit corridor and into a room at the end of the hall. An officer in a tight olive shirt was sitting behind a desk, her documents laid out in front of him.

"Nome!" he barked.

"Giuseppe Rossi." She stood stiffly, her scalp tingling.

He fingered the papers.

"Rank!"

"Private, First Class."

"How did you get on this train?"

My mother was silent. She was determined not to betray Luigi.

"Who were you with?"

"No one."

The officer leapt up from the desk. "Where did you get on this train?"

"Budapest."

"Who were you with?"

"No one."

"You're lying!" he shouted.

He stepped out from behind his desk and approached her slowly. He was a thin man, tall and carefully groomed, with a small mustache and short dark hair. His eyes were a greenish-gray, and they were drilled on her face.

"What were you doing on this train?" he demanded. "Who were you with?"

"No one."

He slammed his fist on the desk. "Private Rossi! Who got on the train with you?"

"No one."

He slapped her across the face. She stumbled backward, then regained her balance and stood without speaking, looking straight ahead.

"Look, punk," he said in a low voice. "We know you were with someone. The other men in the compartment saw him with you. It's going to go easier for you if you tell us the truth. What were you doing on that train?"

She remained silent.

"Where were you going?" he shouted.

She said nothing. By now, she calculated, the train would be heading south. In another few hours it would reach Bologna. Luigi would get out and go home to his family. He would know nothing of this. She would never give him away.

The interrogating officer began pacing, his hands folded behind his back. He knew this soldier didn't belong on that train—the mail guard had tipped off the border patrol. But he didn't yet realize that this was not a soldier. The military papers, after all, were in perfect order. Giuseppe Rossi, Private First Class. Another one of these string-bean, baby-faced recruits. They were dropping like flies at the front.

No one had bothered to look in Private Rossi's knapsack yet.

Luigi was being questioned in another room, but my mother didn't know that yet. She didn't know they'd arrested him, that he'd coughed up the whole story.

Or maybe he changed the story a bit to suit his needs. Or perhaps it's my mother who has made a few changes now, fifty years later, when she tells her daughter, to suit her own needs. Stories always change for a reason. The truth lies somewhere between the reasons and the stories.

The border guards had taken Luigi to the station, where they ripped off his epaulets. They removed his pistol, his gun belt, his officer's rank. They sat him down and interrogated him.

"All right," he said, "all right, I'll tell you. I made up the documents. I obtained the uniform for her."

"Her!?"

"Yes, the girl you arrested."

The interrogating officer looked with alarm at the inspector. "Giuseppe Rossi is a girl?"

Luigi smiled weakly. "Yes," he said. "She's a poor Polish girl. I felt sorry for her. Her parents were killed by a bomb. I—okay, so it was wrong, what can I say? I wanted to help her. She was all alone. She's a good kid. I felt sorry for her. I didn't mean any harm, I just thought I'd help her get to Rome. She has a sister there—a sister who's married to a lawyer. Crozzi is his name, I think, a count. He's a high-ranking government official; you can check this out. The girl's name is Maria Tannen. This is the truth. You see, the girl is, well, she's practically Italian. Her sister lives here. It's the only family she has left."

The interrogating officer was silent. He stared at the papers of the man in front of him. Luigi Balichero Cotulli, thirty-six years old. A wife and two children in Bologna. Second Lieutenant, transportation engineer.

"You're a fool," the interrogating officer said, and left the room to report to his commanding officer.

Postumio Grotto is a little border town in the Italian Alps. The air is iced by glaciers creeping slowly into the valleys. Fresh snow dusts the nearby peaks.

Seven hundred miles away, in Rome, Uncle brought Zosia flowers for her thirtieth birthday. She was three months pregnant. It was October 7, 1942.

My mother had left Lvov a week earlier, hoping to reach Rome and surprise her sister on her birthday. Instead, on her thirtieth birthday, Zosia received word that her sister had been arrested on the Italian border.

My mother, in the meantime, stubbornly stuck to her story: that she was alone, that she was Giuseppe Rossi, Private First Class. Beyond that, she refused to speak.

Her interrogator was called out of the room. She sat quietly, staring at the wall. Soon it would be all over, she thought. They would search her knapsack and find the gold coins. They would find her dress. Sooner or later they would figure out that she was not Giuseppe Rossi, that she was not a soldier, not Italian, and not a man. It was certainly taking them long enough to catch on, but it was only a matter of time. The coins would be a problem. They would assume she was a spy. They would shoot her here on the border, or else they would send her back to Lvov, and shoot her there, as a deterrent to other spies. She didn't care anymore. The escape had been crazy, impossible, and what was most amazing was that she'd almost pulled it off.

Her thoughts drifted to those days before

the war, when she had walked through Mick-iewicz Park on Kovik's arm, among yellow bursts of forsythia, gladiolus shooting brilliant red-and-white spears under sweeping branches of magnificent willows. But suddenly my mother realized it was unlikely that Kovik was still alive. She tried to find comfort in something else; that Luigi had not been caught, that she would never give him away. That Zosia had survived. And perhaps even her parents would survive. It was still possible, after all.

The door burst open, and the interrogating officer returned, his face flaming red. "Stop wasting my time!" he shouted. "Talk!"

She stared at the floor. His boots crunched on the concrete.

"Who are you?" he demanded.

"Giuse—"

He struck her in the face.

"Who are you?" he shouted. He paced around his desk and sat down. "Where did you get these papers?" His fingers drummed the desk; suddenly he stood and threw the papers to the floor. "Start talking!" he said angrily. "Who helped you?"

He leaned over her, hands on his hips. "Well?" he demanded. "Who gave you these papers?"

She stared at his boots, concentrating on the toes. They were elegant boots of fine leather, boots for parlor conversations, for ballroom dancing, afternoon tea.

"You dumbshit!" he shouted. He glanced at the guard standing like a statue by the door. "Go get him," he said impatiently to the guard. "Bring him in here."

The door opened, and she heard footsteps in the corridor. Two guards entered the room, and between them, with his hands cuffed, was Luigi.

My mother's jaw dropped. Luigi's stripes had been ripped, his collar torn, his head hanging in shame. Did their eyes meet? Neither spoke. The walls started spinning. My mother looked at the floor, but the floor seemed to rock. She closed her eyes and heard Luigi being taken away. The door slammed shut.

"Now," the interrogating officer said, "start talking."

She tried to remember to breathe. She felt hollow, empty of thought.

The officer sat on a corner of his desk, staring at her with disgust. "Take her away!" he finally snapped. "Go."

She was led down the hall and through a long corridor into a linked building. Down a series of steps and through another long hallway. The guards unlocked a heavy metal door, and then a second. They pushed her in a cell, closed the door, and locked it.

The silence of the room filled her. She sat on the bench in the corner and closed her eyes. A weight on her chest like an anchor of guilt. Waiting was unbearable. She wished they would finish with her quickly. There was nothing she could do.

"It was the worst moment of my life," my

mother told me. "That was the lowest. You know how I am—I'm hard, I can hold out a long time, but once I reach the end, it's the absolute end. I had nothing left. And that night—I'll never forget it, that night that they showed me Luigi, and I saw that he was arrested because of me—and they took me to that cell—it was the end of me.

"Because it was so clear—he had risked his life for me, now he would be shot. With my parents—the guilt—yes, of course, I felt guilty, but I could still hope. I could still pretend that maybe they were alive some-where, maybe they would survive after all. But here it was open and shut, it was clear. Because of me, Luigi would be killed. He was innocent! He'd done nothing wrong! I couldn't bear it. It was the end of me, the very lowest point in my life.

"And then—I can't explain it—something happened, it was, well, I know that some-thing saved me at that moment. Just before I hit rock bottom—I felt something lift me up—a soaring, calming sense of relief. I don't know how or why—but suddenly, I didn't worry at all; I felt everything would be fine, everything would be all right. It wasn't an act—it wasn't courage. I don't know how else to describe that moment—I'll never forget it. It was something miraculous, although I know that sounds crazy.

"And the guards, the officers, all of them noticed it. They were amazed at how calm I was, how unperturbed. From then on—I was in prison there for months, you know—but nothing bothered me."

My mother was sitting on the couch in the TV room when she told me this. It was the Monday after Thanksgiving, 1992, and we had just watched *To Sir with Love* on the VCR. She had borrowed it from the library. It was fifty years and one month after her arrest. It was forty-six years and five days after her marriage. It was thirty-five years and three months after my birth. Something happens, then something happens, then something happens. This is called a story.

22

Uncle sent a lawyer to the border. He was a friend who owed Uncle a favor, and in accordance with the slippery commerce of connections, Uncle later got him a title of nobility.

The lawyer spent weeks on my mother's case, meeting with officials, shaking hands, smiling, explaining the situation. He moved smoothly from one official to another until he found a soft spot. Favors were exchanged between gentlemen. As my mother put it, "Strings were pulled."

Years later, when I went to law school, Uncle beamed with pride. "The law," he said, "is an excellent and noble profession."

The lawyer persuaded the border officials to pretend my mother had been arrested in Italy, rather than at the border. (Arrest at the border meant a firing squad.) Leaning toward them, he offered the officers a cigarette from a silver case in his breast pocket. "Let her go," he said affably, the citrus scent of cologne wafting from his neck. "She's not a spy, not a saboteur. She did nothing wrong but try to join her sister." In the end, the officials compromised. They decided to send my mother to a concentration camp in southern Italy, but as a deterrent to similar escapades, they sent word back to Lvov that she had been shot.

This is what Jiri heard in Lvov, anxiously awaiting news from my mother. Disheartened, he fled to Warsaw. No one knows how long he lasted, but eventually he was scooped up in a transport to Treblinka. He would manage to jump from the train, but he was shot as he jumped. My mother learned this years later from his cousin who made it to Rome. "I knew he wouldn't survive," my mother said. "You could see he wasn't going to make it."

"How?" I asked.

She thought a moment. "He was too angry," she said finally. "He was too angry to survive."

She turned away from me. "And too hot-tempered," she added, "too impulsive. I knew he wouldn't make it."

We sat in silence for a moment.

"He was in love with me," she said quietly.

My mother finally left the Italian border in the beginning of January 1943, as snow and ice leaked through cracks in the Alps into northern

Italy. She was flanked by two armed guards in olive-green overcoats and earflapping wool hats, boys who had assumed the stone-faced attitude of machine-made men. They had orders to bring her to the concentration camp in Vinchiaturro, in southern Italy.

Before they'd traveled more than a few hundred kilometers, the guards stopped off at Trieste and deposited my mother at the local prison for *Epifania,* the twelfth day of Christmas. While her guards were out celebrating the holiday, my mother endured a grisly night locked up with convicted felons. "It was one of the worst nights of my life," my mother told me without elaboration, in the solemn half whisper she usually reserves for discussion of disability, sexual perversity, or tragedy befalling *others*. I'll never know exactly what happened that night in the Italian prison, except that the prisoners stole everything she had—her toothbrush, her socks, her underwear.

The next day her two guards, hung over from their revels, came to pick her up after her sleepless night. Her knapsack of personal belongings had been held by the prison officials and received better treatment than she had; the knapsack was returned to her upon her release. Her tiger blanket and twenty-five gold coins would miraculously make their way from prison to prison across Italy with her.

My mother boarded the southbound train with her guards, and after settling into a cramped compartment of sleepy soldiers, she dozed off. The train rumbled across coarse winter fields and leafless trees etched against a starless night sky. At midnight they arrived in Bologna, where they had to change trains. The station was deserted, dark kiosks on the platforms like a few teeth left in a mouth. Only the silhouette of a soldier or two smoking a cigarette could be seen leaning against a wall.

"We had some time to kill before catching our next train," my mother told me, "so I asked my guards to call and see if Luigi was working at the station. I told them he was a friend of mine."

"You asked your guards to make a call for you?" I asked.

"Why not?" My mother shrugged. "They were nice boys." She took a sip of coffee, then tapped my wrist with her finger.

"And this," she continued, "this is what was so amazing: Luigi himself answered the phone! He was right there, at the Bologna train station that night!" She leaned back from me, as if my presence interfered with her vision of the past. Her eyes were lit with the magical radiance of memory made visible, past and present melting in watery relief.

The guards led her to Luigi's office, one on either side of her, amused, perhaps, by their prisoner's connections. When Luigi threw open the door, my mother felt her knees go weak and her breath rush out like steam. She barely noticed Luigi slipping the guards some money and telling them to get lost for an hour as he shut the door behind them.

Alone in his office, my mother burst into

tears. "It was a miracle!" my mother told me. "The greatest moment in my life!" Luigi and my mother hugged and laughed and talked for an hour. He reassured her that he was fine, pointing to his stripes, his officer's title, his name sewn above his breast pocket.

"I could see with my own eyes that he was alive!" my mother told me. "I would never have believed it if I hadn't seen him for myself. It was something I can't describe.

"And not only that," my mother added, "not only was he alive, but they'd restored him to his same rank and given him a post in his hometown! Only in Italy," she laughed, her eyes twinkling. "You see, Uncle's lawyer had told the border officials that I was Luigi's girlfriend—that he'd helped me escape because he was having an affair with me. And the Italians—well, once they thought it was a romance, they practically *rewarded* Luigi!"

As it turns out, Luigi was also responsible for the birth of the "bomb" story. He had told the officials at the border that my mother was a Polish orphan, that her parents had been killed in a bombing. "And that's the story that stuck," my mother told me. "The lawyer told me I had to keep my story consistent with his. So that's why I've always main-tained that my parents were killed by a bomb."

Finally her guards knocked at the door. It was time for them to take their prisoner to the southbound connection, and they waited politely, hands folded behind their backs, smiling awkwardly while my mother and Luigi embraced, before walking her to the train platform for the last leg of her journey.

In January 1943 the concentration camp in Vinchiaturro was damp and cold, and there was little food. Most of the women were misplaced and displaced persons, Russian women whose Italian boyfriends had sneaked them onto trains. They spent the days knitting and talking, waiting for liberation.

Zosia sent her sister books and packages, sweaters and gifts for the other women. She also sent gifts for the warden, working on him in her own way, while Uncle explored political connections to try to get my mother released.

Soon after arriving at the camp, my mother wrote to her parents in Busk, to let them know that she had made it to Italy. She worded her letters carefully, so that they would slip through the censors. By now southern Italy was deporting its Jews, shipping them north to internment camps and handing them over to the Germans for "resettlement." In Poland, especially in the east, the cities and towns were all *Judenrein*—cleared of Jews.

"I'm here in Rome with Zosia," my mother wrote her parents, not wanting them to know that she was actually incarcerated. She sent the letter to Zosia, who added a few words and mailed the letter to Busk from Rome.

"You see," my mother explained, "this way it would be postmarked from Rome, without the concentration-camp insignia."

Her parents received my mother's letter. They were still alive in April 1943, and they answered by mail, but I have never seen their response. Zosia saved it for my mother, but later she burned everything—letters, documents, and family photos—when the Nazis invaded Rome.

My mother also wrote Dad's mother, again mailing her letter through Zosia in Rome so that my grandmother wouldn't see the postmark of the concentration camp. Dad's mother wrote a card back to Zosia in April 1943, just before she was killed. This was the postcard full of Easter greetings and Pope's blessings—the card that I first saw last Christmas. Uncle had kept that postcard in his study for fifty years. When Uncle died, Zosia found the postcard written in my grandmother Helen's beautiful handwriting and brought it to my father in 1992.

This card is all that is left of my grandparents, a tiny shard of our past.

Zosia's parents and Checha Godja were killed by the Germans in Busk in May 1943, about the same time that Zosia was giving birth to Renzo in Rome. He was to compensate for his lost grandparents, his lost Checha Godja, a lost world. He was a child of the Holocaust, but with a Mediterranean twist, distilled in Italian sunshine. He was baptized and christened Emilio Renzo Crozzi di Villa Vescovina. This boy would be a new path, the path of no turning back.

Two months later, in July 1943, my mother

was sprung from the concentration camp, thanks to Uncle's diplomatic efforts. A few days later, as it turned out, all the other political prisoners would also be released by the forty-five-day Badoglio government, which came into power on July 25, 1943.

My mother arrived in Rome carrying her knapsack of Russian gold coins and her tiger blanket. She was greeted by her sister, holding the baby my mother had never seen, and Uncle, who smiled sweetly and kissed her on both cheeks. With Mussolini's fall from power, Uncle had lost his job as a government lawyer. But while most Italian Fascists were fleeing north, Uncle, a fair-weather Fascist at best, had no intention of leaving Rome.

Without an income he had no way to support his family, except by doing bits of legal research for friends—a small project here and there. For months he and Zosia stretched their savings, bits of money and jewelry stuffed into brassieres and under mattresses—moist savings that smelled of salt and worry. The family was forced out of their apartment by inflated rents, and they eventually found a smaller, shabbier apartment nearby. They recycled everything in the house. Uncle tinkered with electrical wires, repaired appliances, tables, chairs, plumbing. Even today Zosia's apartment is full of his little makeshift remedies, a hornet's nest of jumbled wires behind every socket.

Fresh out of prison, my mother sat on her sister's terrace, drinking up the blue Roman sky, her fingers curled around a coffee cup, listening for Renzo's cry in the next room. Her hair was growing out, but it was still spiky over her forehead and ears, and she wore a scarf to hide it. She fingered the pen in her hand and wrote her parents in Busk. A careful note, triumphant, a note of inquiry and reassurance. But her parents never responded. And Kovik's mother never responded. This was the beginning of the silence, its first teeth. A silence that slowly ate its way through her heart.

My father, in the meantime, sat on an upturned metal pail in the Gulag, his left arm stuck in a right angle, playing chess with another prisoner. As the years passed he got used to the camps and sealed a part of himself shut. He moved through the Gulag on new muscles, trusting no one but himself. All of his preparation had been a waste—athlete, doctor, musician—all worthless. The Gulag was his ultimate occupation.

23

In November 1992 I finally screwed up the courage to tell my mother that I'm gay. I was home for Thanksgiving, and my mother and I were sitting on the sofa in the TV room. She had just told me about her arrest at the border of Italy in 1942, about how she had seen Luigi taken away, how she thought she would be shot. We had finished watching *To Sir with Love*, and my father had gone to bed.

"Mom," I said, "I feel I should tell you something."

I hesitated, listening to the purr of the videotape rewinding.

"It's something I've meant to tell you for years," I said, "but I was afraid to upset you." The VCR clicked off with a satisfying thunk. "But now that we're finally getting all the secrets out in the open, I think you should know."

My mother nodded.

"I love women," I said. Unable to look at her face, I stared at the carpet and spoke quickly. "Remember Dori? We were more than friends; we were lovers. And I've had relationships with women before that." I finally looked her in the eye. "I wanted you to know that I'm gay."

My mother was calm; she tried to reassure me. "You don't know," she said. "This doesn't mean anything. Dori was dying. And she was a painter, an artist. What you did was for her sake. It doesn't mean you're a lesbian."

"Well, actually—"

"You've always had boyfriends," my mother pointed out. "Boys have always liked you. It takes time. You'll see, give it time."

"I'm gay, Mom," I said. "I think I know by now. I'm thirty-five, I've known for a long time. I didn't want to tell you, because I didn't want to hurt you."

My mother brushed off my remarks with a flick of the wrist. "You don't know," she assured me, offering scores of reasons why I couldn't be gay. Finally I stopped objecting and let her have her way. There seemed little point in arguing the issue. But I was beginning to understand why it had always been so hard for me to figure out who I was, since I could never completely resist my mother's telling me. I knew she only wanted for me what she thought was best. The extraordinary will she developed to survive she couldn't help using in love.

In September 1943, a few months after the fall of Mussolini, the Germans captured Rome. Red and black swastikas flapped from balconies, and Nazi soldiers goose-stepped through central squares, black boots smacking ancient stones. My mother, it seemed, had fled straight into the enemy's arms.

Travel became impossible—British and American planes bombed routes leading to and from the city, choking Rome off like a tourniquet. In the surrounding small towns and villages, fields bristled with swollen tomatoes and sweet cucumbers, pumpkin-sized cabbages and glistening green clubs of zucchini; but in the city, people went hungry, babies cried for milk. Dusty roads linking Rome to the outlying farms were mined and shelled; only a thin stream of food leaked through the black market.

My mother, freshly released from prison, became the family scavenger. Her hair was growing out, and she no longer had to wear a scarf. "I'd ride the tram to the last stop," she told me. "To the outskirts of Rome. Then I'd walk for an hour, sometimes more, into the countryside." She found peasants selling produce by the side of the road, wooden carts, and dusty mules chewing rope bridles. She bought eggs and milk for the baby, cheese, squash, and potatoes. She bartered for food, offering clothes and household items, whatever the family could part with. At the end of the day my mother began the long walk home.

When local supplies grew thin, my mother grew more daring. She went to Nazi headquarters and bummed rides to Abruzzi and Tuscany with military transports. "I went to the ORT," she told me, "the *Organisationstadt*. It was the German military-supply department, and I caught rides out of the city, to Perugia and Siena, where Uncle had friends."

"You went to the Germans?" I asked. "Wasn't that risky?"

"Oh, no," my mother said. She waved her hand absentmindedly, as if shooing a gnat.

I've never been able to imagine the war correctly—my wide-eyed questions, half-whispered reverence scoffed at by her dismissive sweep of the hand, lips pulled back in a mocking pucker. "I spoke fluent German, you know," she said. "And those German soldiers stationed in Rome, they were delighted to have someone to talk to."

She brought back flour, sugar, and fresh fruit to Zosia. "You see, I could do this smuggling openly," my mother said, "because I was not a black marketeer. I was simply getting food for my family."

So my mother hopped rides with the Nazis, who never suspected that she was Jewish. They laughed and shared jokes, made affectionate jibes at the Italians, and talked about what they would do when the war was over. Every so often they had to pull over, jump from the trucks, and throw themselves into ditches, as American and British planes roared overhead, bombing the road. After the planes passed they would pick themselves up, dust themselves off, and continue on their way, resuming their conversation where they'd left off.

These became my bedtime stories, whimsical tales with which my mother tucked me in as a child, turning the gruesome events of her life into my entertainment.

Once, she told me, she used a German military transport to recover Uncle's custom-made prewar dining-room furniture from a cabinetmaker near Florence. She persuaded the driver, a young Nazi soldier, to swing by the furniture factory and haul Uncle's furniture back to Rome, a dangerous trip that took several days. Not only did he complete the trip with her, but he also insisted on helping her carry the furniture up to their apartment.

"Here's the funny part," my mother said with a smile. "Our neighbors had seen the Nazi truck pull up at night and unload furniture into our apartment. And then, over the next few weeks, you know, they saw a car of German soldiers stop in for tea or occasionally for lunch or dinner." Her eyes twinkled mischievously. "So the neighbors suspected Uncle was in cahoots with the Germans!"

Of course, the Count's wife and sister-in-law—far from being Nazi collaborators—were Jewish. While my mother and Zosia offered tea to the German soldier and his friends, across town the Germans were scooping up the Jews in the ghetto like scraps of paper and sending them to Auschwitz.

Although the Americans had already landed in Sicily, it took them almost a year to inch up the coast to Rome. Finally, in June 1944, radios crackled with the news that the American army was approaching the capital. In a matter of hours the German command had jumped into jeeps, trucks, and motorcycles and raced north. Italian collaborators fled with them, running out the door without so much as a change of clothes.

Soon afterward, the first American infantrymen arrived at Fascist headquarters in EUR on the outskirts of Rome and found empty offices. Cigarettes burned down in ashtrays; still-warm coffee sat in cups around a table. As it turned out, Uncle's brother Arturo was the highest-ranking officer left in Rome.

"Arturo was in Mussolini's Special Guard," my mother told me. "He was quite close to him." Broad-chested and long-nosed, Arturo was a fencing champion and avid athlete. He was Uncle's youngest brother, and although he looks nothing like Uncle, he has the same easy smile and sweet disposition.

"But Arturo didn't speak a word of English," my mother said. "So he hopped on his bicycle and pedaled like mad across the city to Uncle's apartment, where I was playing with Renzo. And he just plunked me onto his handlebars and pedaled me back to the waiting American officers.

"And that's how I wound up at the Red Cross," my mother says, laughing. "I translated that first meeting with the incoming American army, and after that the Americans hired me as their translator. They liked me." She shrugs.

The earliest photographs I have of my mother are of her Red Cross days in 1944— playing volleyball with American GIs on leave, or dressed as Santa Claus, handing out treats to the soldiers. There she is, in a dozen photos, too good to be true: grinning ear to ear in an enormous Santa Claus outfit, complete with wide black belt and tall black boots, standing next to a tinsel-smothered Christmas tree. My mother, the Polish office worker, the Italian soldier, in her new disguise: Santa Claus handing out candy to the conquering American soldiers.

In May 1945 the war scraped to a close, and families had broken in pieces. Names filled newspapers and bulletin boards; the Red Cross set up files and searched for missing persons. Thousands were still dying by the minute. Europe was stunned by its discoveries. Remote camps emerged as if from under the earth, skeletons and stick figures on bare feet with hollow eyes, covered with a piece of blanket.

My mother made inquiries about her family and Kovik, posted notices at refugee camps, in local papers, and with the Red Cross. She sent letters to everyone she could think of, to her parents and aunt in Busk, to Kovik's music teacher in Buczacz, to his mother. She put ads in the Polish newspapers in Warsaw and Lvov. No response. She heard nothing.

Eventually news reached her of Auschwitz and Dachau, of Buchenwald, the gas chambers and crematoria. Word came from Americans and the British, soldiers who had liberated the camps and reported what they had seen. My mother finally understood the silence, and feared it more than anything else.

The American Red Cross Rest Center was closing down in Rome; the soldiers were going home. An Italian government official who had worked at the Rest Center offered my mother a job as a translator at the Ministry of Agriculture. A job in Rome in 1945 was more precious than gold. My mother began working at the Ministry in the afternoons and evenings, even before she left the Red Cross. Uncle was still out of work, and my mother was the sole breadwinner of the family. Zosia managed the household expenses, and they lived on air and a little luck.

Renzo was a great distraction for them, a new shoot of life. His aqua-blue eyes were Zosia's; his coffee skin and black hair, Uncle's. He was only two years old when the war ended, but he had a history that went back centuries, from opposite poles of the continent. He was a bridge, a compromise between forces he could not fathom.

24

The days grew longer in Siberia; the summer of 1945 dusted the tundra olive-brown. Snow slipped into streams and sank into the earth. My father continued to drag himself through each day, his head shaved and belly swollen from slow starvation. His skin had wrinkled like an old man's. Bones protruded from his hips and his chest. Around him, men died like flies. They simply lay down and did not get up. My father forced himself to his feet each morning and pushed himself through the days with a burning determination. It was not hope that sustained him, but hatred.

For my father, the war was a distant rumble. It no longer affected him. He was a Soviet prisoner of the Gulag, an enemy of the State under Stalin. He slept on wooden bunks, sucked down fishless broth, and broke his teeth on black bread. He was serving a sentence for being a "Socially Dangerous Element," or anti-Communist. The end of the war was meaningless to him; he had to serve his sentence, regardless of the recent Allied victory.

The summer turned into another winter. Snow fell again, more snow, more wind coating the prisoners with ice. Toes fell off, then feet, then legs. Freezing took no time in winter.

He wondered sometimes where his mother, Helen, was, what she would be doing now. He didn't know yet about Belzec. Or Sobibor. Or Treblinka. He had never heard of Auschwitz. He could not imagine what he had missed. The Gulag took all his concentration. He had no illusions about Batya; five years was a long time, and she was a young woman. He had disappeared, and people did not come back from the Gulag.

My father heard something about Nazi atrocities, but he tried to dismiss them as Soviet propaganda. And yet there must have been prisoners who knew, or relatives who knew, or friends who knew. Word must have reached them. Eventually Kovik must have believed he would never find anyone again. Even if he managed to come out alive.

In 1946 my father was thirty-one. He had spent nearly six years in Siberia. That summer, his status changed. His sentence was commuted from a prison term to exile in Siberia. He was required to report daily to NKVD headquarters, and he would have to live within ten kilometers of the barbed-wire confines of the camp. The first day of his release from the camp enclosure, he escaped.

He had neither papers, possessions, nor

food. He had one good arm, two legs, and an enormous determination to tell the world his experience of Soviet Communism. He made his way to the train tracks and jumped a westbound train. He clung to the side of the train for hours, hiding from guards who patrolled the compartments checking papers.

My father has never said much about his escape, except to mention that by riding illegally he was able to traverse the huge expanse of Russia in a record-breaking four days. "Trains were so jam-packed," he explained, "it was almost impossible to squeeze onto a car even with a paid ticket."

Train stations were mobbed with people— they crowded the platforms and slept on their luggage for days or even weeks, waiting to claw their way onto a train. And it wasn't only in Siberia—the same thing happened when they tried to transfer in other provinces. "If I'd bought a ticket and ridden legally," my father said with a smile, "it would have taken me weeks to get to Buczacz."

He dropped to the ground in his hometown and discovered that Buczacz was now part of Russia. The streets were dusty, the houses dirty, the people suspicious. My father was a ruin of a man, broken, starved, and desperate. He found his home torn apart by a bomb, reduced to rubble. He asked about his mother.

"You're Kovik Buchman?" his neighbors asked, eyes wide with amazement. "It's not possible! How did you survive?"

"Can you tell me what happened to my mother?"

They shook their heads. "They were all taken away."

"Where?"

They looked at the ground or off into the distance. "Not here. Well, a few managed, yes—they went to the city, to Lvov, some went west to Wroclaw—but there is no one left here."

Kovik found his Ukrainian music teacher, Anya Karelewicz, who was in her seventies by then. In 1945, at the end of the war, she had fled from the Soviets and settled in Poland. But now that the Soviets controlled both Poland and the Ukraine, she decided to return to her native Buczacz. Amazingly, my father happened to show up on her doorstep the day after her return to town.

When she answered the door, the old man she saw was a broken bundle of rags, grizzled and gaunt. "Professor Karelewicz," he addressed her formally in Ukrainian. "It's me, Kovik Buchman. Do you know anything about my mother?"

She stood in shock, staring at the man. "Is it you, Kovik?" she whispered. "Is it really you?"

She took him by the arm and led him into the room. He leaned to kiss her hand, but she took his head in her palms and kissed both his cheeks, tears welling in her eyes. She sat him at the kitchen table.

"Here," she said, offering him some bread.

"Let me heat some soup. You must have something to eat."

He tore into the bread, ashamed of his hunger. "Thank you," he said after a moment. "You're very kind." He finished the bread and bit into an onion she pushed toward him. "Mmmm," he murmured, still chewing.

"How did you get here?" she asked.

He waved off her question. "They'll be looking for me," he said. "I escaped. Can you tell me about my mother?"

She heated the soup, which burned his mouth. Turning the spoon in his hand, he recognized it as his mother's silverware.

She glanced at his worn face, then folded her hands in her lap. "Your mother came to live with me," she said. "I took her in. A few months after you left, in the winter of 1941—no, maybe it was later—'42. Under the Germans. She stayed with me a year, almost a year—" Her voice broke off, and she looked away.

"More soup?" she asked. She removed the pot from the stove and filled his bowl.

Outside, the afternoon sun drizzled through the branches of plum trees, casting shadows on the dusty street. A horse dragged a wagon past the house, two silver milk cans clanking.

"It was terrible, what was going on here," she said, looking out the window. "Terrible." She could not look at his face, the deep lines around his eyes, the white stubble on his head.

"They rounded up everyone, all the Jews—men, women, children—" She caught her breath and continued. "The Ukrainian guards, they marched them up to the Fodor, up on the hill." She pointed toward the forested hillside across the river. He nodded. "They forced them to dig huge pits and then shot them all. Thousands of them. Just like that."

"And my mother...?" he asked.

"I took your mother in," she said. "She stayed with me. I hid her."

Silence filled the room. My father wrapped himself in it. He was tired, he wanted to sleep. He did not want to listen anymore, but he could not tear himself away.

"Later the Nazis discovered her. It was in the spring—spring of 1943. There was an informer, I'm sure. They rounded up the rest of the Jews then. Early May, I think. They took them all away."

My father stared at her.

"No one came back."

The walls of the apartment were bare. Everything was still packed in boxes, except a few kitchen utensils. Anya Karelewicz scraped a chair across the floor, startling Kovik.

"Lie down here," she said. "Sleep. You must rest now."

He lay on the cot. She gathered his bowl and spoon and slowly washed the dishes.

He slept all afternoon and all night. In the morning he woke early. Pinpricks of sunlight through drawn shades. Anya Karelewicz was snoring on her cot behind the curtain. The room was stuffy. My father tiptoed out onto the steps. The sun calmed him. A rooster crowed, then a second. The town was silent, indifferent to him. He felt very old. Weeds sprawled over yards; fences rotted and collapsed. Dust coated everything, even the rising sun was shrouded in dust.

Kovik cut across the road to the woods on the hill behind the house, where he would not be seen. He walked aimlessly at first, then realized he was moving in the direction of the Fodor, where the Jews had been killed. He stopped, his heart pounding. Carefully, he turned and retraced his steps. He walked through the town to the opposite hillside, and wandered through the Jewish cemetery. Stones tilted in crazy directions, broken, dug up, crumbling. He searched for his mother, knowing he would not find her. He searched for his grandmother. He had been at her bedside when she died at eighty-six. He had been in medical school then, and he remembered carrying her to this grave. He searched the graveyard, but her stone was missing. He walked back to Anya Karelewicz.

She fed him bread and cabbage, a glass of tea. "Kovik," she said, "I received a card from your fiancée—Batya Tannen—over a year ago now. It arrived a few days before I left for Poland. She wrote right after the war ended."

"Batya!" He had forced himself not to think of her in the last year. Not since reports of the Final Solution had reached the Gulag. He knew that the Jewish problem had been permanently solved in Poland. "Is it possible?"

"It was in the spring, over a year ago now. From Rome. She was living with her sister. I saved the card in case you returned." She went through a folder of papers. "I know it's here somewhere, just a minute."

The card was creased and torn. *Have you heard anything from Kovik?* my mother had written. She gave her sister's name and address in Rome.

Kovik's hands shook. It was her handwriting. She was alive. Or was, only a year ago. He sat at the table, unable to speak. He read the address over and over again until he closed his eyes and saw it clearly, in her own handwriting. Once he had memorized it he tossed the card into the stove and burned it.

"Go to Lvov," Karelewicz advised. "It's a big city; you won't be so obvious. Try to contact her from there."

My father nodded.

"Kovik," she added, "be careful. The walls have ears. Understand? Be careful." She handed him the remaining loaf of bread, a bag of plums, and some money.

"May I take this?" he asked, holding up one of his mother's silver-plated knives.

"Of course," she said.

He walked west beyond the train station and hid in the woods. Toward evening he jumped onto a freight car, holding on with his good arm. With the other he pressed the bread and plums against his chest. He gnawed on the bread and finished it as the train left the outskirts of his hometown.

It was easier to slip through the streets of Lvov unnoticed. The city was now under Russian rule. My father walked to my mother's house on Owacowa Street, but strangers were living in her apartment. A Polish woman answered the door, her head covered in a flowered kerchief. She pushed him quickly out. "No," she said flatly, shaking her head, "no one by that name. Get out."

He wandered down Piekarska Street, remembering how he had walked Batya down these blocks, carrying her books, teasing her, laughing like children. It had been ten years ago that they had started dating. It seemed like a century.

He went to the medical school to obtain a copy of his medical diploma, but the school's records had been partially destroyed. He named his professors, his subjects, his classmates, but there was nothing they could do for him.

My father wandered through the streets, disoriented and strangely detached. He went to the Jewish cemetery and looked for his father's stone, but the cemetery had been leveled by the Germans. He walked down the main street to Platz Mariacki, where he had waited for Batya ten years ago, that day in the rain.

Coming toward him was a man he recognized. A pale pigeon-toed man with a broad forehead and large brown eyes. Gradually, it came back to him. "Janusz Poklowicz!" he cried. A classmate from medical school.

The man stopped, startled.

"Janusz! It's me, Kovik Buchman!"

The man peered at him hesitantly. "Kovik?" he whispered. "Kovik Buchman?"

Kovik smiled, revealing half a mouth of gray-blue teeth. "Yes! It's me!"

"Is it possible? How did you..." His voice trailed off. "Kovik Buchman..." He glanced around him. "Come with me," he whispered. "Come to my office."

Kovik followed him to a small side street near Mickiewicz Park. They climbed the stairs to the second floor and entered Janusz's office, which smelled of freshly polished oak.

"How did you get here? What's happened to you?"

"I have no papers," he said. "My fiancée is alive. She's in Rome. I must contact her."

Janusz drummed the desk with his fingers. He still couldn't believe the change in his classmate. He looked ancient, like an exhumed corpse. All that was left of him were skin and bones and piercing blue-gray eyes.

"It's a problem," Janusz mumbled. "The border was open for six months after the war, people came and went, but it's too late now. Let me see what I can do. Do you have a place to stay?"

Kovik shook his head.

"There's a couch in the other room," Janusz said. "I'll get you something to eat. You must be hungry."

My father wandered the streets of Lvov. Nailed to the walls of buildings at each street corner were new Russian street signs, with black Cyrillic letters— the old Polish street names had simply been translated in some cases, but many streets now sported new Soviet names, the sacred names of the Revolution.

The center of Lvov, for the most part, was unblemished by bombs: patrician homes with marble balconies faced cobblestone squares; the baroque opera house commanded a stately view down the tree-lined Wale Hetmanskie. But the city's churches were boarded up, their onion domes muted green. Synagogues lay in piles of rubble. Zamarstynowska, the Jewish section, had been razed: a field of charred wood and crumbled bricks. People scurried past with drawn faces.

Kovik stepped into a bread line on Krakowska that curved around the block, past the boarded-up entrance to the Boimov Chapel. He fingered the bills in his pocket that Anya Karelewicz had given him. It took a long time to reach the counter, but he was in no hurry. He bought a loaf of black bread and sat on an iron bench in the square. From his pocket he drew his mother's silver-plated knife—the only remaining token from his home in his former life. He would carry it across Europe with him, and it would resurface in our house fifty years later. I still have this knife, an inexpensive piece of flatware—simple, heavy, but elegant. Stamped into the long silver blade is the metalsmith's logo: GERLACH WARSZAWA. My father cut the loaf of bread in half with it and ate.

He wandered back down Krakowska past the

Stary Rynek to his friend's office. In the damp light he took medical texts from the shelf and read them cover to cover. Prewar German textbooks bound in leather, with beautifully drawn illustrations on delicate yellowing pages. He spent days like this, poring over his friend's medical books, gnawing on a loaf of bread, an onion, plums when he found them.

A week later Janusz burst in with good news. A train of Polish orphans was heading across the border to Poland, and Janusz had arranged for my father to accompany them as their physician.

And so my father left Russia for good, on a train full of children—Polish children—without parents and without homes, leaving their city of Lvov. My father was one of them, a homeless orphan swallowed up by Stalinist Russia, now sliding free on the Russian rails for the west.

As soon as he was across the border, he telegrammed my mother in Rome. *I am alive,* he wrote. *Where can we meet? Love, Kovik.*

It was late August 1946. My mother must have been out of her mind with excitement. She dashed back a message to him: *I am waiting for you here. Love, Batya.*

How did my father get from the Russian border to Rome? Without papers, money, or food? The war had ended a year and a half earlier, and borders had been closed, populations reshuffled, languages shifted. My father slept during the day and moved by starlight. He walked across Europe, slept in fields, and foraged for food. When the autumn weather turned crisp, he slept in barns and haylofts. At last he reached Wroclaw on the western edge of Poland. He had a few zlotys in his pocket, and he stepped into a bread line on the street corner. The sun angled lower in the square. He stood with women and children and old tattered men. His clothes hung from him like a scarecrow. The line moved slowly.

"Doctor Buchman!"

My father spun around.

"Doctor Buchman!"

A man ran toward him, waving. "Doc, it's me, Mikhail Tadencyk! Don't you remember? The infirmary in Aktiublag—remember? You saved my life!"

People standing in line turned and stared, murmuring among themselves. "What did he say?" they whispered.

My father racked his brain, but he could not recognize the man. "I'm sorry," he said, "I don't know..."

The man was short and stocky, with bright blue eyes and a toothless smile. He ran up to my father and kissed him twice, on either cheek. "When did you get out?"

"I'm afraid I..." My father hesitated, afraid the man might be an informer, an extortionist, an NKVD agent. "I'm sorry," my father said louder, "I think you must be mistaken. I really don't know you."

The man pulled him gently by the arm. "It's okay, Doc," he whispered in his ear in camp slang. "Come with me, come to my house. I want you to meet my wife." He pulled my father with him, grinning from ear to ear.

My father hung back. He didn't want to make a scene in front of everyone. Was he safer here in the street? Or following the man? He was too tired to think. He let himself be led across the square, his mind racing, looking for a way out.

"Don't you remember?" the man was saying. "It was a couple years ago, winter. I was on a digging crew, freezing my ass off. And I just collapsed. Just like that. My legs swelled up like balloons and just gave out. I was a goner. They dumped me in the infirmary—remember?"

My father looked at him blankly.

"They dumped me in the infirmary for the night, and the next day I felt a little better. I could sit up, you know, I could even walk around a little. But I knew I wouldn't make it through another day in the pits. And you were making the rounds—you had on those crazy feed-bag shoes you used to wear— you examined me, and you realized I spoke Polish— remember? I was a Section 43, criminal code. You were a political, a 58-10, right, Doc?"

My father tried to concentrate on what the man was saying, but his eyes darted across the street, still suspecting an informant.

"—and you said you'd fix it so I could get a little rest in the infirmary. I can't believe you don't remember! You kept me there for two weeks! And you'd come around and talk with me, and bring me extra soup, and even a potato once. I wouldn't have made it, Doc, if not for that. You saved my life."

My father looked closely at the man—his bleached blue eyes, flat nose, tiny ears. Kovik began to nod slowly. The man had put on weight, he looked years younger than the Pole who had been in his infirmary. "Yes," my father said slowly, amazed that this could really be the same person, "yes, I remember you. But don't exaggerate, I was only doing my job. Anyone else would have done—"

The man waved his hand across his face. "You know, you look like hell. Come on, I want you to meet my wife. She's a great little cook! We'll have us a terrific dinner, and we'll drink some vodka and have a good talk! When did you get out?"

And so my father became the houseguest of Mikhail Tadencyk, who apparently was still wheeling and dealing on the black market and still maintained close contacts with the underworld. He was making a good living, running goods back and forth across borders. Five years in the Gulag hadn't shaken his habit, and he seemed to feel relatively safe in postwar Poland.

True to his word, he offered my father vodka and a feast of cabbage and beets, kasha and potatoes. They toasted the West, the free world, their distance from Stalin, the end of the war, and the quality of the vodka. They toasted Kovik, they toasted Mikhail's wife; they toasted the future.

Kovik slept like a pile of bricks.

312

In the morning my father told Mikhail about Batya, about his plan to return to her in Rome. He needed to get across the Iron Curtain, which was three countries thick.

"Don't worry about a thing," Mikhail said, "I know people. I can arrange it, okay? But you're gonna have to beef up a bit, buddy. Crossing those borders involves some hiking. I know good people, don't worry. Give me a couple of days to set things up."

My father's face reddened. "I have no money," he said. "This is all I have." He pulled the zlotys from his pocket, and the silver knife.

Mikhail smiled his toothless smile. "Forget it, pal. I'll take care of it. Okay? Not to worry. I owe you."

A week later my father was walking west with Mikhail's Polish guide. They traveled by night and slept during the day. The nights were chilly—early snow caught them in the hillsides. After several days they climbed into the mountains leading to Hungary. When dawn broke they slept in a field under a haystack and continued across the countryside by night. The guide offered simple food: bread, cheese, apples. At last they reached the border to Austria, and the guide shook his hand. "Good luck," he said.

My father walked through the Austrian fields, sleeping by day in abandoned barns. He was free, although he could not prove it. Within a day or two he found himself in a displaced-persons camp in the American zone of

Vienna. There he bought paper and stamps and wrote my mother a long letter.

Throughout the course of his three-month journey, he would write to her each day, explaining what had happened in the last six years. *I'm a cripple,* he wrote, *I should warn you. I have only the use of one arm.* Whenever he had a few hours free, he wrote—pages upon pages, the story of his last six years.

My mother received his letters, read them, and then destroyed them. None of them has survived. Years before, Zosia had burned all the photographs of their parents, of their home, their childhood, their adolescence. Photographs of their aunts, their relatives, their friends. All that incriminating evidence of their past. My mother wrote Kovik long, reassuring letters, but he never received them. By the time she wrote him back, he had already moved on.

She remembers in particular one letter my father wrote from Zell am See, in the Tirol; he sat by a beautiful lake surrounded by snow-spiked Alps. To my mother, that letter and location mean something I cannot fathom.

Twenty-five years later, in the summer of 1972, she took Lara and me to Zell am See. The three of us stayed in a youth hostel at the rim of the lake, in a spotless pinewood chalet with geraniums bursting from window boxes. We bought hiking boots in town, suede boots with honeycomb soles. It was rainy and cold, and Lara and I hiked up to the glacier through mists and occasional drizzle. A patch of fog whisked off the top of the mountain, revealing its summit, colorful dots of skiers on brilliant white snow. Around us green pines combed and sifted clouds from the sky. Far below us we caught glimpses of sunlight dancing on tiny lakes. Just as suddenly, everything was swallowed up again in gray.

It was raining by the time we got back to town, soaking wet, hair matted to our faces. My mother was waiting on the porch of the hostel, with yogurt and raisin bread, cheese and apples. We showered and sat at the window overlooking the lake, and ate until we were full.

"Dad wrote me from here," my mother said with a sad smile, a faraway look in her dark eyes that made her seem to be both with us and not with us, inviting us in and closing us off at the same time.

"This is like my childhood," my mother murmured. "You know, my family was from Austria-Hungary."

We walked through the streets. She pointed out familiar pastries in the *Konditorei*, pastries she and Zosia had baked for us. Men in green loden coats and wool hats walked by, Tyrolean silver clasps on their jackets and suits. "It's the typical Tyrolean style," my mother whispered. "It's what the Nazis wore."

25

When my father retired from his medical practice in 1987, he finally sat down and wrote his memoirs—six hundred pages of his experiences in the Gulag. Although he was eager for Lara and me to read his manuscript, it would be years before either of us could bring ourselves to finish it. My mother refused to read a single page. It was well written, and the material was gripping, but the problem for both Lara and me was...well, it just sounded too much like our father. We took umbrage at the fact that he had chosen to end his memoir in 1958, the year after I was born. The years after 1958, he wrote, were far more painful than anything he had survived in the Gulag; he could not bring himself to write about us.

Now that Lara and I were researching our family's history, we reread my father's unpublished memoir. "It's amazing," I told Lara over the phone. "He describes everything that ever happened to him in Russia in exquisite detail— yet he completely omits any reference to religion. Or his family, his parents. Do you think he left that stuff out for Mom's sake?"

"He must have," she said. "You know, I actually think he's relieved we found out we're Jewish. I think he's always wanted us to know but promised Mom he'd never tell."

I used to tease Lara about her conspiracy theories about our parents, but now I had to agree with her. "Yeah," I said. "Lately, the minute he's alone with me, he sneaks in a few words about his experiences as a Jew. It's like he's waiting for Mom to leave the room, or get off the phone, to tell an anecdote about being Jewish."

"Mom told me that Dad wanted to tell us when we turned eighteen," Lara said.

"What?"

"He wanted to tell us we're Jewish when we turned eighteen. But Mom wanted to check with Zosia first. So she wrote Zosia in Rome, and Zosia flipped out. It took Mom weeks to persuade Zosia that they *hadn't* told us—that they were just seeing if Zosia had any problem with that."

"And Zosia vetoed it," I said.

"Big time. So they never told us."

"Jeez," I said. "Can you imagine how that must make Dad feel? I mean, it's his life too, right? We're his kids, and if he wanted to tell us who we are, he shouldn't have to get his wife's sister's permission!"

"Yeah, but you know Dad. He gave Mom his word, and his word is like iron, and all that. He probably has always wanted us to know but never wanted to break his promise to Mom."

1946: My father inched across the map of Europe on cracked soles and swollen feet. The liquid steps of his return voyage. In the American section of Vienna, the Red Cross helped him with food and shelter until he could proceed on his journey. He managed to buy two German medical textbooks, perhaps by trading a meal of Red Cross rations for it. He was starving for the written word. After six years in the Gulag he knew his salvation would be what he had in his head, and not in his belly. Scraps of paper, words in print, scribbled from memory and passed along—this was the stuff of survival.

But at the doorstep of Italy his luck suddenly seemed to run out. He waited in the Tirol, trying to finesse a way across the border. He had walked across a whole continent, slipped past half a dozen borders illegally. Now here, at the northern rim of Italy, he was stuck, without documents, money, or an identity. He continued to write long letters to my mother and waited.

It must have been the *Brecha* that finally helped him, I think—the Zionist Underground smuggling Jews to Palestine. My father had no interest in going to Israel; he wanted only to reach Rome, find Batya, and begin a new life. He was thirty-one years old, going on a thousand, and he wanted to catch up on what he had missed: to marry and have children, raise a family, earn a living, have food on the table and a roof over his head, warm clothes and good schools for his children. He wanted, most of all, to be free.

And so he managed to hook up with a Jewish group heading to Palestine. They had hired a mountain guide and set out on foot from the southern Tirol across the Alps. It was already early November, and in the higher elevations they hiked through heavy snows. During the day they huddled together and slept in barns, bribing peasants when necessary or hiding in abandoned shacks in the mountains. Among them was an elderly Jew whose spindly legs could not carry him over the treacherous mountain trails. My father and the other young men took turns carrying him on their shoulders.

"A young healthy man like you," the old man grumbled as my father carried him up steep scree slopes. "This is what our new nation needs! How can you turn your back on your own people? Your own faith! After all that has happened to us?" My father plodded on in silence, sweat dripping from his brow, his shirt soaked through. "A Jew belongs in Israel," the old man said. "Think of your family, your people. Never again! We must build our own nation or be slaughtered by the rest of the world!"

"I'm going to my fiancée in Rome," my father said between gasps for air. "I have no use for Israel."

"Such a lover boy," the old man taunted, "not a speck of respect for your own people. Shame on you."

The trail was unmarked and steep, a rugged climb over ice and rocks. My father wore a ridiculous pair of two-tone wing tips, the prewar shoes of a dandy. He had received them in the displaced-persons camp, since they were the only shoes large enough to fit his feet. On his tall, grizzled frame, with his faded shirt and tattered pants, they looked doubly ridiculous. Still, though not exactly the foot-gear of choice for long hikes and steep climbs, they were a layer of protection between his feet and the ice.

The guide skirted the edge of avalanche slopes and made the group spread out before crossing deep bowls. They moved in darkness, moonlight reflecting off the snow.

My father said little. It was always safer to stay quiet, to listen but not participate. The group had come from camps and cellars, cemeteries, attics, barns. From Placzow, Auschwitz, Treblinka, Bergen Belsen, and Ravensbruck. "You are one of us!" they said. "You have a responsibility to our people!"

But they could not crack through my father's shell. He trudged on, carrying the old man on his shoulders. He was grateful for their food, for their guide, and for their help. But a gulf spread between them. My father was already far removed from the rest of the world. He understood only what it meant to survive in the Gulag. His values and respect for men were limited to that measuring cup.

The group crossed into Italy and descended into the foothills. After resting with an Italian farmer for a day or two, they pushed on.

In Milan my father parted from the others. He went to the makeshift office of a refugee organization and was given a little pocket money and a train ticket to Rome. He immediately sent my mother a telegram, announcing the train he would be taking and the time he would be arriving in Rome the next day. Exhausted, he walked to the station, boarded the train, and fell asleep.

At dawn he grew restless and walked through the cars. He was afraid of what Batya would think of him, a skeleton in rags. In the tiny washroom he stooped and stared at himself in the rusting mirror, ran his hand over his hollow cheeks, eyes stinging from cigarette smoke. Outside, the golden fields of Tuscany whipped by, sleepy towns with tiled roofs, dirt roads snaking over hills of grapes and olive trees. He shaved carefully with the dull razor he had carried from Vienna, leaving only the prickly mustache that he had worn throughout his imprisonment. It was a silly vow he had made to himself—that he would wear this mustache until he was reunited with Batya. It was one of those odd things that a reasonable man cannot explain but cannot give up. He smiled into the mirror—a tired smile, an ancient smile, on a face he no longer recognized.

The Italians in his compartment were talkative and friendly. They broke open sandwiches and passed around oranges and pears, smiling, bubbling with words he didn't understand, offering him food. Their laps became tablecloths, and the compartment burst into colors and smells: red peppers, prosciutto and cheese, flour-dusted rolls, leafy green lettuce. My father accepted a sandwich and a pear and devoured them in two greedy gulps, then closed his eyes.

He had landed in the land of Munchkins.

He towered over them, a benign giant from another world. They were chattering away, instant friends. They wanted to teach him Italian. They wanted him to meet their daughters. They are infected by the sun, he thought.

In Rome, my mother received my father's telegram, and her boss gave her the following day off to meet her fiancé's train. Her colleagues at the *Ministero* buzzed with excitement. Zosia began making preparations immediately. She cleaned the apartment and squeezed a mattress into a corner of the living room for my father. She began baking: first an apple strudel, then *agnelotti,* which she filled with ricotta. She ran to the market and bought onions and oranges, lemons and parsley.

That night my mother couldn't sleep. She twisted in her sheets and flapped her arms on her cot in the little room she shared with Renzo. The train was due to arrive at ten in the morning.

She got up at seven and put on her yellow cotton dress. The day was sunny and warm. She and Zosia waited at the top of the street for the bus to the station. Her heart fluttered like a schoolgirl's. Bicycles and handcarts, cars and trucks, rumbled by. From the bakery at the corner, the smell of fresh bread.

The train station was enormous, an open mouth of steam and noise. People crisscrossed the platforms, carrying briefcases and bundles. Mom and Zosia inquired about the incoming train from Milan. "Delayed," the stationmaster said. "It's due in at noon. Track five."

Three hours. My mother fidgeted, unable to keep still.

"Let's walk," Zosia suggested. They stepped out into the street, relieved to be moving. Bronze-skinned gypsies in bright floral skirts lined the sidewalk in front of the station. Workmen lounged nearby in chalky brown overalls, smoking cigarettes. Zosia decided to celebrate by buying a chicken at the open market. They returned to the station at eleven-fifteen, and waited, listening for the announcement of train arrivals. Half an hour crawled by, then an hour; still no train. At last Zosia inquired and was told that the train from Milan had made up some of its lost time, and had arrived earlier, at about ten-thirty. "What do you mean?" Zosia demanded.

"Signora." The stationmaster shrugged. "It came in at ten-thirty. We thought it would be later. What can I tell you?"

They ran across the station from one track to the other, looking for my father. Pushing past trench-coated travelers lugging suitcases and trunks, sipping espresso at coffee bars. My father was nowhere to be seen. They asked the carabinieri in their starched navy uniforms whether they had seen a tall blue-eyed man, a fair-skinned foreigner, who spoke no Italian. The policemen frowned and shook their heads.

Distraught, Batya and Zosia returned home, the pebble-skinned chicken dangling from Zosia's arm.

When my father's train arrived in Rome, he leapt to the platform, searching eagerly for my mother's face. Crowds of people greeted passengers, and Kovik towered above them, turning slowly, surveying the swarm. He saw a woman whom he thought looked familiar, but she ran to another man and was swallowed in his arms. Minutes passed; the crowd thinned. Kovik grew worried. He looked at the clock—almost ten-thirty; the train was a half hour late, but surely Batya would have waited for him. She had waited six years; half an hour did not seem like too much to ask of her. He walked slowly down the platform toward the terminal, stopping every so often to scan the crowd for my mother's face. He had five lire in his pocket, not even enough for a cup of coffee. He had no idea where her sister's apartment was; he did not even know her sister's married name. All he knew was the address that Batya had sent his music teacher. For a moment he was afraid that something terrible had happened to her or that she had moved and had not received his letters or his recent telegram from Milan. After all, the only time he'd actually heard from her was three months ago; she had responded to his wire from the eastern border of Poland and had said she would wait for him.

Desperate, my father began to wander aimlessly through the terminal. People stared at him and moved out of the way. He knew that he looked gruesome—a tall skeleton with a stomach bloated from years of starvation, one arm stuck at a rigid ninety-degree angle. A pair of ridiculous two-tone wing-tip shoes, tattered pants that ended halfway down his shins, and a torn shirt through which his deformed elbow protruded.

He turned slowly, studying the faces of the women in the terminal.

"*Signore, venga!*" A man's voice startled him, and he spun around. Two armed military police stood before him, one with his hands resting on an automatic rifle, the other holding his hand out toward Kovik. "*Documenti,*" snapped the policeman. Kovik's face froze in panic at the sight of police. He had come so far, escaping from above the Arctic Circle, slipping across borders, only to be arrested in the train station in Rome. He glanced desperately over their heads, hoping to see Batya. "*Documenti!*" snapped the policeman again.

My father clutched his small brown paper package against his ribs and held out his empty palms to show he had no papers.

"*Venga, signore,*" the policemen said curtly, and, gripping him by his good arm, escorted him across the station. People turned and stared at him. The police brought him into an interrogation room and closed the door.

They frisked him and found his five-lire coin and the silver knife from his mother's kitchen. They took his parcel from him and laid it on the table. He had no documents, no identifying papers.

"Name," they asked.

"Kovik Buchman."

"What are you doing here?"

He shook his head, not understanding. "Where are you from?"

"I don't speak Italian," he said in Polish.

The policemen looked at each other, puzzled.

"*Parlez-vous français?*" one of them offered.

Kovik shook his head. "*Deutsch?*" he countered.

The policemen nodded. One of them left the room to call a translator. A few minutes later another policeman entered and addressed him in shaky German.

"Where are you from?"

"I am a displaced person," Kovik said, "from Poland originally. My fiancée was to meet me at the train, but my train was late. She lives here with her sister, in Rome. Her sister is married to an Italian; I don't know his name. My fiancée is Batya Tannen. She is at via Torino 20."

They looked up her name in the phone book, but there was no Batya Tannen listed at via Torino or anywhere else in the city of Rome. They turned toward their prisoner suspiciously.

"And who are you exactly?"

"My name is Kovik Buchman. I am a doctor by profession."

The policeman burst out laughing. "Oh, yeah, and I'm the Virgin Mary!"

"I'm a physician," he repeated seriously. "I have a medical degree from the University of Lvov."

"Let's see it!" the carabinieri said, hooting.

Kovik pointed at the parcel. "Open that, you'll find two medical texts I purchased in Vienna. That's why I have no money. See for yourself."

Still grinning, the police opened the parcel. To their amazement they found a textbook on anatomy and one on histological bases of disease. The policemen looked at him differently now, less sure of themselves.

"This fiancée of yours," they said, "how do you know she's here?"

My father told them about their exchange of telegrams. He did not dare tell of his illegal entry into Italy, or of his escape from the Soviets. He saw that they were beginning to get tired of him. One of them looked positively bored by now.

"Can you help me find via Torino?" he asked.

The policemen shrugged, and looked it up on a map. "Here it is, up here," they said, "it's a good distance away. Take the number 12 bus to Piazza Donati. That's right here, see? Then you just walk three blocks, take a right on via Torino. Got it?"

Kovik nodded, and they released him. He didn't have enough money for bus fare, so he walked. After an hour he finally reached via Torino. The bald-headed *portière* of number 20 stopped him in the doorway and refused to let him in.

"Batya Tannen," Kovik said.

The *portière* looked dubious. *"Non c'e nessuno,"* he said. *"Sono partiti."*

The *portière* rang the apartment, but no one answered. He indicated the staircase in the hallway with obvious distaste. *"Aspette qua."*

My father sat on the stairs and waited. Outside, the sun beat down on the pavement, but inside the hallway it was cool. After half an hour or so an impeccably dressed gentleman in a three-piece suit entered the building and picked up his mail from the *portière*. He gingerly stepped past my father and mounted the stairs. As he rounded the first floor, he hesitated and retraced his steps.

"Kovik Buchman?" he asked hesitatingly.

My father rose to his feet, his face brightening. He looked down at the little man. "Yes." He nodded. "Kovik Buchman."

The gentleman smiled with such genuine warmth that even my father was disarmed. *"Sono Giulio, il marito di Zosia,"* he said, extending his hand. *"Venga, venga,* I'm sorry you were kept waiting."

And so Kovik was led into the count's little apartment, an opulent gem from another world. High ceilings, walls covered with portraits of the count's ancestors. Hand-carved furniture filled the dining room. Kovik and the count managed to communicate a bit in the only language they shared, ancient Latin, embellished with sign language.

After an hour or so my mother and Zosia burst into the apartment, their plucked chicken dangling forlornly from Zosia's arm. Kovik and Uncle jumped up at once, and for an imperceptible moment everyone froze. Then my mother ran to my father and hugged him. "Kovik," she cried, "Kovik." He stood stiffly, holding her with his good arm, and suddenly felt impossibly old.

It was November 14, 1946, the day my father walked across Rome and found my mother. Zosia made lunch. Uncle prepared the table. My mother and father held hands and talked. What did they say? They had not seen each other in six years. Their homes were gone. Their parents, their friends, their past. They had crawled out on ashes. How did they find words? What could they talk about? There was too much and nothing to say. After the meal Kovik went into the bathroom and shaved off his mustache. Then he lay down on the cot in the corner of the living room and fell asleep.

Everything happened quickly. My parents wanted to marry on November 24, the tenth anniversary of their first meeting, but there were a few snags. First, although they were both Jews, they would have to marry as Catholics to maintain Zosia's cover. Since Uncle was a Roman Catholic count, everyone in Rome assumed that his wife, Zosia, was a Polish Catholic. Therefore, her sister must also be Catholic, and surely her fiancé would be Catholic as well.

"I knew Dad wouldn't care," my mother recently told me. "He hadn't been the least bit religious, even before the war."

So within a few hours of his arrival my

mother pulled my father aside and explained the situation. First, she told him that her name was not Batya, would never again be Batya, but that she was now Maria. Second, they would have to marry as Catholics to protect Zosia's Catholic identity and that of her son.

"No problem," my father said without giving it a second thought.

But there was another problem: Catholic banns required a three-week delay from the date of the formal announcement of marriage to the ceremony. If my parents were to wait the required period, they would be too late for their ten-year-anniversary date.

Uncle agreed to try to work something out. He had friends in the Vatican, bishops with whom he'd gone to school. Perhaps, he thought, they could persuade the Pope to issue a papal dispensation, allowing the marriage to take place prior to the running of the banns. That two Jews would have to get permission from the Pope to marry is one of the delicious ironies of my parents' lives.

In the meantime, Zosia went ahead and planned their honeymoon. "You'll go to Ospedale, of course," she said, "on the Riviera." Zosia and Uncle had honeymooned there in 1936, in a little hotel on the ocean. "It's magical," Zosia said. "You'll love it. Leave everything to me."

Uncle, however, dragged his heels on his assignment. He became consumed with other projects, and although he had every intention of helping his sister-in-law, he kept postponing his visit to the Vatican. Finally, in exasperation, Zosia told him she would send my parents off on their honeymoon on November 25, whether they were married or not.

That did the trick. Uncle rushed to the Vatican and asked for help.

The days rolled by in anticipation. Such strings are delicate and must be pulled with care and expertise. In the meantime, my mother left each morning for the office, bringing home her small salary, on which four adults and one child now lived. Zosia carefully monitored Kovik's diet, measuring out small portions of plain foods, gradually coaxing him back from starvation; little by little, he would lose the swelling around his stomach and ankles and gain some weight.

Zosia hired a tailor to make my father a suit for the wedding. It would be his only clothing in Rome. "The tailor came and took his measurements," my mother says. "You know, in those days our clothes were all sewn by hand. And the tailor walked in the apartment, and took one look at Dad, and nearly fainted. He'd never seen anyone so tall. He was used to Italians—you know, Uncle's size—and here was Dad, this giant."

My mother smiles. "So he took the measurements and went home to cut the cloth. A few days later he came back for the first fitting. But when Dad tried the suit on, it hung off him in huge folds—it was three or four sizes too big! So I asked the tailor, 'But didn't you take his measurements last time?' and he was terribly embarrassed. 'Yes,' he said, 'but when I got home and went to cut the material, I couldn't imagine that my measurements had been correct. They were so small compared to my impression of the man! He seemed so enormous! I couldn't believe that he was only a few centimeters larger than most men.' "

And so the tailor had to remeasure and recut the cloth, returning to fit the suit again.

As for my mother, she was married wearing a black wool business suit made from Uncle's fascist uniform. The same tailor had made the suit for her years before, when she was released from the concentration camp.

Since they had no idea when the papal dispensation might come through, my mother went to work each morning, waiting for word as to whether she would be marrying that day. She and Kovik watched the twenty-fourth come and go, without the Pope's blessing. Then the twenty-fifth. At last, on November 26, Uncle received word from the Vatican. He called my mother at work and ran to notify the priest. In the meantime, Zosia found two witnesses, another displaced person and his wife—both White Russians who had escaped the Bolsheviks. Everyone rushed to church on a moment's notice. My mother was married during her lunch break.

Zosia, Uncle, and the two Russians were the only witnesses at the wedding, just enough to make it legal. My mother told me that the priest baptized her and Dad immediately before marrying them. Two Catholic rituals for the price of one, a bargain.

As it turned out, the priest who married them would later become the first Catholic priest to be excommunicated for leaving the Church and marrying a nun, which my parents feel is a fitting finale to the story of their marriage.

They spent their wedding night on the little cot in the corner of Renzo's room. Renzo was three years old at the time, and my father has never quite forgiven my cousin for sharing their wedding-night suite. The next night was even worse, my father says. They spent their honeymoon eve in a train compartment together with two nuns.

My parents finally arrived in Ospedale late at night, in the pouring rain. They inquired at the station for the hotel that Zosia had written on a slip of paper. "Oh, that was bombed out during the war," they were told. "There's nothing left."

So my parents spent the week of their honeymoon in the train-station hotel, the only place with overnight accommodations in town. Every few hours they woke to the lurching rattle and whistling of trains.

It was an inauspicious start to a marriage, but they did not take the hint. They had too much riding on it.

26

In 1982 I joined the Peace Corps. Less than a year had passed since I'd milked long-lashed, dreamy-eyed cows on the Vermont dairy farm. In the meantime, I had completed law school, passed the bar exam, and vowed never to be a lawyer. Now I found myself teaching English and science in a remote mountain village in southern Africa. Once again my parents were shocked by my reckless refusal to settle down and practice law; once again I was inexplicably drawn by the promise of physical and emotional hardship—this time in a remote land, chock full of racial and political strife.

I reveled in the extremity of my assignment: I lived alone in a hut perched on a mountainside eight thousand feet above sea level, without heat, electricity, or plumbing. A four-hour hike across rugged terrain brought me to a small camp where I could purchase cabbage, tinned pilchards, flour, and lard. Political tensions ran high; a nearby hut was blown up one night by rebel forces. Men were armed with old-fashioned rifles. I was one of the few white people within a day's travel, if the weather was good and the mountain passes and rivers fordable.

It took me months to realize that I had set out to imitate—or approximate— aspects of my parents' lives. I had marooned myself on a distant continent, among people who were suspicious of me because of my race. I learned a new language and new customs, and I had to adjust to being cut off from friends, family, and anyone with whom I could communicate easily. I was conscious of the dangers inherent in walking alone as a woman, as a white person, as an inhabitant of a country mired in violence.

What was the lure that had drawn me here? I was twenty-five years old, and I had come to Africa to test myself, to prove my endurance, my ability to withstand privation. I found myself trying to imagine what my parents had experienced— the bombings of buildings and random killings, the desperate conditions of the Gulag, the loss of friends and family. I was trying to reenact, in some strange way, their lives under the duress of war and also their adjustment to a new country as refugees. Without fully understanding it, I had traveled halfway around the globe in order to be closer to my parents— who, at the time, were furious with me for my abandonment of them in the States.

Ironically, my Peace Corps stint was shortened when I gradually tore all the ligaments in my knee until I could no longer walk twenty-five yards without suddenly falling down. I was flown home for surgery, and with a sinking feeling I realized that I had managed to do to my knee the equivalent of what my father's fellow prisoners had done to his elbow.

December 1946. Without proof of his Polish medical degree, my father now began studying for an Italian medical degree. Within a few months of his arrival and wedding in Rome, he had mastered the language and passed his first barrage of medical exams. At the same time, Uncle arranged for him to enter the hospital for surgery on his left arm.

The orthopedists removed his elbow, cut a groove in the remaining bone of the forearm, and attached the upper arm to it, creating a primitive hinge-type joint. My father had not moved the arm in over two years, and he had to break in the new joint by repetitive motion.

"He had a bar over his bed," my mother says, "and he would exercise his arm until he passed out from the pain. Then, the minute he came to, he would exercise it again." After weeks of this, my father managed to carve a new joint out of the junction of two bones. To everyone's amazement he regained enough strength and range of motion to play the violin.

The violin he played, incidentally, was an antique from a collection of rare instruments that belonged to Uncle's uncle, Evan Gorga, the opera singer for whom Puccini had written the role of Rodolfo in *La Bohème* in 1896. After my father got out of the hospital in 1946, Uncle brought him to meet the eighty-year-old opera star. Evan Gorga listened to my father play the violin, and gave it to him on the spot.

"It's the same violin I have today," my father says proudly. "It was worth the pain of making a new elbow."

Soon after my father's arrival in Rome, my mother showed him the gold coins she had smuggled out of Poland for him. He was stunned to discover that his mother had been saving these coins throughout his childhood. Half of them made it to Italy on my mother's shoulders.

My father suggested that Zosia use the gold coins as a security deposit to buy a larger apartment for the family; they could no longer fit in their cramped quarters near Piazza Donati. Within a few months Zosia found a spacious penthouse apartment on via Castagna, with three bedrooms and two terraces. A price was negotiated, and the family moved in.

For the next several months, Zosia saved the family's earnings and finally scraped together enough to pay off the security deposit. But when she presented the money to the owner and asked for the return of the coins, the man shrugged his shoulders. He had already sold the gold coins, which were worth far more than the down payment. Those gold coins, my grandmother Helen's life savings, went into a new home, the apartment that Zosia still lives in today.

In 1947, my father passed his final exams and earned his Italian medical degree. Jobs in postwar Italy were nonexistent, but since my father had survived tuberculosis as a child, he was offered a job at a TB sanatorium in Merano, in the Italian Alps. My mother, however, could not afford to leave her job in Rome, since she was the sole breadwinner for Zosia's family. So within months of their reunion and marriage, the newlyweds were separated again, this time by simple economic necessity.

Once a month my mother took the train north to Merano and spent a weekend with my father. They bicycled along the sparkling streams that wound through the valley, and took long walks in the mountains. They bought fresh rolls and hard cheese and ate picnics in alpine-flowered meadows. The weekends seemed to evaporate in the mountain air, and before they knew it it was Sunday, and my mother had to take the train back to Rome.

For three years my parents lived like this at opposite ends of the country. The separation was especially hard on my father, after his imprisonment in Siberia. He wanted children instantly. He wanted an adoring wife who would give him bouncing baby boys; they would worship him and respect him and grow into strong young men.

But he didn't marry that woman; he married my mother. He married his memory of a twenty-year-old girl with a Mozart hairdo and straight *A*'s on her report card. He married a fantasy—a symbol of everything he missed, everything he'd lost. That had been six years earlier, before she had dodged bombs and dressed as a soldier, before she had swallowed soul and self for survival. She'd hardened, he realized, and now she was sharp and resourceful, determined, silent.

He kept looking for the old Batya, the Batya he'd dreamed of for the past six years; he kept hoping to come upon her in an unprotected moment, picking buttercups by the river or daydreaming in the sun. But this Maria didn't care for flowers and didn't daydream. She worked, saved money, and scouted the coast for an opportunity, a ledge on which to climb. She did not look back but moved forward with a joyless, energetic will. It frightened him to see how much she had become like him, how much they had in common. He tried to gather all their lost potential, wrap it quickly in a bundle, and present it to her like a bouquet of wildflowers. But she was already two steps ahead of him, plucking the petals and making jam, stripping the stalks and building a future.

My parents had applied for permission to emigrate to America, and at last in 1950 they were accepted. A Liberty ship of refugees would be leaving from Hamburg for New York City, and they were scheduled to board a train for Germany.

The departure was agonizing for my mother and Zosia. The two sisters believed they would never see each other again; separation meant extermination in their experience, and America seemed so far away—another planet. It seems crazy that Zosia and my mother should separate like this. They did not know when to stop—a survival instinct run amok. They did not know when they had survived enough, and when they could begin to live.

Why didn't my parents stay in Italy? My

mother said it would have been impossible for my father to obtain Italian citizenship; Italy would not accept refugees as citizens.

"That's not true," Zosia told me recently. "Plenty of displaced persons, including Poles, applied for Italian citizenship after the war and were accepted. Your mother was fluent in seven languages," Zosia pointed out, "she was an experienced translator. And your father, a physician, would have been a very desirable candidate for citizenship. They could have applied and been granted citizenship without any problem."

"Especially with Uncle's connections!" I mused.

"No," Zosia said solemnly, "no, it was I who thought they should go to America." She shook her head. "I knew your father, I knew that he would not be happy in Italy. He did not have the temperament. He could not tolerate the inefficiency, the slow pace, the laziness. And Italians would not know what to make of him.

"Besides," Zosia added, "I could see that Italy was having its own problems. It was not the country of hope and promise that America was. I pushed them to go to America."

I mulled this over for a moment. Zosia, it seems, was once again catapulting her little sister to heights she couldn't have reached alone. Zosia, with the long arm of their mother, lobbing Mom across the ocean.

"What about Mom?" I asked. "What did she want to do?"

Zosia smiled, that all-knowing smile of

hers. "Your mother stayed quiet," she said. "Your mother didn't say anything." Her smile sweetened. "Because, of course, your mother wanted to stay here. To be with me."

"And my father? Did he want to stay in Italy or go to America?"

"He had just come out of Siberia. He didn't know anything. He'd never been in Italy before. He didn't know what it was like. He relied on me to tell him."

My mother stood in line in the displaced-persons camp, waiting to be registered prior to boarding the train for Hamburg. My father struck up conversations with other refugees; he played chess. He covered his head with a T-shirt or sat in the shade. Children clung to women's skirts. Pregnant women blushed under my father's longing gaze. He was hungry for children, family, a home.

The train ride north through Germany was long and hot. They passed gutted buildings, factories charred to rubble. Inching along station platforms, hollow-faced Germans begged for scraps of food from passing trains. So this, my mother thought bitterly, this is what has become of the majestic Aryan race, the glorious Third Reich. Germany could not even lift its head to receive her rage. My mother found herself robbed of her fury. She tried to hate them, but she couldn't, feeling only pity and disgust.

My parents finally left Europe and rolled across the sea, three weeks. Everyone got seasick except my mother, who marched the decks in aggressively good health. "Even the sailors got sick," she says proudly. My father came up for air once the whole trip, looking stiff and green as a tree. He went back to his bunk and tossed and turned and moaned for days.

My mother quickly became the captain's favorite, helping the crew, tending to the sick. After three weeks of rough seas and storms, the captain motioned her to follow him above deck. "I think you'll want to see this," he said, smiling. The ship tilted at a crazy angle, lurching through thirty-foot waves that crashed over the deck. In the distance, nearly swallowed by sea swells, stood the Statue of Liberty. The captain shouted in her ear, and she grabbed on with both hands to the ropes on deck. My mother stood with her feet squared and smiled at the Statue of Liberty, eyeing it like a competitor. Perhaps she allowed herself a margin of hope.

At last the ship sat quietly in its moorings after the storm subsided. Refugees slowly wobbled onto the strange solid ground of their new land. Relatives ran to them and cried, waved caps, banners, shouted names, and hugged them. My parents walked to the end of the pier carrying their two suitcases and smiled.

They had gained passage to the States under my mother's name, as head of the household. By then she'd changed identities so many times, her name carried no import beyond the convenience of a moment's survival. A label to be peeled off and reapplied, like a picture pasted on a crate of fruit.

When my parents later applied for American citizenship in 1955, they would change their names again. Uncle would find us our name this time, pulling it out of his magic hat of genealogical research: Bocard. Not the least bit Jewish.

My parents spent their first weeks in America camped in the basement of Simon Getz, a sweet-faced, bow-tied son of a New York financial wizard. My mother had met Simon when he was a GI on leave at the Rest Center in Rome, and he invited my parents to stay with him until my mother got a job. With her first paycheck, my parents moved into a studio apartment in Ossining.

"This was New York City in 1950," my mother reminds me. "You could get a job faster than you could hail a taxi. Within a week I got four or five job offers, and Simon helped me pick the best one."

She took a job as translator for an import-export firm in Manhattan, earning fifty dollars a week, an outlandish amount of money for her. My father, in the meantime, studied English from a college textbook Simon had given him; he memorized grammar books from the library, read street signs, shop signs, advertisements, newspapers. With a dictionary in one hand and an English medical textbook in the other, he began studying medicine again, preparing for his American board exams.

Within a few weeks, my father began a residency at the Mount Sinai hospital, earning a token forty-five dollars a month, enough for shaving cream, underwear, and a pair of shoes. Every morning my mother took the commuter train to New York; after work she attended courses in typing and shorthand, business and secretarial skills. They squeaked by on her salary and even managed to save enough money so that a few years later they bought a used Ford, which Simon taught my father to drive.

"I didn't have a child on either hip in the DP camps, as all the other women did," my mother says with obvious disdain for the procreative impulse. She didn't have us in Italy, and she didn't bear us on the boat, or in the little studio apartment in Ossining. She waited till she'd put my father through his third country's medical exams, until he passed the Michigan state boards, and until he put out his shingle before she settled down and made babies.

PART
Three

27

I'm sitting at the foldup table in Uncle's study, surrounded by leather-bound volumes of nineteenth-century Italian law. January 1993: I've taken a leave of absence from my job as a lawyer in Boston and come to Rome to write, to sit in Zosia's penthouse apartment and trace the outline of silence into a story.

Uncle would be ninety-three now if he hadn't been run over by a car five years ago. He used to sit in this room, amid skyscrapers of documents, researching titles of nobility and tracing genealogical histories. Impeccably dressed in a pin-striped suit, with gold watch and chain, a silk tie, and sixty-year-old Florentine shoes, he sorted the papers on his desk with delicate, perfectly manicured hands. Each morning he selected a matching silk foulard for the breast pocket of his suit and brought a demitasse of espresso to his wife's bedside.

"Uncle was born two hundred years too late," my mother has always said of him, but she says it with such affection that I can tell she wishes she could have seen him in his proper element.

The day he was hit by the car, he was going for the morning paper, or to the bank, or for milk for his coffee. He was in a coma for months, while Zosia tried to understand how it could have all come to this—to a hit-and-run blow in his beloved city. He adored Zosia, he loved

Rome, and he worshiped women, placing them all—regardless of age, intelligence, and beauty—on a pedestal high above the earth.

"You know," Zosia said yesterday, apropos of nothing in particular, "truth is not all it's cracked up to be. Sometimes one lie is worth a thousand truths." She was repairing the electrical wires in her bedroom at the time. She abruptly turned, then skated down the hall on mismatched rags, polishing the marble floor as she went.

She is not your ordinary eighty-year-old countess. In her home-sewn pants (my mother made them from a Very Easy-Very Vogue pattern) she marches eight blocks to the market, where she sniffs the ricotta, pinches the figs, and argues with the street vendors over the freshness of the broccoletti. She returns, rustles, chops, strips, and minces her purchases into a cast-iron pan, two pots, and a pie tin in the kitchen. From there she hits the closet, emerging with pliers and screwdrivers, nuts and bolts. I find her balanced on two toes, straddling the porcelain edge of the bathtub, yanking at the dripping shower head with a pair of pliers. No leaks in her apartment.

Two weeks ago I was home with my parents for Christmas. Lara gave me a menorah, but she didn't have the guts to put it under the tree. We went to church with our parents on Christmas morning, the first Christmas our family has celebrated since we all know we're Jewish. The four of us crushed into the last pew, forcing an old man to move over. Our family always sits in the very last row in church, an admission of our marginality—no one can see us from behind, and no one will notice when we leave Mass early, before Communion.

I hadn't been to church with my family in decades—and, trying to understand, I watched closely now. Before entering the pew, my father dropped dramatically from the height of over six feet to one knee—one bony seventy-seven-year-old knee—and made a rapid and large sign of the cross over his broad chest, with bowed head. This act was so forceful, so elaborate, so elegant and graceful that I couldn't help being alarmed. My father the cocky decathlete, falling in obeisance to a higher being. This is what startled me—that humility that I have never before witnessed in my father.

"Now, listen," my mother told me the day before I flew to Rome, "you are not to breathe a word of any of the family history to Zosia. Remember—not a word! Promise?"

I promised. After all, my parents and Zosia have lived fifty years with their secret, and their identity is blended with it. Pull away the secret and you tear apart the fabric of their lives. I could never survive the guilt, I would never get the blood out.

On the other hand, wasn't it dishonest of me to pretend that I didn't know the truth about my aunt?

"Helen," my sister told me over the phone before I left. "You have to talk to Zosia about this, okay?"

"I know, but—"

"Keep me posted, will you?" she said. "I'll call you every week or two. You have to talk to her."

"Yeah," I said. "Okay."

January 8, 1993: Zosia's son, Renzo, and his wife, Bea, picked me up this morning in their little red Yugo—the size of a ladybug—to spend the day with them in their house outside the city. Renzo is a stunning aqua-eyed, olive-skinned man with ink-black hair and a boyish smile that makes him look half his age of fifty. Sitting behind the Cheerio-sized steering wheel, he smiled shyly at me, while Bea climbed out of the front seat. She seemed to be emerging from a suitcase, her long legs unfolding onto the sidewalk. When she finally rose to her full height, she towered over me— erect, bristly, and British. We hugged—a hard-edged sticks-and-ribs hug, and then I climbed into the backseat, while she folded her legs back into the tiny space below the dashboard.

Twenty-five years ago Bea left the drizzle of her youth in Scotland and allowed herself to be lured south by Italian sunshine and my Roman cousin. That was before she had learned Italian, so Renzo courted her in French—"the language of love," my mother likes to say, almost misty-eyed. Perhaps this accounts for the intensity of Renzo and Bea's adoration of each other a quarter of a century later.

Within forty minutes we arrived at their home, a sharp-angled house jackknifing up from a surly lawn of couch grass and palm trees. Inside, soaring ceilings, walk-in fireplaces, and windows you could fly an airplane through.

"What did you and Lara discover on your trip to Ukraine last summer?" Bea asked the minute we had sat down in the living room. "Did you find out any more about your parents and your background?" She said it with such innocence, I nearly fell off the sofa. According to my family's unwritten rules, one did not ask direct questions about the past. I was not prepared for such forthrightness from my own cousin.

I crunched my eyebrows and tried to come up with an answer. "Well," I began cautiously, "the trip was...well, it was very emotional...." I stalled for time. What should I tell her? My mother had cautioned me that Renzo was anti-Semitic, and although I had trouble believing this, I really didn't know my cousin well at all.

"We were...we went to their hometowns," I continued, "and it was very upsetting, you know. It was a hard trip." Bea nodded. How could I begin to explain it? What would happen if I tried? "But, no," I said quickly, "we didn't find anyone who remembered our parents."

Okay, so it was a lie. It seemed appropriate at the time.

Bea opened a cabinet and pulled out a huge folder of her family documents— birth and death certificates of her father and her grandfathers and grandmothers in Scotland—pages and pages of county records, church records, photographs, and histories. And the contrast between our families hit me like a King James Version falling from the sky. The only evidence of my family's existence was a handful of pages written by two survivors telling how everyone had been killed.

"You see," Bea was saying, "you can find these sorts of records, you know. Poland is a Catholic country—all you'd have to do is go to the church in your parents' locality, and you'd find all the records like this! The churches keep these records, you should start there."

I stared at Bea's carefully handwritten papers, yellow with age, discreetly recording the sex of her father at birth as *boy*.

They don't have a clue, I thought. Not the faintest idea.

"See, I have all the names of my relatives and the names of the towns, so I'll know exactly where to go when I begin my research!" She proudly showed me the marriage certificate of her grandparents.

Or I think it was her grandparents. I was having a hard time concentrating, and my heart was pounding. I managed to remain quiet, but I was in agony over it. How could she not know anything about us?

The next morning Bea showed me around the little village of Bocchio near their house. Walking through the open market, I screwed up my courage.

"Bea," I said, absurdly serious. "There's something I want to talk to you about."

She looked at me, eyes sparkling.

"Well," I said, wondering how to begin. "I don't know how you'll take this— but I wanted you to know I'm gay." Start with the small stuff, I thought, and see what happens. "I want to be honest with you after all these years."

Bea shrugged. "No problem," she said. "Does Zosia know?"

I smiled sheepishly, shaking my head. "I want to tell her, but—" I shrugged. "I told my mother in November, and I'm not sure how much sank in. I think she's working on it."

Bea nodded. "Your mother is a very wise woman," she said. "And she has a big heart. She'll come around."

"It's funny," I said. "Everyone else knows I'm gay—my friends and Lara, my work colleagues, my neighbors—I'm out to the whole world. The only ones I never told were my parents—and you, Zosia, and Renzo."

Bea smiled. "Well, it's fine with me," she said.

We walked in silence. I realized, of course, that I *wasn't* out to the whole world—that there were others I'd been careful to hide my sexual identity from. I had never come out to the rabbi in Israel, for example, who had helped us with our research, and with whom I corresponded regularly. And I had not come out to the Janiczeks or other survivors who had been so helpful to us. I good-naturedly shrugged off their questions about my plans for a husband and children. And I shyly declined their efforts to set me up with a nice young Jewish man.

The fact is, now that I was ready to think of myself as Jewish, I didn't believe Jews would want to accept me—the real me, a queer—as one of them. I'd had a run-in with a rabbi in Boston over this very issue. After weeks of studying Judaism with him, I finally told him I was a lesbian.

"Let's just put that aside," he told me. "You've been in the dark about who you are for a long time. Now you have a chance to reclaim your Jewish identity. Once you do, things will fall into place for you. You'll find a Jewish man whom you'll love. Don't worry about it."

He smiled serenely and leaned back in his chair. Behind him towered a wall of thick books, dusty brown-and-black jackets with gold lettering.

"Well," I said, "to tell the truth, I kind of doubt it. I mean, if that happens, fine. But I sincerely doubt it." I smiled. "Look," I said. "I've been through too much of a struggle already over all this—it's taken me years of therapy to get to this point." I felt my face reddening. "I mean, no one could accuse me of not *trying* to be straight," I said. "But I'm gay."

He crossed his ankles and began rocking gently in his chair. "Once you embrace the faith," he assured me with a wise, all-knowing smile, "you won't need that anymore."

I tried to keep a calm face. "You know," I said, "this doesn't exactly enamor me to Judaism, if I have to give up who I am sexually to become who I am spiritually. What does God want from me?"

"Abstain from practicing," the rabbi said simply. "You can be a lesbian, but just don't act on it."

I sighed. The point was purely academic, because I hadn't "acted on it" in over a year, not since my lover had died. Having sex was the last thing on my mind. But it didn't prevent me from arguing the principle of the matter. I was determined to find a way to reclaim my faith as a Jew without giving up my life as a lesbian.

The rabbi and I continued to meet every few weeks to argue and discuss feminism, spirituality, and religion, but I could never get past this obstacle. Now that I had found out I was Jewish, he insisted, I would want to renounce my lesbianism. In a strange way I began to appreciate why my parents had been so quick to dump their religion—albeit for different reasons than my own.

Bea and I were walking now along a cypress-lined road back to the car. I was absorbed in my thoughts, and we hadn't spoken for some time. "Is that all?" Bea asked after a few minutes.

"What?"

"Is that all you wanted to tell me," she said. "That you're gay?"

I swallowed. "Well, actually—" I said,

"there's a lot more that Lara and I found out about our family."

Bea's eyebrows perked up, and her mouth popped open impishly. "Have you!?" she exclaimed.

I began to feel uncomfortable. "Yes," I said, "but first I have to find a way to talk to Zosia. Because there are an awful lot of secrets that they've kept from us about our family."

Bea was intrigued by the idea. We had climbed into the Yugo, strapped ourselves in, and pulled into traffic heading back to Rome.

"And you finally found out in Ukraine?" she asked. Bea has a disarmingly forthright presence—dazzling eyes, a quirky mouth, and exquisitely erect posture. She should be a basketball player, a forward or center. A leaner, sweeter Larry Bird.

"Even before," I said, "but the trip to Ukraine was the first time we really understood our parents. It's the first time we could really see what they went through."

I was still unsure how to talk about this. "In Ukraine we saw that there is nothing left, none of their family, their friends, or their community. It's the first time I could really see and understand what they went through in the war."

"They were all killed," she said solemnly.

"Yes." I nodded, wondering whether maybe she, too, had ever suspected they were Jewish. "It was devastating to see." Outside our window, gold grasses whizzed by. "I began to see why they would keep so much from us, why they could never talk about it, why the past is so painful. And everything about them began to make sense." I took a deep breath. "Because we discovered that we're Jewish."

Bea's crystal-blue eyes went wide in amazement. "Oh my!" she said. "Of course! Of course!"

I liked her reaction—she seemed thrilled and relieved and amazed all at once—it was a good reaction, and I felt encouraged.

"Zosia is Jewish," I continued. "Completely Jewish. My mother and father are both Jewish, but they've never told us a thing."

"This explains *everything*!" Bea exclaimed. "Of course, that's it! That explains *so* much!"

And so I told her all about it. I hadn't exactly meant to, but once I started talking, the whole story just sort of flopped out like a huge slippery fish that I couldn't hold on to. I told how Lara wrote to Yad Vashem and how we got the pages of testimony and then how we decided to tell Mom and Dad. And how Mom made me promise not to tell Zosia.

"Of course!" Bea exclaimed. "This makes so much sense! I never understood why she fell apart when Giulio died. Of course, I expected grief—but she almost fell to pieces—it was as if she didn't know who she was anymore."

I knew that Zosia had suffered some sort of breakdown when Uncle had died five years earlier, but it was something we never spoke of in our family. Bea, I realized, had seen it firsthand.

"—she has always read so much about the Holocaust!" Bea was saying. "And she's so vehement about Israel! You know, Renzo has gotten into heated arguments about Israeli politics with her," she said. "And Zosia is absolutely passionate on this subject—she is rabidly pro-Israel—sometimes I think she has no sympathy for the Arabs whatsoever."

Before we knew it we were driving down the cobblestones of via Salaria, a few blocks from Zosia's apartment.

"Let's go for a coffee," Bea suggested. "There's too much to say."

We went to a little bar in the corner of Piazza Farulli, found a table, and sat down to talk.

"You know," Bea began, "Zosia and I have a reasonably good relationship now. There are ups and downs, of course, but basically we get along. But when Renzo and I first met, Zosia treated me with utter disdain.

"And it didn't matter what I did or how I acted—she was ice. But the turning point in our relationship came a few years after my marriage, when one of Zosia's closest friends, Elsa Sonderling, came to Rome to visit."

Bea laughed. "Elsa liked me," she continued. "And after Elsa's visit, Zosia became much more civil to me, and I knew that Elsa had talked with her and had spoken highly of me." Bea's eyes widened. "And I knew that Elsa was Jewish and was from Israel, but of course I thought nothing of it."

I smiled. Elsa Sonderling was the woman who

in 1955 had written the pages of testimony outlining how both my grandmothers had been killed during the war.

It's evening now, moonlight skidding across the rooftops, and I'm hunched over my little desk by Uncle's window. By now, I suppose, Bea has told Renzo everything. How is he taking it? My dashing cousin, the fifty-year-old Count Emilio Renzo Crozzi di Villa Vescovina, son of the legal scholar and nobleman, raised in exclusive private Jesuit schools since his First Communion. How will he react to the news that he is Jewish?

Sooner or later I must tell Zosia about this, that we know that we are Jewish, we know what happened to our family. I want to end the secrets, the tiptoeing around, the lies and self-sacrifice and fear of exposure. I want to tell her I finally know who I am, that I understand. It's just too important for me to hide from her. And it seems absurd for me to protect her from her own secret.

Two weeks have gone by like water through fingers. Zosia has finished her cooking for the morning, hung up her apron, and skated down the hallway. It just occurred to me now what I am hearing from her room. It's Sunday, and the streets are quiet. It's past noon. I thought she was listening to a concert of Gregorian chant, but now I realize that what she is watching is the Sunday Catholic High Mass. She also watched it on New Year's

Day. Renzo says that she has begun going to church recently.

The priest is saying a blessing now. Silence. Now he is saying, "This is my blood." Silence. Now he's giving some speech. This is all in Italian, and I can't make out everything since my door is closed. I thought watching golf on TV was coma-causing, but watching Mass on TV is probably a close second. But now I'm fascinated that Zosia, my proud, brash aunt, a radical activist who is Jewish, is sitting in her room watching the Catholic High Mass on TV. I'm intrigued and touched and don't want to blow it, whatever it is, this life she has carefully constructed out of the ruins of the Holocaust.

Bea came into the city yesterday and we ran some errands together. She has told Renzo everything.

"He's a little shaken up," Bea admitted as we walked to the post office, "but he's glad you told us." We crossed via Ussolino, narrowly missing a Fiat 500 that appeared out of nowhere. "Not about being gay," she said quickly. "He's fine about that."

I nodded, relieved.

"But about the family," she continued. "Everything is starting to make sense. For example, he said Zosia knows Hebrew!"

"She knows Hebrew?" I asked, amazed.

"He never understood why—he assumed that it was part of her classical high school curriculum. After all, she's fluent in six or seven languages, so he never thought much of it."

I shook my head.

"And you know Renzo was supposed to be named Adolf, after his Italian grandfather Adolfo!" Bea continued. "But Zosia put her foot down, and refused to name her son after Hitler. So they came up with Renzo."

"Adolf ?!"

Bea's arm shot out and caught me in the collarbone just as I was about to step into the street. A motorcycle buzzed by, inches from us.

"You have to be careful, eh," Bea said, raising her eyebrows. She nodded and we crossed the street, picking our way among stray cats and cars. The sun glinted off rearview mirrors, shooting spikes of white light into the arms of trees, which leaned over walled-in courtyards.

"And Zosia had a few Jewish pieces of silver in the apartment," Bea continued, "—spice boxes or something—something she brought with her from Poland. Renzo remembers them from his childhood; they were in the dining room, and he never knew what they were for. A few years ago, when he and I were on holiday in Prague, we saw the same sort of silver spice boxes in the Jewish Museum, and Renzo immediately recognized them as the silver boxes Zosia had in the apartment."

We forded the street and climbed over bumpers of parked cars to get to the sidewalk. Empty Fiats and Alfa Romeos hugged the edge of the road, nose to tail like caterpillars.

"When we got back from Prague, Renzo looked for those spice boxes in his mother's house, but he couldn't find them anywhere. He asked Zosia what happened to them, and she just shrugged and said that she'd given them away years ago.

"And now," Bea continued, "he understands why Zosia always made so many trips to Israel! She used to visit her friends there every year and left Renzo with Giulio. They've never been to Israel, she always went alone."

We finally reached the post office, where a homemade sign hung outside the entrance: *sciopero*. Postal workers on strike. We turned back home.

"What did Renzo think happened to his grandparents?" I asked Bea.

"Zosia always said that she had come from Polish Catholic aristocracy. And that under the Russian Communists the whole family estate was packed up and deported to concentration camps in Soviet Russia. Their family and all the servants, she said, died in Russian concentration camps."

Servants? I thought. *Aristocracy?* This took a moment to sink in. It was so different from my mother's version of what happened to their parents. My mother had always told us that her family was very poor. We grew up with the bomb story.

I grabbed Bea's arm. "I can't believe it!" I said. "The two sisters never even got their stories straight, yet they managed to keep the secret from their own children for fifty years!"

Bea nodded. "Renzo has never suspected a thing."

"Me neither," I said. "I had no idea."

28

Renzo and Bea know?" Lara asked with surprise. "You told Renzo and Bea?" She had telephoned me for our weekly chat while Zosia was out playing bridge.

"Well, I didn't plan it exactly," I said. "They asked me. And it's amazing how much stuff is coming out when we compare notes."

"When are you going to talk to Zosia?"

"I don't know," I said. "I'm scared to approach her about this. I just don't know."

"Look, Helen. You have to talk to her. She knows more than Mom, I'm sure of it. Zosia's the only one left who can fill in the gaps. I bet she knows more about our family than anyone else! You have to talk to her."

I shifted uneasily. "Yeah, I'll talk to her," I said. "But I don't think I'm going to ask any questions. I'll just tell her that I know the truth, and that's it. If she wants to talk, fine. But I'm not going to push it."

A month later, in February 1993, I had finally gathered my nerve. "Zosia," I said, holding my breath, "I want to talk to you about something."

We were sitting in her bedroom, sipping tea after lunch. She held a hard candy wedged between her teeth. Every so often she rattled the candy from one side of her mouth to the other.

"I promised my mother I wouldn't," I said,

"but I can't go on pretending—" I glanced up and tried to read her face, but she sat like a Buddha in the armchair in her bedroom, serenely calm.

"I think this may upset you," I said slowly, "and I understand if you don't want to talk about it, but I need to let you know that I know." My voice began to teeter. I reached for a Kleenex and struggled to regain my composure.

Zosia sipped her tea quietly while I told her about the research Lara and I had done during the past year.

"Where did you inquire?" she asked.

"We wrote to Yad Vashem and the American Red Cross."

"Ah, yes," she said, "I know Yad Vashem." She spat the piece of candy into its little cellophane wrapper, saving it for tomorrow's tea.

"We received pages of testimony written by family and friends, including your friend Elsa Sonderling."

Zosia shrugged and glanced out the window. On the rooftop terrace across from us, pink sheets flapped in the February wind and a woman struggled to peg them to a clothesline.

"We found survivors who remember my father."

"Who?" she asked.

"A man named Saul Rosenfeld in Chicago."

She shrugged again. "Never heard of him." Just then a gust of wind whipped the sheet from the clothesline into the woman's face. A spark jumped into Zosia's eyes as she watched the woman, clothespins in teeth, muscling the sheet back into position.

For some reason I thought of the first time I'd been here at Zosia's apartment, more than thirty years ago. I'd been content to sit on the tile floor of the terrace then, dark-eyed and open-mouthed, watching the people who were my world. They were laid out on the terrace like figures in a chess game: My mother basked like a tulip in her sister's presence; Uncle sat smiling, his eyes pressed to slits in the blistering sun; and my aunt commanded the terrace, hands on hips, now watering the lemon tree, now snapping off wilted leaves from the cyclamen plants, now scowling, now smiling. Already then I knew Zosia was the leader of our family; she bent all wills to hers. My mother adored her, and instinctively, Lara and I did too, sensing that it was impossible to do otherwise. The ferocity of our aunt's love for us nearly eclipsed our own mother's.

"We discovered a lot about our parents' past," I said, "and about your past. We found out how your parents were killed. We know we're Jewish."

Zosia's eyebrows shot up, her mouth drawn in a tight line.

"You see," I added quickly, "it was important for us, Zosia. We needed to know about this, to understand our family, to know who we are."

Her face darkened perceptibly, a trace of a storm gathering around her eyes. "So what are you saying?" she said, a hint of threat in her voice. "All this research, all this history, has it changed anything?"

"No," I reassured her, "nothing has changed on the outside. I'm still the same person. But on the inside it's a big change, it's a big relief."

"Good for you," she said.

In the hallway, Uncle's moody ancestors stared from mahogany frames on the walls. He and Zosia were such opposites—how had they managed to live together for sixty years?

"But I was afraid to upset you," I told her. "All year Lara and I were worried about how to tell you."

The lines around her mouth seemed to loosen, and she smiled. "Upset me? Why should I be upset? What difference should it make to me?"

"I don't know," I said. "It upset my parents." I remembered how agonizing it had been to talk to my parents less than a year ago. I could still see my mother's outstretched hands shaking as she exclaimed, "What happened? What happened to my parents?"

"Ah, you told them?"

"Yes," I said, "we finally told them last May, and they were devastated at first. Mom said we shouldn't tell you."

Zosia shrugged again and took a sip of tea.

A few weeks before, walking down viale Libia, Zosia and I had passed a young woman. "Excuse me, signora," Zosia had said, stopping her on the street, "but you dropped something." Zosia pointed to the pavement with a sweet smile on her face. I hadn't seen what the woman had dropped, but I was impressed with Zosia's concern, her attentiveness, and I was surprised by the woman's irritation at having to retrace her steps and pick up the slip of paper. We walked on.

"She was throwing it away," Zosia had confided to me with a sly smile. "It wasn't that she dropped it inadvertently." Zosia winked. "I just wanted her to pick it up."

I looked now into Zosia's swimming-pool-blue eyes. How could I convince her of the importance of our discovery? Was I merely asking her to pick up the past that she had willfully dropped?

"For Lara and me," I said, "all our lives we've felt that something didn't fit, that there was a great secret that we weren't supposed to know about."

Zosia looked impatient.

"And this year," I said, "our research finally seemed to lift a wall between our parents and us."

"So," Zosia said coolly, "are you satisfied with what you discovered?"

"Yes, it was important for us."

Zosia nodded. "So you found out what you wanted to know. You found out your roots. No big deal. No one was a killer. No one was a thief or a murderer, right?"

"No one was a Nazi," I added.

Zosia's head jerked up. "No, that—for sure not!" She lowered her voice. "So you can relax now."

Who knows, I wondered, what other secrets of the past remain hidden, beyond the reach of my research?

Zosia looked at me a little sadly, still smiling. "Listen," she said gently, "after what we went through, you know, your mother and I—I have completely forgotten everything."

I nodded.

Her face sagged, and little half-moons bunched under her eyes.

"It's a defense," she said. "I literally cannot remember anything from before. A complete blank."

"Maybe it's a good thing," I offered.

"It's not entirely good," she said slowly, "because I have no roots. They are wiped out. I have nothing."

I was silent.

"When I returned here to Italy, I remembered nothing."

Zosia, I knew, had managed to get out of Lvov in April 1942, and return to Italy, after being separated from Uncle for two and a half years. In the meantime she had survived both the Russian and German occupations.

"I went to a doctor about it," she said.

"When?"

"When I got back to Italy. I couldn't remember anything. There was a certain day, when the Germans first entered Lvov, and there was such a massacre in the streets, that you can't imagine—from that day on, I remember nothing. Nothing. To the point that sometimes I can't even remember my sister's name."

"My mother?" I asked.

"Your mother." She nodded. "I don't even know what her name was. And the doctor told me, 'Signora, it's a defense, it's nature's protection.' "

Petlura Day, I thought—the massacre that Zosia was talking about was Petlura Day. And suddenly I realized that the only name Zosia has ever called my mother is "Cucca," Uncle's nickname for her. That's the name Zosia called my mother in the Lvov courtyard on Petlura Day, when she saved my mother from the Ukrainian killings.

"But this enables you to live," I said, repeating what a psychologist in Boston had once explained to me. "Otherwise you couldn't continue. If you remember, you cannot go on."

"No," she said. "One must remember. It's vital. One needs to remember. One needs one's roots. For me"—she waved her hand helplessly—"I have nothing. I have no roots."

She looked past me, at the oval mirror on her dresser where the 1945 picture of my mother sat propped in a silver frame. "Giulio had roots," she said, "but I don't. I've been living in Italy for nearly sixty years, but I'm not Italian, I don't feel Italian. And I come from Poland, or you could say so, but I'm not Polish. Because when my parents lived there, it was Austria. But it kept changing. I don't have roots. And I don't remember anything. I live from day to day." Her voice drifted off.

I thought of Zosia's daily stream of bridge games and social activities she has assembled to fill her life. Every few days, when it's her turn to play hostess, she opens the door at four-thirty and the bridge players enter, all three at once, in their little fur coats and gray hair, painted lips and cheeks. They bend at the waist, peck lips to faces, and gather around the card table. On a china plate in the little kitchen, Zosia's freshly sliced ricotta pie sits plumply powdered, waiting to be served. The ladies' voices rise and fall, then disappear into the game. To keep things interesting, they play for money. Zosia nearly always wins, and she brings me her spoils, a few hundred lire a day, which I use to buy stamps.

"You see," she continued, "I wish I did remember my past. But what can I do? Some people in the war lost an arm, or a leg. It's like that. I lost my past."

We were silent for a few moments.

"Zosia," I said, "there's something else, something I wanted to tell you about me."

She smiled. "Yes?"

I told her about my girlfriend Dori, whom Zosia had met before she died of cancer. I told her I was a lesbian.

"Did you love her?" she asked.

I nodded.

"And she loved you?"

"Yes."

"Were you happy?"

I nodded.

"Well then, wonderful!"

"Really?" I said. "It's really okay with you?"

"Of course," she said. "Why wouldn't it be?"

She leaned toward me, smiling. "Look," she said. "By the time you get to be my age—eighty—you start to realize how precious and rare love is. That's all that matters, that you loved each other, that you were happy. Who cares whether you love someone in a skirt or in pants or—"

She glanced at the clock. "Oh, no!" she said suddenly, bringing her hand down on her thigh. "Look at the time! I'll be late for bridge!" She hopped up and brushed her hair, then put on her clip earrings.

I laughed.

"So everything's solved," she said breezily as she headed for the door. "You don't have to worry about anything. Your father was not a robber or a murderer. He wasn't in prison, or—"

"Yes, he was," I said with a grin.

"Well, don't tell anyone!" Zosia quickly scolded, feigning alarm. "Don't tell anyone; otherwise, our reputation's shot!" She threw on her coat. *"Ciao, bimba!"*

A few days later Zosia and I walked in T-shirts to Sta. Emerenza, the butterscotch brick church where my parents were married fifty years ago. The congregation was mostly white-haired men and women, with a smattering of younger people; a few children twisted around, making faces and sticking their tongues out at one another.

Zosia made the sign of the cross, selected a pew toward the rear, and sat down, although the entire congregation was standing up. I waffled, unsure what to do, and finally sat next to her. Zosia tapped me on the knee, pointed to her ears, and wagged her finger back and forth, shaking her head to indicate that she does not listen to what the priest says—she doesn't pay attention to the service. I nodded.

Everyone else murmured various blessings and responses to the priest. Two middle-aged women walked around with baskets and Zosia threw in a few thousand lire. Eventually everyone got up to get Communion. Not everyone; Zosia and I sat still. And there were others in the church who did not get up to get Communion. Maybe they'd already gotten it at an earlier Mass; maybe they couldn't be bothered. Maybe they were Jewish.

"Uncle was her roots," I said. "He was what anchored her to this country, to a sense of belonging. Now she's adrift, she's lost him. And she doesn't have her own past; she lives from day to day. She doesn't remember her childhood. She doesn't even remember my mother's name!"

Renzo and I were walking around the block by his office, which, as it turns out, is in the heart of the Jewish ghetto of Rome.

"What do you mean?" he said.

"My mother—her name is not Maria, that's an invented name."

Renzo seemed miffed.

"No," I continued, "Lara and I know that she changed her name to Maria as part of her Catholic cover. But we still don't know what her original name was as a child. When Lara and I talked with her last year and asked her what her real name was, she insisted it was always Maria. But when we asked my father what it was, he got nervous and hedged for a moment and finally blurted out, 'I think—I think it was Berta!' "

Renzo laughed, amazed. "And my mother?" he said. "What was her version?"

"Ah, your mother, she said that her loss of memory is so complete that she cannot even remember what her sister's name was."

Renzo was silent.

"So we don't really know," I said.

"That's serious," Renzo said after a while. "I can understand forgetting a particularly brutal time in your life, like when the Germans came and massacred people in the streets. But to completely forget your childhood, to forget your *name*—this is deep, indeed."

We rounded the corner by the enormous old Jewish synagogue. Paramilitary police stood outside the building, carrying machine guns.

"There have been some recent incidents," Renzo explained. "Some beatings, arson attempts. Anti-Semitic violence."

We continued to Portico d'Ottavio.

"Maybe after so many years," Renzo said, "hiding is second nature for our mothers. Perhaps they can't change. But you know what I hope?" He looked at me. "After all these years of hiding, perhaps now we can all be a little more open about it—a little more relaxed.

Maybe they won't feel so constrained, so on guard." He shrugged. "Who knows."

"Your mother will never talk about it again," I said. "She seemed pretty defensive, neither confirming nor denying anything. She simply said, 'You think you know? Fine, let's not talk of it anymore. End of discussion.' "

Renzo walked in silence, brooding. "And you didn't tell her that I know?"

"No," I said. "I was too chicken! If she'd asked me I would have told her, but she didn't ask, and I didn't get that far. I didn't exactly *lie*, I just didn't tell her."

Renzo laughed. "Ah, listen, that's not quite honest, all the same! I'm raised as a Jesuit, you know! With Jesuit principles!" He shook his head. "And so you have kept a secret from her, I see! It's not quite honest, not completely!"

He's right. We both know that Zosia will be furious. He's probably wondering whether and when to talk with his mother about it.

29

I woke at night to hear Zosia's angry voice yelling into the telephone. She was shouting so loud, I could hear her two rooms down, with both our doors closed. I looked at my watch. It was two in the morning. Would she be talking to Renzo this late? Maybe she's talking to my mother, I thought. It would be about 7:00 P.M. back home, so perhaps she had called my mother. But why? I tried to listen, but all I could hear was *"Che c'entra lei?"* which she repeated at an alarming decibel level. "What does she have to do with it?"

The next morning when I brought her our morning espresso, I asked her whom she had been talking to. She shrugged as usual when she doesn't want to answer. "Everything all right?" I asked.

"Yes," she said brusquely, and changed the subject.

Renzo invited me to his high school reunion—a private Jesuit school for boys, where he spent his youth from eleven to seventeen, and where Uncle, too, went to school as a boy. It's a regal building—Massimo Massimus, something like that—a majestic palazzo that was converted thirty-three years ago into the National Archaeological Museum.

I was amazed to see so many priests at the reunion. Elegant white-haired men in long black robes and little black caps, strolling the courtyard arm in arm. "Are they professors?" I whispered to Renzo.

"Oh no!" he said. "They're alumni!"

Renzo showed me the room that used to be the chapel, in the center of the building, up a colossal flight of stairs. "We had to go to chapel every morning," he said. "First thing, at eight o'clock. This Jesuit business is serious stuff. No one who comes out of this school takes Catholicism lightly," he added. "You're affected for life. Either you become a priest, or you devour priests!" He grinned diabolically, curling one black eyebrow up, a gleam in his aqua-blue eyes. Renzo is a priest-eater.

We found his class picture—Renzo at eighteen in black suit and skinny tie, standing in the top row of his 1961 graduating class, among priests sitting calmly with their hands on their laps, patient and long-suffering, their faces suffused with peace and purpose. Surrounding them, in poky adolescence, is a flock of black-and-white-suited boys, arrested in a moment's flash of the camera in their headlong leap into the next minute. Boys of the Italian aristocracy and upper-middle class with a respect for brains, learning, God, and the Church.

After spending the night with Bea and Renzo, I caught a lift into the city the next morning on Renzo's motorcycle. He dropped me at eight o'clock outside Zosia's apartment on his way to work. I crept into the kitchen, just in time to make Zosia our traditional morning espresso in the forty-year-old screw-top espresso maker. When I brought it into her bedroom, the shutters were sealed tight, the room erased in black.

Hearing my footsteps, Zosia bolted up in bed and greeted me with a sleepy smile. I raised the window blinds, and dusty yellow sunlight spilled in. We listened to the morning news until Zosia flipped off the radio and turned to me for our usual discussion of world events and local politics. I'd grown fond of this ritual, which we'd followed every morning for the past four months.

But this morning, when it seemed we'd run out of things to say, Zosia's eyes narrowed as if squinting down twin gun barrels. "Tell me," she said in a strange quivering voice, "why have you come here?" Her words seemed poised on a thin wire. She drilled her ice-blue eyes on mine.

"What do you mean?" I asked, puzzled.

She began to shake now with a barely suppressed fury. "You're here to spy on me!" she said.

I stared at her, bewildered.

"You've come to spy on me!" Her eyes flashed.

"What...?"

"How could you do it?" she shouted. "Torturing your mother like that! After all they've been through!" Her face was white with rage. "What does it matter, I was baptized in 1936 and they were baptized in 1946 and you were baptized in 1957! Who cares if I go to church or synagogue or whatever?"

"Zosia, I—"

"You don't care about me or anyone else but yourself! You're sick! Crazy!"

I sat stunned, trying to wade through her words. Gradually, they began to take on meaning. I felt dizzy. Dread sloshed in my stomach. What had triggered this? I'd been expecting Zosia's outburst months ago, when I'd first spoken to her about my discovery that we were Jewish. Now the room seemed to spin. Zosia sat rigid, her half-buttoned pink pajama top tucked into mismatched brown-striped bottoms.

"You're a Nazi!" she cried. "You're worse than Hitler! Hitler at least had a noble purpose—or thought he did. He believed he was doing it for the purity of the race! But you—you're doing it for no other reason than sheer cruelty! You're a beast!"

My jaw dropped, but nothing came out. I sat in silence, letting her words wash over me. A few weeks earlier I had received a letter from the rabbi at Yad Vashem. "Be careful," he had warned. "There is definitely a deep-seated need on your aunt's part to protect her offspring from the 'next edition' of racial-purity laws or genocide as well as survivor guilt. Be careful."

"You don't think they've suffered enough?" she cried. "You don't think that at their age, at my age, you can leave us in peace? You have to torture your own parents like that for years? For years!"

I shook my head.

"You went behind my back! You've been lying! You went behind my back and talked to Renzo! You had no right to talk to my son about this! *Non hai il diritto!*"

I was blindsided. Scrambling for words, I finally found my voice and shot back. "Why?" I said, "What, is he your property?"

"He's my son! You're interfering with my relationship with my son!"

"He's my cousin!" I said. "And they *asked* me, they *wanted* to know the truth!"

"You should have come to me first!"

"Bea asked *me*! You know when? Months ago,

378

January! Before I even talked with you about it."

She drew her head back, her lips pinched together.

"They wanted to hear all about our trip to Ukraine—they kept asking, 'What did you find out about our family?' and at first I denied, I told him nothing, I made up excuses. But finally I thought, this is nuts! Why am I hiding this from them? They want to know the truth! He's my cousin! He's the only cousin I have."

"You're lying!" she snapped.

I held out my hands in protest.

"Then you're the devil," she said coolly.

I searched her face for something familiar, a glimpse of recognition, but she was a sealed door. My blood was boiling now. The shock had worn off, and all that was left was anger.

"Right," I said, nodding with sarcasm. "That's right. I live to hurt you, to torture Mom and Dad, that's obviously my only goal, right."

"Yes!" she said, incensed by my tone. "That's obvious!"

"Uh-huh," I said, lowering my voice, trying to regain my composure, "I see...so...what do you make of it? How do you explain it?"

"Well, you're sick!" she spat out.

I knit my eyebrows together and concentrated, holding myself in check. "Yes, I see," I said, unable to keep the sarcasm from my voice. "Aha. I'm sick, yes, terribly sick." I nodded. "What should I do about it?"

She pushed me away. "*Cura ti!* Get help! Leave us alone! We have our own lives!"

I stared at her. "I don't think—"

"Oh, I understand perfectly," she shouted, "You're out to destroy us! You've done nothing but sneak around and spy on me the whole time you were here!"

What had happened? I wondered. The phone call in the middle of the night two days ago must have been to my mother. My mother must have told her about how we questioned her, how she told us of her past.

"What did you talk about the other night with Mom?" I asked.

"Affari miei," she snapped. None of your business.

"All right," I said, "what do you want? Do you want me to go? If you don't want me here, I'll leave. I'll do whatever you want."

She pursed her lips. Still sitting up in bed, she reached for a box of bobby pins, and busily arranged her hair now, combing it and pinning white flyaway wisps to her head.

"I'm not upset for my sake, you know," she said coolly, taking a bobby pin from between her teeth and fastening it to the back of her head. "I don't care for me, but for him, for Renzo."

"Renzo understands," I said, "he's not upset."

"I will have to talk to Renzo now," she said. "I will tell him, and if he doesn't approve, too bad, it's who I am, I'm his mother, too bad."

"But he *does* approve," I said.

"Well," she said brusquely, "never mind." She patted her hair back. "I have to get up and go shopping." She swung her feet to the floor, marched to the closet, and began dressing.

"Go on," she said flatly, "go wash your face. Never mind. All right. Go."

In the bathroom I stared at the mirror for a long time, but I wasn't sure who I had become, or what she had seen in me. I went back to my room and made my bed in a daze. I heard the door shut behind her as she went out to the market.

"She called me two days ago," Renzo told me over the phone. "I was at work, it was around noon. She asked me something about electronics, about the kitchen sockets, something like that. And then just before I hung up she said, 'Did Helen tell you about her family?' And I said, 'You mean *our* family?' She was a little thrown off by that, you know, and then she quickly said, 'Yes.' So I told her, 'Yes, she did.' So my mother said, 'We'll talk about it sometime.' "

"That's all?" I asked.

"That's all."

The full moon was hanging like a blood orange over the rooftop outside my window. Night like blue violets, and the moon rising orange, lifting itself over the gold-stained building, spinning a tale across the sky.

I heard Zosia in the kitchen, chopping vegetables and putting them in the blender for a *minestra*. It sounded like a forest coming down. I must be careful, I thought, about unraveling the lies of loved ones. Except they had already unraveled.

Neither Zosia nor I were able to sleep the next few nights. We listened to the news on the *telegiornale* and talked about world politics in a strange, meticulous way, trying to be nice to each other.

One night on the news, as we ate our dinner of leftovers, a long story on the Warsaw Ghetto Uprising. The Pope had a huge memorial gathering at St. Peter's. The square was packed with people wearing prayer shawls and yarmulkes. They were interviewed by television reporters, and one by one, they vowed never to forget.

Two weeks later, after our midday meal, Zosia and I were sipping tea on the little kitchen terrace. Zosia had splashed blood-red vinegar on the tiles to scare off the local cats, and now it looked like the scene of a small massacre.

"I don't know what you're doing here," Zosia calmly said to me, apropos of nothing in particular. "Why are you here?"

I placed my teacup on the saucer and took a deep breath. "We've been through this," I said. "What can I tell you? Do you want me to leave?"

"I want to know why you're here! You do have access to logic, don't you?" she sneered. "Logic, right? Do you know how to use logic?" She clutched her cup of tea with a white-knuckled hand. Behind her, on the roof deck across the street, a helpless white shirt hung from its shirttails upside down on the line, its arms flung down in a desperate gesture of— what? of grief, of acquiescence, renunciation?

"You have no right to interfere in my private life!" Zosia shouted suddenly, slamming her teacup on the table. "You have no right! You are obsessed! We have nothing in common. You are a stranger."

Struggling to regain her composure, she took a sip of tea. "Pack your bags and go," she said quietly.

I stood and walked to my room. I opened drawers and emptied my books and belongings into my two suitcases. *What have I done? I wondered. What has gone wrong?*

"Get your writing out of the apartment," Lara advised me over the telephone that night. "Get it out of there and transfer it to Renzo and Bea's. Zosia has been reading your journals."

I nodded. Of course, I thought. For weeks now, perhaps longer, she'd been reading my writing, my efforts to piece together the story of our family. "Bea is coming for me tomorrow morning," I said.

"Mom is furious," Lara said. "She talked with Zosia, and they both think you're sick. That you're obsessed with the Holocaust. They want to have you institutionalized."

"What?"

"Don't worry," she said. "Just get out of there."

I went out for a walk and returned late. When I came in the apartment I thought I saw Zosia's light on, but by the time I'd locked the door and turned out the hall light, her light was off, and only the painful wail of a soprano on the radio reached me through the darkness. I heard her again, the soprano, in a flight of panic, with the orchestra swelling beneath her, a tenor crying in alarm, and the rest of the city below me dead.

30

Two weeks later Lara flew to Rome to join me at Renzo and Bea's house. My mother, Lara said, had been calling Zosia day and night, frantic with worry. Zosia had fallen into a black depression and had not left her apartment for days.

"I know," I said. "We've been calling her too. She sounds terrible. Very weepy."

But the morning after Lara arrived, Zosia invited us all for lunch. Her voice was bright and cheerful, as if nothing had happened. Renzo, Lara, and I drove into the city and squeezed into the tiny elevator on the ground floor of Zosia's building. A bead of sweat crept down Renzo's cheek as we rode in silence to the penthouse. Zosia stood in the foyer waiting for us, holding open the heavy oak door leading to her formal living room.

I had never entered Zosia's apartment through this door in my life. Her apartment is shaped like a horseshoe; one entrance is the "family" entrance, which leads past the kitchen and a small scrub sink to the bedrooms; the other entrance is strictly for guests. It was in this doorway that Zosia now stood, smiling sweetly, as if greeting her bridge friends.

She wore a sleeveless light blue dress I'd never seen before, gold clips in her ears, and a bracelet on her wrist. She had brushed her hair and made up her face with lipstick and powder, as she did for social events.

Smiling, she led us through the living room to the terrace, where she politely asked if we'd like anything to drink. Lara started crying. It was surreal to be treated as formal guests by our aunt; the leap was too much for Lara. Zosia waited patiently while Lara dried her eyes, then asked again if we'd like anything to drink—water? Tea?

Renzo stared at his shoes. His fingers grazed his jacket pocket where he'd stashed a fresh pack of cigarettes. He had started smoking again in the last few weeks but didn't want his mother to know.

Zosia asked Lara about her work, about her flight, the weather in San Diego. Renzo talked a bit about his office, and I stayed quiet, studying Zosia, flawless in her role as hostess. She led us to the dining room and seated us at a brightly set table; then she disappeared into the kitchen and served a stream of exquisite dishes she must have spent days cooking.

After a while we managed to relax a bit. We spoke of things one speaks of at a luncheon—pleasant things, daily things. Zosia let me clear the table and do the dishes while she made tea and served her fresh-baked *apfelschnitten*. At the end of the meal Zosia escorted us out of the apartment, this time through the family door.

Everything, Zosia seemed to want us to believe, was fine. Nothing had happened. Nothing would ever be spoken of again.

I returned to Boston at the end of the summer and resumed work as a public defender. My mother and I maintained a cautious but cordial relationship, discussing books and movies, work and weather. My father occasionally dropped hints of his life before the war but rarely within earshot of my mother.

One evening in early October 1993 my mother surprised me during one of our telephone conversations. "Have you seen *Schindler's List*?" she suddenly asked. "It's an excellent movie! You must see it!"

"I have," I said, amazed that my mother had broached the subject of the Holocaust.

"You know, we had no idea what was happening to the Jews," my mother said with wonder. "None whatsoever."

I remained quiet, afraid to challenge her. Was she aware at that moment that she is Jewish? Did she think I didn't know? The gaps in her mind frightened me.

A few months later, after visiting my parents for Christmas in 1993, I offered to drive the son of family friends back to Boston. My mother pulled me aside before I left the house. "Don't tell him anything," she warned in a low voice. "Don't mention a word about our family."

I looked at her with surprise. "Of course not, Mom."

She touched my elbow. "It wouldn't be a good idea for you to invite him over," she said. "If he met your friends, Kari or Saul...well, they're Jewish, and he might get ideas."

I stared at her in disbelief. "Mom," I said, "look, he'll probably never meet my friends, but even if he did, he wouldn't care whether they're Jewish. Or whether I'm Jewish. No one cares."

"If my friends found out," my mother said, "I'm not afraid that they would drop me—you don't understand. It's that I want to spare them the embarrassment, don't you see? They will begin to worry whether they've ever said anything bad about Jews in my presence in the past thirty years! I don't want to do that to them!"

I glanced across the room at my father, who was sitting on a kitchen stool. He watched me attentively.

"Mom," I said, "why are you protecting your friends from their own anti-Semitism?"

"They aren't anti-Semitic!" my mother said, exasperated. "But they would feel I've betrayed them! I couldn't face them!"

"I think you underestimate your friends," I said. "Maybe they'd feel even closer to you if they knew the truth."

My father shifted abruptly in his seat. "It's always good to underestimate your friends," he piped in, a word of warning to me. "You're safer *not* trusting your friends."

For the next few years I was plunged into self-doubt. I seemed to have lost track of the shape of my own life, and I dragged myself from home to office and back in a fog. I agonized over my relationship with my parents and family. My allegiance was to them, and I could not understand how I could carve my own path without disturbing theirs. Years went by, but the story and the secret gnawed at me, refused to let me be.

Could I follow my heart without breaking theirs? When I visited my parents, I began to see them through a different lens. My father, white-haired and clear-eyed, with deep lines carved into his face, had learned to live by trusting no one. He would never let his guard down, sacrificing his connection to others for safety. And my mother had survived by dancing from one foot to the other, spinning and twirling her way out of danger.

Perhaps the war had not changed them so much as selected their strengths, reinforced them, and made them rigid. Their secret was their armor, but it was a mask of silence imposed on all of us. Was it possible to be loyal to them and to myself at the same time? To honor them without exposing them? Families always bind loved ones in ways both supportive and constrictive.

"If you look at history," my mother told me a few years ago, "every century has its massive slaughter of the Jewish people. And after what I lived through, I decided it would be irresponsible to be Jewish and have children. If I wanted children, I could not be Jewish."

But to what extent did her bond with Zosia determine her decision? Zosia, after all, was married to a Roman Catholic count. She raised her son in a country steeped in Catholicism. If my mother had chosen to remain Jewish after the war, would she have risked losing her relationship with her sister? And what about my father—did he have reservations about pretending to be Catholic?

My parents do not say, and I am left to puzzle over these questions myself. Eventually I have come to accept that I will never know exactly what happened to them or why they made the choices they did. I cannot undo what was done fifty years ago. And so I have learned to avoid mentioning the past to my parents. We now talk of other things—work, friends, books, movies—leaving the rest unspoken. They hope I will let the past slip out of sight like a ship sinking off a rocky coast. And let them do what they have always done— survive, move forward, carry on.

"When I grow up," I told my parents when I was eight years old, "I'm going to write the story of your lives." My mother smiled. At the time I knew almost nothing of their lives—the past was a mystery, part romance, part war. But what little I knew captured my imagination with such force that I have never been able to shake free. Theirs was a barely spoken narrative that led, I somehow felt, directly to my soul.

Families are intricate, multiheaded creatures, moving in many directions at once but perhaps with an internal logic. My family is greater than just my parents and Zosia—my family extends backward in time and space. I want to put them on record, however imperfectly—I want them to be seen and heard.

And strangely enough, on the page I begin to recognize myself in my parents—a gesture here, a question there. My attachment to them grows stronger with each sentence that arranges itself before me. Perhaps this is the ultimate irony of my family: I express my love for them in ways that are invariably the opposite of what they would wish.

1994: Lara pumped up the tires on the bicycles and loaned me a pair of gloves and bike shorts. "Here," she said, fitting a water bottle onto each frame.

We pedaled south on narrow winding roads, through a countryside checkered with farms. Smell of sweet grain and seasoned cow manure. The valley opened before us, a rippled blanket of yellow wheat. After a few hours we rested along a stream and drank.

"Sometimes," Lara said, "I wish we hadn't found out all that stuff."

"What stuff?" I asked. "About being Jewish?"

She swatted at a mosquito and raised the bottle to her lips. Her face was bathed in sweat. "About Mom and Dad."

"Why?"

Lara shrugged and wiped her face with her forearm. "What good did it do?" she said. "All that anguish." She touched her calf, tracing the line where her bicycle chain had left its imprint in a delicate filigree of black grease. "For nothing."

The sun punched a hole in the blue plate of the sky. We drank. Water spiders danced on the surface of the stream. I closed my eyes, and the sun felt sumptuous; the water was cold, and the stream gurgled in a singsong way that made me smile. "Lie back," I said. "Close your eyes."

We lay under the shattered sky for some time. A gentle breeze ruffled the leaves of the red oaks.

"Here we are," I said. "Right here."

Lara turned her head toward me. Salt had stained the edges of her eyebrows a faint white.

"We have our own lives," I said. "I'm beginning to think we can live our own lives."

It was a radical thing to say in our family. No one had the right to his own life; the family was the smallest unit of identity.

"No, we can't," Lara said, smiling. "You're just suffering from the delusion of individuality."

I threw a twig at her and missed. She's probably right, I thought. Still, the delusion

391

felt good. Maybe nothing had changed in my family; maybe my parents were still victims of their past, maybe Lara and I were still trapped in the aftermath. But something else was happening. Gradually, I was beginning to discover my own shape, to inhabit my own life.

"It doesn't matter," I said. "I get to be me. For the first time, maybe. You know, with my own take on things."

"So who are you?"

I closed my eyes and felt the warmth of the sun sprinkled through the leaves of the trees.

"Someone I just met," I said. "Give me time."

"Suffering," my mother once told me after a childhood fight, "is a great glue." I felt comforted by her words then, believing our family was bound together by our suffering. Today I feel tied to my family less by pain or obligation than by love. In spite of all that has transpired, or perhaps because of it, our devotion to each other seems to have deepened.

My family's past held me in its grip all my life. Now I tell the story, I suppose, because it is the only way to loosen the knot that has held us captive for so long.

Acknowledgments

I am lucky to have had the help of so many generous people in researching and writing this book.

Thanks to the faculty and alumni of the Warren Wilson MFA Program for Writers for keeping me going, and for their tireless reading and rereading of early drafts. Ali Dor-Ner provided the inspiration for this book, and Charlie Baxter and Mary Elsie Robertson offered sage advice at crucial times. Special thanks to Allan Gurganus for his generous support and encouragement. Michael Ryan was a godsend; I couldn't have done this without him. To Stratis Haviaras, thanks for your guidance and for believing in me.

Eliza McCormick Feld gets a Purple Heart for her friendship, blistering wit, and editorial acumen. Helen Epstein and Holly Metz sustained me for years, offering advice, support, and four-hour lunches.

I thank my lucky stars for Jackie Cantor, my editor, whose insight, intelligence, and dedication to the work have been invaluable. I'm also grateful to Linda Steinman for her thorough and thoughtful legal advice. My agents, Elise and Arnold Goodman, have been wonderfully supportive, wise, and generous.

For helping me understand my new (old) identity, I am indebted to David and Helen Jakubowski, Bernie and Roberta Marcus, Max and Clara Mermelstein, Joseph Polak, Henry Rosen, Mina Rosner, Meylach Scheiched, Mark Solomon, and the women of JLDHS and the West End House. Heartfelt thanks to Joseph Schachter—without you, I'd still be in the dark about much of my heritage.

To Lisa Rubinstein, thanks for your infinite patience and guiding hand in helping me find this book in me, and me in this book.

Thanks to my colleagues, past and present, and friends at the Committee for Public Counsel Services who have lived with this book nearly as long as I have. You've stretched far for lawyers, and I'm grateful.

My deepest gratitude to my partner, Donna, whose love and unwavering support have been my lifeline.

Finally, thanks to my family, to whom I owe everything.